9/11 UNMASKED

AN INTERNATIONAL REVIEW PANEL INVESTIGATION

DAVID RAY GRIFFIN AND ELIZABETH WOODWORTH

OLIVE
BRANCH
PRESS

An imprint of Interlink Publishing Group, Inc.
www.interlinkbooks.com

First published in 2018 by

Olive Branch Press
An imprint of Interlink Publishing Group, Inc.
46 Crosby Street, Northampton, MA 01060
www.interlinkbooks.com

Library of Congress Cataloging-in-Publication data available:
ISBN-13: 978-1-62371-974-6

Printed and bound in the United States of America

Contents

Acknowledgments

As co-founders of the 9/11 Consensus Panel, we would first like to extend our great thanks to the 23 expert reviewers who accepted our invitation to join an exacting review project in 2011, most of whom have served it each year until the present.

They are: Dr. Robert Bowman (1934–2013) (former Director of Advanced Space Programs Development, ["Star Wars"]); David S. Chandler (physics and mathematics teacher); Giulietto Chiesa (Italian journalist, former member, European Parliament); Jonathan Cole (professional civil engineer); Dwain Deets (former aerospace research director, NASA); Tod Fletcher (1952–2014) (former geography and environmental science instructor at Berkeley); Dr. Daniele Ganser (Swiss historian); Lt. Col. David Gapp (US Air Force retired pilot and aircraft accident investigator); Dr. Niels Harrit (Associate Professor Emeritus of Chemistry, Copenhagen); Dr. Steven E. Jones (Professor Emeritus of Physics, Brigham Young University); Commander Ralph Kolstad (retired US Navy fighter pilot, airline pilot); Dr. Graeme MacQueen, Professor Emeritus Peace Studies, McMaster University, Canada); Massimo Mazzucco (award-winning filmmaker, screenwriter, journalist); P. Dennis McMahon (attorney for 9/11 families); Aidan Monaghan (B.S. in electronic engineering); Rowland Morgan (former journalist, *The Guardian* and *The Independent*); Frances Shure (Licensed Professional Counselor); Lou Stolzenberg (retired physical therapist); Daniel Sunjata (American actor in film, television and theater); Tony Szamboti (B.S. Mechanical Engineering); William Veale (attorney, retired instructor at UC Berkeley School of Law); Dr. Matthew Witt (Professor of Public Administration, University of La Verne, CA); Dr. Jonathan B. Weisbuch, M.D. (former senior public health officer in Arizona and Wyoming).

We further wish to thank the seven Honorary Members who lent their considerable weight to supporting this project: James W. Douglass, Christian theologian, author, and peace activist; Mathieu Kassovitz, French director, screenwriter, producer, and actor; William F. Pepper, former barrister for the Martin Luther

King family; Andreas von Bülow, German writer, lawyer, and politician; the late Ferdinando Imposimato, Honorary President of the Italian Supreme Court; the late National Medal of Science-winner Lynn Margulis; and the late Hon. Michael Meacher, who had been the longest-sitting member of the British House of Commons.

We extend special thanks posthumously to Dr. Timothy E. Johnstone (1939-2018), former provincial epidemiologist of British Columbia, who recommended the Delphi Method as a model for achieving best-evidence consensus.

Finally, we thank our wonderful publisher, Michel Moushabeck, for once again supporting ongoing research into the events of 9/11; his most helpful assistant, Pamela FontesMay, who brought the book to completion; and David Klein, who conscientiously did the first edit of the manuscript in a surprisingly short time.

Both of our lives have been impacted for seven years by the time requirements of this project, and we wish to thank our families and friends for their patience and support.

Introduction

The 9/11 attacks of 2001 have had powerfully destructive global effects. The nature of these effects is shown by ongoing headlines in the mainstream press:

- "The 9/11 Decade and the Decline of U.S. Democracy."[1]

- "9/11 Used to Demonize Muslim World, Justify NSA Spying of US Citizens."[2]

- "The Tyranny of 9/11: The Building Blocks of the American Police State from A-Z."[3]

- "Since 9/11, We've Had 4 Wars in the Middle East. They've All Been Disasters."[4]

Given these disastrous effects, and the many people who have raised questions about the attacks, one would suppose that the press would have thoroughly explored the question of how they were carried out and who organized them. But this did not happen. Rather, the press for the most part simply repeated the official account and attacked those who questioned it. But deep and pervasive contradictions in the official reports made questioning necessary.[5]

According to the official account, the attacks were engineered by al-Qaeda under the inspiration of Osama bin Laden. As researchers outside the mainstream press began studying the evidence, they discovered more and more facts that seemed to conflict with the official account.

As a result, a movement evolved—which came to be called the "9/11 Truth Movement." The main focus of this movement has been to investigate evidence that does not square with the official story. But some of this evidence has, beyond showing problems in the official account, also suggested that the attacks were organized by people within the US government, specifically the Bush-Cheney administration and its Pentagon.

Under this interpretation, 9/11 was a "false-flag attack," in which a government attacks itself while providing evidence implicating some other government or group, thereby providing a basis for attacking it. And there were certainly motives to organize attacks. For example, the neoconservatives, led by Dick Cheney, had in the 1990s expressed their desire to attack Iraq.[6] Moreover, in 2001, at the first meeting of the Bush-Cheney administration's National Security Council, the focus was on how (not whether) to eliminate Iraq's president, Saddam Hussein.[7]

However, although 9/11 scholars pointed to possible motives for a false flag attack, in addition to reasons why the official account of 9/11 cannot be true, the mainstream press dismissed these arguments as irrational, unsupported "conspiracy theories," and instead suggested personal shortcomings that make people susceptible to conspiracy theories. Rather than investigating the claims of the 9/11 research community, a writer for Accuracy in Media wrote, "What needs to be investigated is the 9/11 'truth' movement, its members, and those abroad who continue to promote it."[8]

The public debates about the credibility of the claims of the "9/11 Truth Movement" have been generally dismissive, and superficial at best. One of the main reasons for this has been the lack of any basis for saying what the movement's beliefs are. Reporters sometimes take statements by various people claiming that "9/11 was an inside job" as summarizing "what 9/11 truthers believe." Using that basis, they have often portrayed people who question 9/11 as ignorant and irrational.

This portrayal has blocked public access to solid investigative research into the defining political event of this century.

The two of us, therefore, decided to offer the media and the public a body of scientific information constituting "best evidence" that contradicts the official position about 9/11.

Forming the 9/11 Consensus Panel

The best way to do this, we decided, would be to form a panel of twenty-some independent researchers well-versed on 9/11 with a broad spectrum of expertise. Dubious claims embedded in the official account of 9/11 would be presented to the panelists separately to see if they, with no consultation among themselves, would reach consensus on whether there was sufficient basis to declare the claim false.

In response to our invitation to potential members, a panel of twenty-three people with varying professional backgrounds came together to apply disciplined analysis to the verifiable evidence about the 9/11 attacks. The 9/11 Panel includes people from the fields of physics, chemistry, structural engineering, aeronautical engineering, piloting, airplane crash investigation, medicine, journalism, psychology, and religion. The members are named on the Acknowledgments page.

The Purpose and Goal

The panel members have approved the following statement of purpose and goal:

> The purpose of the 9/11 Consensus Panel is to provide the world with a clear statement, based on expert independent opinion, of some of the best evidence opposing the official narrative about 9/11.

> The goal of the Consensus Panel is to provide a ready source of evidence-based research to any investigation that may be undertaken by the public, the media, academia, or any other investigative body or institution.

The Procedure

Applying a standard best-evidence consensus model used in science and medicine, the 9/11 Consensus Panel examined a growing number of claims made in the official account of the 9/11 attacks.

Each chapter examines an official claim. The chapter is divided into "The Official Account" and "The Best Evidence" about some aspect of the 9/11 attacks. The Official Account especially includes statements by (a) the White House, the FBI, and the Pentagon, usually as conveyed in the mainstream media; (b) statements in reports by U.S. agencies, especially *The 9/11 Commission Report* and reports by the National Institute of Standards and Technology (NIST) about the Twin Towers and WTC 7, and reports by other U.S. agencies, such as the Federal Emergency Management Agency (FEMA) and the Federal Aviation Administration (FAA), unless contradicted by a higher government authority; and (c) reports by the mainstream media, unless corrected by the government.

(Please note that "The Official Account" is always stated from the perspective of the agencies involved.)

The examination of each claim received three rounds of review and feedback. According to the panel's investigative model,[9] members submitted their votes to the two of us moderators while remaining blind to one another. Proposed points had to receive a vote of at least 85 percent to be accepted. Although most of the proposed points we presented to panel reached that threshold, some failed. In the present book, the points are now called chapters.

This model carries so much authority in medicine that medical consensus statements derived from it are often reported in the news. They represent the highest standard of medical research and practice and may result in malpractice lawsuits if not followed.

Similarly, the crime of 9/11—which was never properly investigated by any official body[10]—requires that an approach something like that employed in medicine be used for an open investigation. Consensus 9/11 has provided evidence against official claims in nine categories:

- The Destruction of the Twin Towers
- The Destruction of WTC 7
- The Attack on the Pentagon
- The 9/11 Flights
- US Military Exercises on and before 9/11
- Claims About Military and Political Leaders
- Osama bin Laden and the Hijackers
- Phone Calls from the 9/11 Flights
- Insider Trading

This book grew out of a project on the Internet, Consensus 9/11—which is available online in English as well as in Dutch, French, German, Italian, and Spanish—thanks to six excellent and hard-working translators: Erick van Dijk, Christophe Terrasson, Wolf Dieter Aichberger, Wibren Visser, Massimo Mazzucco, and Manuel Aliaga. However, we had decided some time back that when we reached fifty points or more, we would, to increase the reach of this research, turn Consensus 9/11 into a book, with each point becoming a chapter.

In turning the fifty-one points into chapters, we made a few changes. Except for trivial editorial changes, all changes suggested by the editors of this book were approved by the 9/11 Consensus Panel.

David Ray Griffin, Ph.D.
Elizabeth Woodworth, BA, BLS
Co-founders, Consensus 9/11

I.

THE DESTRUCTION OF THE TWIN TOWERS

Introduction

After the World Trade Center was destroyed, the first investigation of the destruction of the Twin Towers was arranged by the Federal Emergency Management Agency (FEMA), which released a report, prepared by some volunteers from the American Society of Civil Engineers. But these engineers were barred from Ground Zero (except for a brief examination described by one of them as a "tourist trip").[11]

Also, according to *City in the Sky: The Rise and Fall of the World Trade Center* by *New York Times* reporters James Glanz and Eric Lipton, FEMA refused to give the engineers "basic data like detailed blueprints of the buildings" and "refused to let the team appeal to the public for photographs and videos of the towers."[12] The editor of *Fire Engineering* magazine called the "investigation" a "half-baked farce that may already have been commandeered by political forces."[13] The report, published in 2002 as the *World Trade Center Building Performance Study*, served as the official report on the Twin Towers for several years until the NIST report (see below) was issued in 2005.

To be sure, *The 9/11 Commission Report,* which was issued in 2004, made comments about the Twin Towers, but these comments were not based on a new investigation. For one thing, there was not a single scientist on this commission. Also, the 9/11 Commission's report made some obviously false claims, such as its claim that each tower suffered a "pancake" collapse, which was possible (it claimed) because the "interior core of the buildings was a hollow steel shaft, in which elevators and stairwells were grouped"[14]—as if the 47 massive steel columns in the core of each tower did not exist. The Commission's report also failed to mention that, in addition to the

Twin Towers, a third massive building, WTC 7, also came down.

The task of developing a plausible explanation for the destruction of the Twin Towers was given to the National Institute of Standards and Technology (NIST). NIST's scientific explanations were to be provided by a team of scientists under lead investigator Shyam Sunder. NIST issued its *Final Report on the Collapse of the World Trade Center Towers* in 2005.[15]

This report has often been treated as if it were produced by an independent institution. NIST itself, in fact, seemed to make this claim, saying, "Since NIST is not a regulatory agency and does not issue building standards or codes, the institute is viewed as a neutral, 'third party' investigator."[16] However, NIST is an agency of the US Department of Commerce, and while writing its WTC report, it was an agency of the Bush administration. The name of Carlos Gutierrez, Bush's secretary of commerce, was on the first page of NIST's *Final Report*, and all of NIST's directors were Bush appointees.[17]

Moreover, a former NIST employee, who had worked on the WTC project, reported in 2007 that NIST had been "fully hijacked from the scientific into the political realm." As a result, scientists working for NIST "lost [their] scientific independence, and became little more than 'hired guns.'" With regard to 9/11-related issues in particular, this whistleblower said:

> By 2001, everyone in NIST leadership had been trained to pay close heed to political pressures. There was no chance that NIST people "investigating" the 9/11 situation could have been acting in the true spirit of scientific independence. . . . Everything that came from the hired guns was by then routinely filtered through the front office, and assessed for political implications before release.[18]

However, although NIST's report on the WTC is arguably more of a political than a scientific document, the 9/11 Consensus Panel has evaluated how its claims hold up from a scientific point of view.

Another NIST whistleblower spoke out in the summer of 2016. *Europhysics News,* known as "the magazine of the European physics community," had published an article titled "15 Years

Later: On the Physics of High-Rise Building Collapses." Written by physicist Steven Jones and three other researchers, the article concluded, "[T]he evidence points overwhelmingly to the conclusion that all three buildings were destroyed by controlled demolition."[19]

Because *Europhysics News* is a magazine, not a peer-reviewed journal, some writers dismissed the paper as unimportant. However, a letter to the editor by Peter Michael Ketcham, a former NIST mathematician who worked in its Scientific Applications and Visualization Group, made it undoubtedly important. Reporting that he had not contributed to NIST's WTC investigation, Ketcham said that in August 2016 he began looking at some of NIST's reports on the World Trade Center and watching documentaries challenging its findings. In summarizing his response, he said:

> I quickly became furious. First, I was furious with myself. How could I have worked at NIST all those years and not have noticed this before? Second, I was furious with NIST. . . . The more I investigated, the more apparent it became that NIST had reached a predetermined conclusion by ignoring, dismissing, and denying the evidence.[20]

The Claim That No One Reported Explosions in the Twin Towers

The Official Account

No one—including members of the Fire Department of the City of New York—gave evidence of explosions in the Twin Towers.[21]

The Best Evidence

Over 100 of the roughly 500 members of the FDNY who were at the site that day reported what they described as explosions in the Twin Towers.[22] Similar reports were given by journalists, police officers, and WTC employees.[23]

Conclusion

The claim by NIST was clearly false.

2

The Claim That the Twin Towers Came Down
Rapidly Without Explosives

The Official Account

On 9/11, the Twin Towers came down because of damage produced by the impact of the planes combined with fires ignited by the jet fuel. After burning for 101 and 56 minutes, respectively, the North and South Towers came down rapidly but without the aid of explosives.[24]

The Best Evidence

The Twin Towers were built to withstand the impacts of airliners having approximately the size and speed of those that struck them.[25] And office fires, even if fed by jet fuel (which is essentially kerosene), could not have weakened the steel structure of these buildings sufficiently to collapse as suddenly as they did.[26]

Only the top sections of these buildings were damaged by the airplane impacts and the resulting fires, whereas their steel structures, much heavier toward the base, were like pyramids in terms of strength.[27] So the official account, which ruled out explosives, cannot explain why these buildings completely collapsed.

Conclusion

The official account fails through being inconsistent with the evidence, so a new investigation is needed.

3

The Claim That the Twin Towers Were Destroyed by Airplane Impacts, Jet Fuel, and Fire

The Official Account

The Twin Towers were brought down by airplane impacts, jet fuel, and office fires.[28]

The Best Evidence

Experience, based on physical observation and scientific knowledge, shows that office fires, even with the aid of jet fuel, could not have reached temperatures greater than 1,800 degrees Fahrenheit (1,000 degrees Celsius).

But multiple scientific reports show that metals in the Twin Towers melted.[29] These metals included steel, iron, and molybdenum, which normally do not melt until they reach 2,700°F (1482°C), 2,800°F (1538°C), and 4,753°F (2,623°C), respectively.

Conclusion

The official account does not stand up to scrutiny and hence needs to be investigated.

4

The Claim That the Twin Towers Were Destroyed by Impact, Fire, and Gravity Alone

The Official Account

The Twin Towers were destroyed by three, and only three, causes: the impacts of the airliners, the resulting fires, and gravity.[30]

The Best Evidence

During the destruction of the Twin Towers, huge sections of the perimeter steel columns, weighing many tons, were ejected horizontally as far as 500 to 600 feet, as seen in multiple photographs[31] and maps.[32]

These high-speed ejections of heavy structural members cannot be explained by the fires, the pull of gravity, or the airplane impacts (which had occurred about an hour earlier).

Human bone fragments approximately 1 cm long were found in abundance on the roof of the Deutsche Bank following the towers' destruction,[33] which points to the use of explosives. Pancaking or tamping of floors from above would tend to trap bodies, not hurl splintered bones more than 500 feet horizontally.

Conclusion

The official account is refuted by relevant evidence. The use of explosives requires further investigation.

5

The Claim That There Were Widespread Infernos in the South Tower

Background

The importance of this chapter is that a Fire Department of New York radio report unmistakably refutes the official account's claim that there were widespread fires in World Trade Center 2 (the South Tower) the morning of 9/11.

The official story's claim of the vast fires in the South Tower (as cited below) has been told without taking into account radio reports from firefighters ascending the building, which had been struck at approximately 9:03 AM.

An examination of a seventy-eight-minute radio transcript, which was found in World Trade Center 5 and publicly reported in November 2002, shows that firefighters in the South Tower could be heard speaking over their radios while ascending to and arriving at the seventy-eighth floor using various stairways, until the building collapsed at 9:59 AM.

This transcript is related to the official claims that the floors in the vicinity of the airplane strike[34] were all "infernos," and that the fires were of such a nature as to initiate the collapse of the building.

The Official Account

1. *The 9/11 Commission Report* (2004) stated:

   "From approximately 9:21 on, the ascending battalion chief was unable to reach the South Tower lobby command post because the senior chief in the lobby had ceased to communicate on repeater channel 7."[35]

2. The National Institute of Standards and Technology (NIST) reported:

   "On Sept. 11, 2001, the jet-fuel-ignited fires quickly spread over most of the 40,000 square feet on several floors in each tower.

This created infernos that could not have been suppressed even by an undamaged sprinkler system."[36]

The Best Evidence

These claims about the South Tower are negated by two types of evidence:

1. *Regarding the claim of a breakdown in fire communications:* On 4 August 2002, the *New York Times* reported (20 months before the 9/11 Commission published its findings in 2004) that a seventy-eight-minute radio tape of FDNY firefighters ascending to the seventy-eighth floor of the South Tower had been found but not released to the public.[37]

    On 9 November 2002, a *New York Times* article by Jim Dwyer and Kevin Flynn,[38] which reported about the tape's release, included a transcript containing the following segment:

    9:25 AM: Ladder 15 Irons: "Just got a report from the director of Morgan Stanley. Seventy-eight seems to have taken the brunt of this stuff, there's a lot of bodies, they say the stairway is clear all the way up, though."

    9:43 AM: Battalion 9 Chief: "What stairway you in Orio?" Battalion 7 Chief [Orio Palmer]: "The center of the building, boy, boy. [Stairwell B]"

    9:48 AM: Ladder 15: "What do you got up there, Chief?" Battalion Seven Chief: "I'm still in boy [B] stair seventy-fourth floor. No smoke or fire problems, walls are breached, so be careful."

    9:52 AM: There was an extensive discussion:
    *   Battalion Seven Chief: "Battalion 7 ... Ladder 15, we've got two isolated pockets of fire. We should be able to knock it down with two lines. Radio that, seventy-eighth floor numerous 10-45 Code Ones [Deceased]."[39]

    *   Ladder 15: "Chief, what stair you in?" Battalion 7 Chief: "South stairway Adam [Stairwell A], South Tower."

    *   Ladder 15: "Floor seventy-eight?"

- Battalion Seven Chief: "Ten-four, numerous civilians, we gonna need two engines up here."

- Ladder 15: "Alright ten-four, we're on our way."

- Battalion Seven Chief: "I'm going to need two of your firefighters Adam stairway to knock down two fires. We have a house line stretched we could use some water on it, knock it down, 'kay."

- Ladder 15: "Alright ten-four, we're coming up the stairs. We're on seventy-seven now in the B stair, I'll be right to you."

- Ladder 15 Roof: "Fifteen Roof to 15. We're on seventy-one. We're coming right up." [40]

9:57 AM:

- Battalion Seven Operations Tower One: "Battalion Seven Operations Tower One to Battalion Nine, need you on floor above seventy-nine. We have access stairs going up to seventy-nine, 'kay."

- Battalion Nine: "Alright, I'm on my way up Orio."

According to Dwyer and Flynn, this tape "flatly contradicts" the claim that the "devastating breakdown in fire communications at the World Trade Center was largely caused by the failure of an electronic device in the complex called a repeater, which was designed to boost radio transmissions in high rise buildings."[41]

2. *Regarding the claim of the vast extent of fires in the South Tower:* The radio transcript shows that:

- Firefighters had reached South Tower floors 71, 77, 78, 79 (and possibly 80), high up in the building.

- At 9:52 AM, seven minutes before the South Tower collapsed rapidly and completely at 9:59 AM (*The 9/11 Commission Report* gives the collapse duration as ten seconds[42]), Battalion 7 Chief Orio Palmer said from the south stairway:

    "Battalion 7 ... Ladder 15, we've got two isolated pockets of fire. We should be able to knock it down with two lines. Radio that, seventy-eighth floor numerous 10-45 Code Ones."

- The firefighters were able to climb to Floor 78 on at least three of the stairwells.

- As Dwyer and Flynn note, at 9:56 AM (three minutes before the sudden collapse), the firefighters finally encountered fire at the seventy-eighth floor in both stairwells A and B:

  > "Ladder 15 had finally found the fire after an arduous climb to the seventy-eighth floor, according to the tape. They were in the B stairwell. On the other side of the fire were hundreds of people, blocked from fleeing by smoke and flame on the stairs. Chief Palmer was facing similar fires in the A stairwell, across the floor."[43]

- The firefighters were calm and unafraid:

  > The voices, captured on a tape of Fire Department radio transmissions, betray no fear. The words are matter-of-fact.... But nowhere on the tape is there any indication that firefighters had the slightest indication that the tower had become unstable or that it could fall.
  >   "Chief, I'm going to stop on 44," Stephen Belson, an aide to Chief Palmer, tells him at 9:25 as he ascends.
  >   "Take your time," the chief responds.[44]

  > Debbie Palmer, whose husband, Battalion Chief Orio Palmer, can be heard on the tape ... said the recording gave her some peace about her husband's last moments.
  >   "I didn't hear fear, I didn't hear panic," she told the *Times*. "When the tape is made public to the world, people will hear that they all went about their jobs without fear, and selflessly."[45]

Conclusion

There is incontrovertible evidence that the firefighter teams were communicating clearly with one another as they ascended WTC 2.

The fact that they went about their work calmly is not surprising, because in their professional experience a fire—even a fire caused by an airplane impact— had never resulted in the collapse of a steel-frame high-rise building, not even a single floor.

The incontrovertible evidence of firefighter teams operating calmly, methodically, and with confidence that they could easily defeat the fires in the South Tower refutes the official claim that floors in the vicinity of the airplane strike were all "infernos," and that the building was unstable and about to collapse.

The evidence from the radio transcript supports chapters 1–4 in affirming that the Twin Towers did not come down from airplane impact and fires, as the official narrative alleges.

6

The Claim That There Was No Molten Steel or Iron in the WTC Debris

Introduction

According to the official account, the Twin Towers were brought down by airplane impacts and fire, and in the case of WTC 7, by fire alone. One implication of this account is that the destruction would have produced no molten steel or molten iron (which is produced in a thermite reaction). But there was evidence in the debris of molten steel or iron.

The Official Account

There is no evidence that any molten steel or iron was found in any of the WTC buildings. The NIST report showed that the Twin Towers were brought down by the airplane impacts and the resulting fires, which were ignited by jet fuel.[46] WTC 7, which was not hit by a plane, was brought down by fire alone.[47] There would, therefore, have been no reason for molten steel or iron to have been produced.[48]

Molten steel or iron was not mentioned in the *9/11 Commission Report*,[49] the NIST report about the Twin Towers,[50] or the NIST report about WTC 7.[51] This silence about molten steel or iron implies its absence.

The existence of molten steel (or iron) was inexplicitly denied by one of the authors of the NIST reports, engineer John L. Gross.[52] At a lecture at the University of Texas in October 2006, Gross was asked a question about "a pool of molten steel," to which he replied:

> Let's go back to your basic premise that there was a pool of molten steel. I know of absolutely nobody—no eyewitnesses said so, nobody's produced it.[53]

In a post-report publication (September 2011), NIST wrote:

> NIST investigators and experts from the American Society of Civil Engineers (ASCE) and the Structural Engineers Association of New York (SEONY)—who inspected the WTC steel at the WTC site and the salvage yards—found no evidence that would support the melting of steel in a jet-fuel-ignited fire in the towers prior to collapse.

Moreover, this publication said:

> The condition of the steel in the wreckage of the WTC towers (i.e., whether it was in a molten state or not) was irrelevant to the investigation of the collapse since it does not provide any conclusive information on the condition of the steel when the WTC towers were standing.

Finally, this publication said:

> Under certain circumstances it is conceivable for some of the steel in the wreckage to have melted after the buildings collapsed. Any molten steel in the wreckage was more likely due to the high temperature resulting from long exposure to combustion within the pile than to short exposure to fires or explosions while the buildings were standing.[54]

In summary:

1. The collapses were caused by jet-fuel fires, which were not hot enough to produce molten steel or iron.

2. There was no evidence for molten steel or iron, and no reason to expect it.

3. Even if there had been molten steel or iron in the debris afterward, it would have been irrelevant to the cause of the collapses.

The Best Evidence

Not one of those claims can be maintained:
1) The evidence of molten steel or iron cannot be called "irrelevant," given the fact that the building fires, as NIST pointed out,

cannot explain it. The only explanation NIST suggested was that, if there was molten steel or iron, it would have been "due to the high temperature resulting from long exposure to combustion within the pile." But NIST claimed that the buildings were brought down by building fires, which at most could have reached 1,000°C (1,832°F). So the idea that burning debris from these buildings could have reached anywhere close to the temperature needed to melt structural steel (1,482°C, 2,700°F),[55] without the help of explosive or incendiary material, is implausible.

It is also unscientific. Physicist Steven Jones has written: "Are there any examples of buildings toppled by fires or any reason other than deliberate demolition that show large pools of molten metal in the rubble? I have posed this question to numerous engineers and scientists, but so far no examples have emerged. Strange then that three buildings in Manhattan, supposedly brought down finally by fires, all show these large pools of molten metal in their basements post-collapse on 9-11-2001. It would be interesting if underground fires could somehow produce large pools of molten steel, for example, but then there should be historical examples of this effect since there have been many large fires in numerous buildings. It is not enough to argue hypothetically that fires could possibly cause all three pools of orange-hot molten metal." The fact that the pools of metal had an orange color was crucial, Jones explained, because something had raised the temperature of iron to more than 2,000°C (3,632°F).[56]

2) There were two types of evidence for molten steel or iron in the debris:

    I. Physical evidence, which was presented in a 2002 report by FEMA and elsewhere.

    II. Reports from many credible witnesses, including firefighters and other professionals.

I. Physical Evidence

I-A. The 2002 FEMA Report

New York Times journalist James Glanz, writing near the end of 2001 about the collapse of WTC 7, reported that some engineers said that a "combination of an uncontrolled fire and the structural damage might have been able to bring the building down," but that this "would not explain," according to Dr. Barnett, "steel members in the debris pile that appear to have been partly evaporated in extraordinarily high temperatures."[57]

Glanz was referring to Jonathan Barnett, a professor of fire protection engineering at the Worcester Polytechnic Institute (WPI). Early in 2002, Barnett and two WPI colleagues published an analysis of a section of steel from one of the Twin Towers, along with sections from WTC 7, as an appendix to FEMA's 2002 *World Trade Center Building Performance Study*.[58] Their discoveries were also reported in a WPI article titled "The 'Deep Mystery' of Melted Steel," which said:

> [S]teel—which has a melting point of 2,800 degrees Fahrenheit—may weaken and bend, but does not melt during an ordinary office fire. Yet metallurgical studies on WTC steel brought back to WPI reveal that a novel phenomenon—called a eutectic reaction—occurred at the surface, causing intergranular melting capable of turning a solid steel girder into Swiss cheese.

Stating that the *New York Times* called these findings "perhaps the deepest mystery uncovered in the investigation," the article added:

> A one-inch column has been reduced to half-inch thickness. Its edges—which are curled like a paper scroll—have been thinned to almost razor sharpness. Gaping holes—some larger than a silver dollar—let light shine through a formerly solid steel flange. This Swiss cheese appearance shocked all of the fire-wise professors, who expected to see distortion and bending—but not holes.[59]

In discussing "the deepest mystery," the *New York Times* story said: "The steel apparently melted away, but no fire in any of the buildings was believed to be hot enough to melt steel outright."[60] That was an understatement, because a building fire, even with a perfect mixture of air and fuel, could at most reach 1,000°C (1,832°F).[61] In fact, Professor Thomas Eagar of MIT estimated that the fires were "probably only about 1,200 or 1,300°F [648°C or 704°C]."[62]

I-B. The RJ Lee Report

In May 2004, the RJ Lee Group issued a report, titled "WTC Dust Signature," at the request of the Deutsche Bank, in order to prove (to its insurance company) that the building was "pervasively contaminated with WTC Dust, unique to the WTC Event."[63] The report listed five elements in this signature, one of which was: "Spherical iron and spherical or vesicular silicate particles that result from exposure to high temperature."[64] This was the only statement about iron being modified by high temperature in this 2004 report.

However, RJ Lee had written an earlier report in 2003, titled "WTC Dust Signature Study," which contained much more about iron. It said: "Particles of materials that had been modified by exposure to high temperature, such as spherical particles of iron and silicates, are common in WTC Dust . . . but are not common in 'normal' interior office dust."[65] This 2003 version of the report even pointed out that, whereas iron particles constitute only 0.04 percent of normal building dust, they constituted an enormous amount of the WTC dust: 5.87 percent (meaning that the dust contained almost 150 times more iron than normal).[66] This earlier version also explicitly stated that iron and other metals were "melted during the WTC Event, producing spherical metallic particles."[67]

In addition, whereas the 2004 report did not use the word "vaporize," this earlier version spoke of temperatures "at which lead would have undergone vaporization."[68] Accordingly, whereas the 2004 report referred to "high temperatures," the earlier report indicated that the temperatures were not merely high but *extremely* high, because for lead to boil and hence vaporize, it must be heated to 1,749°C (3,180°F).[69]

I-C. The USGS Report

In 2005, the United States Geological Survey (USGS) published a report titled "Particle Atlas of World Trade Center Dust," which was intended to aid the "identification of WTC dust components." Among the components, it reported, were "metal or metal oxides" (which could not be distinguished by the USGS's methods). "The primary metal and metal-oxide phases in WTC dust," the report said, "are Fe-rich [iron-rich] and Zn-rich [zinc-rich] particles."[70] The report included a micrograph of an "iron-rich sphere."[71]

These iron-rich spherical particles—or "spherules," as they are sometimes called—can only come about if iron is melted and then "sprayed into the air so that surface tension draws the molten droplets into near-spherical shapes."[72]

Accordingly, the USGS report mentioned (without explaining) the existence of particles in the dust that should not have been there, according to the NIST explanation of the collapses.

I-D. Report by the Steven Jones Group

NIST also ignored another scientific report describing phenomena in the WTC dust that could have been produced only by extremely high temperatures. Entitled, in fact, "Extremely High Temperatures During the World Trade Center Destruction," this report, written by Steven E. Jones and seven other scientists, pointed out the existence of particles in the dust that required even higher temperatures than those implied by the RJ Lee and USGS reports.

Jones and his colleagues performed tests using their own samples of WTC dust, which had been collected shortly after the destruction of the WTC—either very shortly afterward or from the inside of nearby buildings (which means that the dust could not have been contaminated by cleanup operations at Ground Zero). They reported finding "an abundance of tiny solidified droplets roughly spherical in shape (spherules)," which were primarily "iron-rich . . . and silicates." The iron-rich spherules would have required a temperature of 1,538°C (2,800°F). The silicates often contained aluminum, and aluminosilicate spherules, which were found in abundance in the dust, would have required a temperature of 1,450°C (2,652°F).[73]

Iron could not have arisen from the steel alone and should not have been found in the rubble. The iron, which needs to be accounted for, is a byproduct of the thermite reaction.

Still more remarkable, the Jones group reported, was a spherule found in the dust that was not mentioned in USGS's "Particle Atlas," and which was obtained only through an FOIA request, namely, "a molybdenum-rich spherule," which had been observed and studied by the USGS team. This information is remarkable, because molybdenum (Mo) is "known for its extremely high melting point": 2,623°C (4,753°F).[74] NIST did not mention the presence of this molybdenum-rich spherule in the WTC dust, although it could have learned about it from the article by the Jones group or directly from the USGS.

II. Testimony

II-A. Testimony from Firefighters

- New York Fire Department Captain Philip Ruvolo said: "You'd get down below and you'd see molten steel, *molten steel*, running down the channel rails, like you're in a foundry, like lava."[75]

- Joe O'Toole, a Bronx firefighter who worked on the rescue and cleanup efforts, reported that one beam lifted from deep below the surface months later, in February 2002, "was dripping from the molten steel."[76]

- In the 2003 documentary film *Collateral Damages*, New York firefighters recalled heat so intense they encountered "rivers of molten steel."[77]

Testimony from Other Professionals

- Leslie Robertson, a member of the engineering firm that designed the World Trade Center, said, twenty-one days after the attack: "When we were down at the B1 level, one of the firefighters said, "I think you'd be interested in this," and they pulled up a big block of concrete and there was a, like a little river of steel, flowing."[78]

- Ron Burger, a public health advisor at the National Center for Environmental Health who arrived at Ground Zero September 12, 2001, said, "Feeling the heat, seeing the molten steel, the layers upon layers of ash, like lava, it reminded me of Mount St. Helens and the thousands who fled that disaster."[79]

- In late fall 2001, Dr. Alison Geyh of the Johns Hopkins School of Public Health reported: "Fires are still actively burning and the smoke is very intense. In some pockets now being uncovered, they are finding molten steel."[80]

- Joe Allbaugh, the director of FEMA, said in an October 2001 interview on CBS: "It's just too hot for rescuers to get into [some] areas. So we do not know yet what's in those areas, other than very hot, molten material."[81]

- Dr. Keith Eaton reported in *Structural Engineer*: "They showed us many fascinating slides . . . ranging from molten metal which was still red hot weeks after the event, to 4-inch thick steel plates sheared and bent in the disaster."

- Don Carson, a hazardous-materials expert from the National Operating Engineers Union, said six weeks after 9/11, "There are pieces of steel being pulled out from as far as six stories underground that are still cherry red."[82]

II-B. Testimony from Other Credible Witnesses

- Greg Fuchek, vice president of a company that supplied computer equipment used to identify human remains, reported that "sometimes when a worker would pull a steel beam from the wreckage, the end of the beam would be dripping molten steel."[83]

- Sarah Atlas, of New Jersey Task Force One Urban Search & Rescue, arrived at Ground Zero on September 11 and it was reported that "fires burned and molten steel flowed in the pile of ruins still settling beneath her feet."[84]

- Tom Arterburn, writing in *Waste Age*, reported that the New York Department of Sanitation removed "everything from molten steel beams to human remains."[85]

Rebuttal of Official Claims: Summary

1. Three scientific reports, one from a government agency (USGS), strongly refute the claim that no evidence of any molten steel or iron was found in any of the WTC buildings.

2. John Gross's claim that "no eyewitnesses said" there was molten steel (or iron) was strongly and repeatedly contradicted.

3. As for the claim that molten steel or iron would be irrelevant because it could have been produced in the combustion pile: This would mean claiming, with no scientific evidence and no plausibility, that combustion in an oxygen-starved pile of rubbish could have heated steel to at least 1500°C (2800° F).

4. With regard to the NIST claim that molten steel or iron is "irrelevant to the investigation of the collapse" because "it does not provide any conclusive information on the condition of the steel when the WTC towers [including WTC 7] were standing": Given the fact that the molten steel or iron in the debris could not have been produced without incendiaries or explosives, the presence of molten forms of either of these metals indicates that some of the steel was melted before, or during, the final moments of the collapses.

5. With regard to NIST's statement in its post-report publication that there was no evidence for "the melting of steel in a jet-fuel ignited fire in the towers": This statement is truly irrelevant. The presence of melted steel and/or iron is a clear indication that the buildings must have been brought down by something other than fire.

Conclusion

None of the official claims about the nonexistence of molten iron or steel in the destroyed WTC buildings withstand scrutiny. The fact that the rubble contained steel or iron that had been melted shows that the buildings were destroyed by something other than fire and airplane impact. Especially dramatic evidence was provided by several facts: that the original RJ Lee report showed that there was almost 150 times more iron in the dust than normal; that the rubble contained steel with gaping holes, manifesting a "Swiss cheese appearance" that shocked the three "fire-wise professors" from Worcester Polytechnic Institute; that lead had been vaporized; that molybdenum had been melted; and that the metal pools contained iron that had been heated, as shown by the orange color, above 2,000°C (3,632°F).

 When all of this physical evidence is combined with the

testimony about explosions from many types of professionals, the claim that the Twin Towers were brought down by nothing other than the airplane impacts and resulting fires is simply not credible.

The Claim That the World Trade Center Dust Contained No Thermitic Materials

The Official Account

Having conducted an experiment to test the idea that explosives or incendiaries (such as thermite) might have been used to bring WTC buildings down,[86] NIST "found no evidence of any blast events."[87]

The Best Evidence

The "experiment" NIST claimed to have performed was only a hypothetical experiment,[88] so it cannot refute actual evidence at the site for any explosives and/or incendiaries. Unreacted nano-thermite was found in four independently collected samples of the WTC dust.[89] These discoveries were reported in a multi-author paper in a peer-reviewed journal.[90] Energetic nano-materials "can be tailored[91] to behave as an incendiary (like ordinary thermite), as a propellant, or as an explosive."[92]

Conclusion

The official account, according to which the buildings could not have been brought down by nano-thermite, is contradicted by evidence found in WTC dust gathered from four sites.

8

The Claim That the Detected Seismic Waves Were Caused by the Airplane Attacks and the Collapses of the Twin Towers

Introduction

Seismic waves were detected at seismograph stations in New York and four neighboring states on September 11, 2001, during the period when WTC 1 and 2 (the North and South Towers) were struck by airliners and collapsed. Scientists at the Lamont-Doherty Earth Observatory (LDEO) at Columbia University published analyses of the seismographic data from the WTC, based on raw data from the Palisades, NY, station. The Federal Emergency Management Agency (FEMA) and the National Institute of Standards and Technology (NIST) relied upon the LDEO analysis in their publications on the events at the World Trade Center.[93] *The 9/11 Commission Report* also cited the LDEO analysis,[94] although it did not confirm LDEO's analysis of plane-impact times, basing its own conclusions on ground radar data instead of seismic wave data.

But independent analyses have disputed LDEO's conclusions and thereby the conclusions reached by FEMA and NIST. These independent analyses cast even further doubt upon the conclusions of the 9/11 Commission.

The Official Account

The seismic waves were caused by the airplane impacts into the Twin Towers and the resulting collapses of the buildings.[95] The magnitudes of the airplane impact shocks at WTC 2 and WTC 1, respectively, were 0.7 and 0.9. The collapse of WTC 2 caused a shock of magnitude 2.1; the collapse of WTC 1 caused a shock of magnitude 2.3.[96] The signals were used to determine accurately when the plane impacts and collapses occurred.[97]

The Best Evidence

The results of independent research conflict with the conclusions by LDEO (Lamont-Doherty Earth Observatory) that the waves were caused by airplane impacts and resulting building collapses.

In 2006, engineers Craig Furlong and Gordon Ross showed that the plane impacts could not have caused the seismic signals attributed to them by LDEO because they originated several seconds *before* the 9/11 Commission's radar-based times of impact.

The seismic events, therefore, must have resulted from different causes. The best (and probably only plausible) explanation for these causes would seem to be explosions in the basements of the Twin Towers, for which there is abundant physical and testimonial evidence.[98] (See the physical and testimonial evidence in Chapter 9.)

The conclusion of Furlong and Ross—that seismic evidence does not fit the official story (in any of its versions)—was reinforced in 2012 by a French geophysicist, Dr. André Rousseau, who reanalyzed the seismic wave data.[99] Rousseau concluded that the LDEO report is flawed in three significant respects:

- The radar-based timing of the airplane impacts does not match the origin-times of the seismic waves (as indicated by the data).

- The lack of explanation of why, although the two towers were destroyed in essentially the same way, the data show large differences between them in terms of released energy.

- The frequencies of the waves are much too low to have been caused by plane impacts and building collapses (although they match those of underground explosions, evidence for which is documented in Chapter 9).

The Timing of the Wave Origins: LDEO in 2001 published a report giving the times at which four wave signals began.[100] It correlated these times with the two airplane impacts and the two collapses. The LDEO researchers stated that these times were derived by calculation from the times the signals were received at the Palisades station. *The 9/11 Commission Report*, however, published very different impact times, based on ground radar data, which tracked the airplanes' approaches to, and collisions with, the buildings. The differences are greatest with regard to WTC 1 (which was hit first): Rousseau, like Furlong and Ross, pointed out that the radar-based times, being approximately 15 seconds later than the times that could be plausibly inferred from the Palisades data, do not support the correlation of the seismic waveforms with the plane impacts.[101]

Event Magnitudes: "[I]t is strange that identical events . . . at the same location," said Rousseau, "would have generated seismic sources of different magnitudes."[102] This discrepancy occurred both for the plane impacts and the building collapses. For the two waves attributed by LDEO to the impacts, the magnitudes of the signals[103] are different (0.9 for WTC 1, 0.7 for WTC 2), despite the similarity of the two plane crashes into the virtually identical buildings. The signals assigned to the collapses of the Twin Towers also display significant differences (magnitudes 2.1 for WTC 2 and 2.3 for WTC 1), again despite the similarity of the events resulting in the disintegrations of the two essentially identical buildings. Although the difference between 2.1 and 2.3 might seem minor, the unique (logarithmic) way in which seismic events are measured means that a shock that registers a magnitude of 2.3 releases *twice* as much energy as a magnitude 2.1 event, so the discrepancy is too large to have been due to an error.[104] Rousseau concluded that the waves had to have been caused by something else (which, given the evidence provided in Chapter 9, points to explosives).[105]

Wave Frequencies: The frequencies of waves caused by plane impacts, reported Rousseau, are typically much greater—one to two orders of magnitude higher—than the frequencies of the waves that were, according to LDEO, caused by the plane impacts into WTC 1 and 2. That is, the frequencies of waves typically caused by plane impacts range from (roughly) 10 to 100 Hertz (Hz), whereas the waves that were said by LDEO to be caused by the plane strikes are on the order of only 1Hz. The idea that the seismic waves in question were caused by plane impacts was, therefore, highly unlikely. Furthermore, the recording equipment at Palisades had a range of only 0.6-5Hz, so it was incapable of recording waves generated by typical plane impacts.[106]

Conclusion

The discrepancies described above indicate that the LDEO conclusions about the nature of the events that generated the signals recorded at Palisades cannot be correct. Most strikingly, the ground radar data, which are very precise, showed WTC 1 to have been struck fifteen seconds *later* than the Palisades-recorded seismic activity, which LDEO scientists attributed to an airplane impact. The radar also shows WTC 2 to have been struck later than the seismic activity attributed to it. The seismic activity, therefore, must have been produced by something other than the crashes of the airliners into the two buildings.

Rousseau, like Furlong and Ross, provided reasons to conclude that the signals attributed to airplane impacts in the official story had actually been caused by something else, which, as evidence documented in Chapter 9 suggests, was shocks, explosive in nature, that had occurred at the bases of the buildings. Rousseau further demonstrated that the wave details were characteristic of such explosions, not of plane impacts or building collapses.

9

The Denial of the Existence of Physical and Testimonial Evidence That the Towers Were Brought Down by Controlled Demolition

Introduction

According to the various official versions of the destruction of the Twin Towers, the buildings were brought down by the impact of the airplanes and the resulting fires. But independent evidence—both physical and testimonial—challenges this conclusion.

The Official Account

The Twin Towers collapsed solely because of the impact of the airliners and the resulting fires. This conclusion was first reached by the Federal Emergency Management Agency (FEMA) report of 2002.[107] It was reaffirmed by *The 9/11 Commission Report* of 2004.[108]

And it was then confirmed by the most extensive report, which was issued in 2005 by the National Institute of Standards and Technology (NIST),[109] which later added, "NIST found no corroborating evidence for alternative hypotheses suggesting that the WTC towers were brought down by controlled demolition." In particular, NIST said, "there was no evidence . . . of any blast or explosions in the region below the impact and fire floors." (This qualification was important, because there could have been explosions caused by fires on floors where they were burning.)[110]

The Best Evidence

A combination of testimonial and physical evidence shows the official story—in any of its versions—to be false. Mark Loizeaux, the head of Controlled Demolition, Inc., has said, "If I were to bring the towers down, I would put explosives in the basement to get the weight of the building to help collapse the structure."[111]

A combination of testimonial and physical evidence suggests that this was what happened.

Testimonial Evidence

Many firefighters and others reported explosions below the impact and fire floors. For example:

- Genelle Guzman, the last survivor to be rescued from the WTC 1 rubble, reports that when she got down to the 13th floor, some 20 minutes before the North Tower collapsed, she heard a "big explosion" and "[t]he wall I was facing just opened up, and it threw me on the other side."

- Firefighter Edward Cachi said: "As my officer and I were looking at the South Tower, it just gave. It actually gave at a lower floor, not the floor where the plane hit. . . . [I]t went in succession, boom, boom, boom, boom, and then the tower came down."[112]

- Firefighter Kenneth Rogers said: "[T]here was an explosion in the South Tower [WTC 2]. . . . Floor after floor after floor. One floor under another after another, and when it hit about the fifth floor, I figured it was a bomb, because it looked like a synchronized, deliberate kind of thing."[113]

- Stephen Evans, a New York-based correspondent for the BBC, said: "I was at the base of the second tower . . . that was hit. . . . There was an explosion. . . . The base of the building shook. . . . [T]hen there was a series of explosions."[114]

- Firefighter Louie Cacchioli reported that upon entering the lobby of the WTC's North Tower, he saw elevator doors completely blown out. "I remember thinking," he said, "how could this be happening so quickly if a plane hit way above?" When he reached the twenty-fourth floor, he encountered heavy dust and smoke, which he found puzzling in light of the fact that the plane had struck the building over fifty stories higher.[115]

There were also reports of explosions in the buildings' basements. For example:

- William Rodriguez, a janitor, reported that he and fourteen others in the North Tower heard and felt an explosion below the first sub-level office before the aircraft impact. He said the floor beneath his feet vibrated and "everything started shaking." Seconds later, he added, "I hear another explosion from way above. . . . Although I was unaware at the time, this was the airplane hitting the tower." In any case, he said, coworker Felipe David, who had been in front of a nearby freight elevator, came into the office with severe burns on his face and arms yelling, "Explosion! Explosion! Explosion!"[116]

- Rodriguez's account was corroborated by José Sanchez, who was in the workshop on the fourth sub-level. Sanchez said that he and a coworker heard a big blast that "sounded like a bomb," after which "a huge ball of fire went through the freight elevator."[117]

- Engineer Mike Pecoraro, who was working in the North Tower's sixth sub-basement, said that after an explosion he and a coworker went up to the C level, where there was a small machine shop. "There was nothing there but rubble," said Pecoraro. "We're talking about a 50-ton hydraulic press—gone!" They then went to the parking garage, but found that it was also gone. Then, on the B level, they found that a steel-and-concrete fire door, which weighed about 300 pounds, was wrinkled up "like a piece of aluminum foil."[118]

Moreover, if there were explosions in the basements of the towers before they came down, we would expect them to have caused the ground to shake. And several people did, in fact, report shaking.

- Medical technician Lonnie Penn said that just before the collapse of the South Tower, "I felt the ground shake, I turned around and ran for my life. I made it as far as the Financial Center when the collapse happened."[119]

- Fire patrolman Paul Curran said he was standing near the North Tower when, "all of a sudden the ground just started shaking. It felt like a train was running under my feet. . . . The next thing we know, we look up and the tower is collapsing."[120]

- Lieutenant Bradley Mann of the Fire Department saw both buildings come down. "Shortly before the first tower came down," he said, "I remember feeling the ground shaking. I heard a terrible noise, and then debris just started flying everywhere. People started running." After they returned to the area, he said, "we basically had the same thing: The ground shook again, and we heard another terrible noise and the next thing we knew the second tower was coming down."[121]

Physical Evidence

In addition to the testimonial evidence about explosions in the towers, there was physical evidence provided by the nature of the collapses that involved features generally consistent only with intentional collapses brought about via controlled demolition. For example:

- **Sudden Onset:** In controlled demolition, the onset of the collapse is sudden: One moment, the building is perfectly motionless; the next moment, it suddenly starts coming down. But when steel is heated, it does not suddenly buckle or break, but bends and sags. So if heat could induce a collapse, the onset would be gradual. But, as videos show, the buildings were perfectly motionless up to the moment they began their collapse.[122]

- **Straight Down:** The most important thing in a controlled demolition of a tall building that's close to other buildings is that it comes straight down. Mark Loizeaux of Controlled Demolition, Inc., has said that careful planning is needed in setting the charges "to bring [a building] down as we want, so . . . no other structure is harmed."[123] If the 110-story Twin Towers had fallen over, rather than coming straight down, they would have caused an enormous amount of damage to buildings covering many city blocks; but they did not.[124]

- **Rapid Constant Acceleration:** Measurements show that when the North Tower collapsed, it accelerated constantly at approximately two-thirds the rate of gravity.[125] Such acceleration is incompatible with the official explanation of the building collapse. The official explanation of the collapse of each of the towers claims that the top part of the building, above where the planes struck, came down on the structure below and initiated total collapse. If that were what happened, the lower stories would have provided significant resistance and a deceleration of the top section would have been observed, had there been an impact. As videos show, and as careful measurements of the motion of the top section confirm, the upper stories of the building fell down through the lower stories with a high rate of constant acceleration and no associated deceleration or impact. This means that the official explanation is false.[126] It is clear that most of the columns of the lower stories must have been destroyed by some force other than gravity, such as explosive force, so that when the upper stories came down they encountered little resistance. This analysis has been validated by measurements of the Verinage technique of building demolition, which actually uses the momentum and kinetic energy of a falling upper section to break up the lower section without the use of explosives. In those cases, deceleration of the top section is clearly observed.[127] A further analysis showing that the columns of the North Tower could not have been involved in resisting the collapse was published in June 2013.[128]

- **Total Collapse:** These 110-story buildings collapsed into piles of rubble only a few stories high, even though the core of each tower contained 47 steel box columns, which in the lower floors were massive.[129]

- **Pulverization and Dust Clouds:** "At the World Trade Center sites," said Colonel John O'Dowd of the US

Army Corps of Engineers, "it seemed like everything [except the steel] was pulverized."[130] Although this was an exaggeration, much of the non-metallic contents of the buildings were indeed pulverized into tiny particles of dust, giving rise to enormous dust clouds, which impeded visibility of the buildings for a half hour after each collapse—even though, according to the official theory, the only physical forces involved, after the impact of the airplanes, were gravitational acceleration and fire.[131]

In disputing the view that the destruction of the towers was the result of controlled demolition, NIST said, "Video evidence . . . showed unambiguously that the collapse progressed from the top to the bottom."[132] NIST's implicit argument was based on two presuppositions: (1) Controlled demolition must begin from the bottom. (2) The collapses of the Twin Towers began at the top. However, both of these presuppositions are false.

(1) As the first statement by Mark Loizeaux quoted above indicates, controlled demolition usually begins from the bottom. However, as physicist Steven Jones has pointed out, the top-down destruction of the towers "is unusual for controlled demolition, but clearly possible, depending on the order in which explosives are detonated."[133] Conversely, a natural gravitational top-down collapse replicating the observed phenomena is impossible.

(2) Although the collapses *appeared*, to people watching them on TV, to have begun with the impacts and resulting fires, they mostly began, as testimonies above indicate, with explosions in the basements. It is also notable that they initiated just above the impact damage.

Seismic Evidence

Seismic waves provide one more type of evidence that the buildings were brought down by explosions below ground when the planes struck. The previous chapter explored that issue.

Conclusion

Defending its claim that the Twin Towers were brought down solely by the plane impacts and the resulting fires, NIST argued that there was no evidence that they were brought down by controlled demolition and that, in particular, no explosions occurred below the floors on which fires burned. However:

- Multiple witnesses reported hearing explosions below the fire floors, including massive explosions in the basements, and others reported that the ground was shaking outside.

- In addition to this testimonial evidence, the collapses exemplified various features characteristic of controlled demolitions that could not plausibly be explained in any other way.

- One more type of physical evidence, provided by seismic graphs, was discussed in Chapter 8.

It can safely be concluded, therefore, that the position presented by FEMA, the 9/11 Commission, and NIST—that there is no evidence of explosions in the Twin Towers before their collapses occurred—is indefensible.

II.

THE DESTRUCTION OF WTC 7

Introduction

World Trade Center 7 was a forty-seven-story steel-framed building that was like the Twin Towers in two fundamental ways: First, all three buildings came down on 9/11 (although unlike the Twin Towers, which came down in the morning, WTC 7 did not come down until late in the afternoon). Second, the three buildings shared the distinction, according to the official account, of being the first steel-framed buildings to have collapsed without explosives.

But there were also crucial differences among the building collapses. First, WTC 7, unlike the Twin Towers, was not hit by an airplane.

Second, the buildings were treated very differently by the government and the press. The airplane strikes on the Twin Towers and their subsequent collapses were shown by the television networks over and over again. But after 9/11 itself, the destruction of WTC 7 was seldom if ever shown on TV. Moreover, *The 9/11 Commission Report*, which appeared in 2004, did not even mention WTC 7. This treatment by the networks and the government evidently prevented many people from knowing about this third collapse: A Zogby poll in May 2006 found that 43 percent of the American people were still unaware that WTC 7 had come down.[134]

The treatment of the buildings by the National Institute of Standards and Technology (NIST) constitutes a third difference. NIST announced in 2002 that it would issue reports on both the Twin Towers and WTC 7 in 2004. It did finally release its report on the Twin Towers in 2005, but NIST's report on WTC 7 was very slow in coming. Months after NIST issued a preliminary report on this building, in 2005,[135] it announced that the final WTC 7 report would be delayed until 2006. In 2006, however, NIST said: "It is anticipated that a draft report will be released by early 2007."[136]

But it was 2008 before the draft and final reports on WTC 7 were released.[137]

It would appear that the answer to these two questions—why the Twin Towers and WTC 7 were treated so differently by the government and the media, and why it took NIST so much longer to issue a report on WTC 7—is the same. The fact that the Twin Towers were hit by airplanes provided an explanation for their collapses that was plausible to people who knew nothing about steel-framed buildings and controlled demolition.

By contrast, the fact that WTC 7 was not struck by a plane left officials without any seemingly obvious reason for its destruction. In November 2001, James Glanz of the *New York Times* wrote, "[W]ithin the structural engineering community, [WTC 7] is considered to be much more important to understand [than the Twin Towers]," because engineers had no answer to the question, "Why did 7 come down?"[138]

This was a very good question, given NIST's assertion that explosives were not used. And there was no good answer to this question. In fact, many people consider NIST's explanation of the destruction of WTC 7 one of its weakest explanations. One of these people is former NIST employee Peter Ketcham, whose criticism of NIST's report was discussed in the introduction to the section on the Twin Towers. Right after stating that "NIST had reached a predetermined conclusion by ignoring, dismissing, and denying the evidence," Ketcham said:

> Among the most egregious examples is the explanation for the collapse of WTC 7 as an elaborate sequence of unlikely events culminating in the almost symmetrical total collapse of a steel-frame building into its own footprint at free-fall acceleration.[139]

10

The Claim That WTC 7 Collapsed from Fire Alone

The Official Account

NIST originally suggested that World Trade Center 7 (WTC 7) was brought down by structural damage combined with a raging fire fed by diesel fuel.[140] However, in its *Final Report* (of November 2008), NIST declared that neither diesel fuel nor structural damage played a role in this building's collapse, and that this building, which was not struck by a plane, was brought down by fire alone.[141]

The Best Evidence

Before or after 9/11, no steel-frame high-rise building had ever collapsed due to fire.[142] If fire were to cause such a building to collapse, the onset would be gradual, whereas the videos show that WTC 7, after being completely stable, suddenly came down in virtual free fall. This building's straight-down, symmetrical collapse, with the roofline remaining essentially horizontal, shows that all eighty-two of WTC 7's support columns had been eliminated by the time the top started down.

Conclusion

In addition to the fact that fire had never brought down a steel-framed building, the official account is also refuted by the facts about the destruction of WTC 7.

11

The Claim in NIST's Draft Report That WTC 7 Did Not Come Down in Free Fall

The Official Account

Having denied for years that WTC 7 came down at free fall acceleration, NIST repeated this position in August 2008, when it issued a report on WTC 7 in the form of a *Draft for Public Comment*.[143] Shyam Sunder, the head of NIST's WTC project, said—speaking within the framework of its claim that the building was brought down by fire—that free fall would have been physically impossible.[144]

The Best Evidence

Scientific analysis[145] by mathematician David Chandler shows that WTC 7 came down in absolute free fall for a period of about 2.25 seconds. NIST's *Draft for Public Comment* had been challenged by Chandler and physicist Steven Jones in a public review, and NIST then re-analyzed the fall of WTC 7.

In its *Final Report*, NIST provided a detailed analysis and graph that conceded that WTC 7 came down at free-fall acceleration for over 100 feet, or about 2.25 seconds, consistent with the findings of Chandler and Jones.[146]

Conclusion

Challenged in public by physical evidence, NIST admitted that its first account was false.

12

The Claim in NIST's Final Report That WTC 7 Came Down in Free Fall Without Explosives

The Official Account

In its *Final Report* on WTC 7, issued in November 2008, NIST finally acknowledged that WTC 7 had entered into free fall for more than two seconds. NIST continued to say, however, that WTC 7 was brought down by fire, with no aid from explosives.[147]

The Best Evidence

Scientific analysis[148] shows that a free-fall collapse of a steel-framed building could not be produced by fire, that is, without explosives—a fact that NIST's lead investigator, Shyam Sunder, acknowledged in his discussions of NIST's *Draft Report for Public Comment* in August 2008.[149]

Conclusion

After having argued that WTC 7 could not have come down in free fall without explosives, NIST's Shyam Sunder ended up admitting that it did come down in free fall for over two seconds, but still insisted that no explosives were involved. In doing so, he contradicted his earlier statement, with no explanation of how what had previously been deemed impossible had become fact.

13

The Assumption That NIST's Computer Simulation of the Fall of WTC 7 Matched the Observed Collapse

Introduction

The sudden fall of WTC 7, a massive forty-seven-story steel-framed building two blocks from the Twin Towers, has been a troublesome issue for the official narrative. The imminent demise of the building was predicted repeatedly during the afternoon of September 11. Police and firefighters cleared a radius of several blocks, and people, including several reporters, were told that this was "the building that would come down next"[150]—even though no steel structure had ever collapsed due to fire prior to 9/11. Hundreds of people witnessed the event and documented it with cameras.

At about 5:20 PM, the East Penthouse of WTC 7 collapsed into the building, accompanied by window breakage on multiple floors.[151] A few seconds later, the West Penthouse began to collapse into the building, but before it disappeared the entire building underwent a sudden transition to free fall, which lasted for over two seconds.[152]

In its initial report on the building collapses, the National Institute of Standards and Technology (NIST) discussed only the Twin Towers, omitting WTC 7. A separate report on this building was repeatedly delayed because, in the words of project director Shyam Sunder, "We've had trouble getting a handle on building No. 7."[153] NIST released its *Final Report on the Collapse of World Trade Center Building 7* in November 2008 (when the Bush administration was in the midst of leaving office). NIST offered a computer-generated graphical simulation in a final attempt to explain the collapse.

The Official Account

WTC 7 collapsed because of fire alone.[154] Here are the central features of the collapse:

- Intense heating on the twelfth floor caused an overhead

beam to lengthen, due to thermal expansion, and to push a thirteenth-floor girder off the seat that had connected it to interior column 79.

- This failure propagated for several floors, leaving column 79 unsupported, thereby causing it to buckle. Nearby columns were unable to absorb the transfer of load. This inability initiated a progressive collapse, which led to catastrophic failure of the entire building.

- Computer simulations are provided to support this account of the building's collapse.

- The mechanism behind the collapse is supported by graphical output, which is included in the NIST *Final Report*[155] and explained by animations posted on the NIST website.[156]

The Best Evidence

1. A building undergoing progressive collapse would come down in a sequential manner. Sections would be expected to fail as they lost support. However, from measurements of the collapse time, the collapse could not have been progressive or sequential:

- From the time of the collapse of the East Penthouse to the onset of global collapse, the building appeared, from all external signs, to retain its overall integrity. The transition from total support to free fall was sudden. The building fell with a horizontal roofline, implying that catastrophic failure across the entire width of the building (100 meters east to west) occurred virtually simultaneously, within a fraction of a second.[157]

- The building buckled horizontally near the middle about 1.5 seconds prior to the onset of free fall, but this was not accompanied by downward motion. The building retained its full height until the onset of global collapse. The initial downward motion, measured at the northwest corner of the building, was a sudden transition to free fall.

2. In addition to the fact that the collapse of a steel-framed building entering into free fall in the absence of explosives to remove the steel supports is inherently implausible, the graphical output from NIST's computer simulations does not match the actual observations at all. The two cases presented in NIST's *Final Report* represent two, very different, scenarios:

- In one of these, damage caused by debris from the North Tower collapse was a contributing factor.

- In the other, no mention is made of debris-caused damage.

The scenario that included debris-caused damage to the south face of WTC 7 somewhat resembled the observed fall, but NIST concluded that debris-caused damage was not a significant factor in the collapse. Even on casual inspection, it is clear that the simulation does not account for the following observations:

- The simulated building shows marked deformations that would be easily detectable from exterior views.[158] These were not observed.

- The actual building did not even undergo window breakage during the interval leading up to the free fall collapse, whereas window breakage was quite conspicuous during the much smaller local collapse under the East Penthouse. If, as NIST reported, the interior collapse of the majority of the building had been actually occurring, one would expect window breakage to be at least as evident as what was observed in the smaller collapse event.

- When the simulated building starts to collapse, it does not enter free fall, whereas free fall is the most notable aspect of the actual collapse and the feature most in need of explanation.

- The animation depicting the collapse of the simulated building is cut short. It does not cover the entire period of observed free fall.

Therefore, NIST cannot justify its claim that free fall was consistent with its sequential collapse model. In fact, free fall is not consistent with any collapse model that does not involve the sudden removal of all supports across the entire width of the building.

3. In statements following the release of NIST's *Final Report*, project director Shyam Sunder still failed to come to terms with the reality of the observed period of free fall. His claim, presumably speaking for NIST, was that we are not seeing the actual collapse, but only the north facade of the building. According to this explanation, the interior collapsed first (in progressive collapse, as described by NIST's model), leaving the facade to free-fall as a separate event. This explanation does not pass scrutiny, however, for four reasons:

- Video footage shows the north and west faces of the building, along with the corners connecting to its south and east faces, appearing stable and intact until the sudden onset of free fall.

- The West Penthouse, and therefore the interior structure supporting it, did not fail until about a second before the onset of free fall. Therefore the interior of the building got no more than about a half-story head start.[159]

- Even though the smaller collapse of the East Penthouse brought about a brief period of window breakage, no further windows were broken until the onset of free fall, so it is not believable that total internal collapse was occurring.

- The roiling clouds of debris that raced down the street, often likened by professionals to pyroclastic flow, did not occur until the visible collapse of the building. If the interior of the building had collapsed earlier, the flow of debris would have started earlier as well.

Conclusion

We can conclude that the computer simulations do not correlate to the key features of the building collapse. NIST's attempt to "decouple" developments in the unseen interior of the building from what happened to its easily observable exterior is, therefore, contrary to evidence. NIST's position appears to be no more than an attempt to evade legitimate questions. This conclusion is reinforced by NIST's refusal to release its computer models, combined with the fact that progressive collapse resulting in free fall could never be replicated experimentally—for the simple reason that a progressive collapse involving free fall is physically impossible.

14

The Assumption That NIST's Analysis of the Collapse Initiation of WTC 7 Is Valid

Introduction

In its reports on WTC 7, the National Institute of Standards and Technology, or NIST, claimed that, for the first time in history, fire caused the complete collapse of a large, fire-protected, steel-framed building. In 2008, NIST published analyses purporting to show that fire-induced thermal expansion caused the collapse-initiation of the building.[160]

The reliability of the NIST analyses would obviously depend upon the inclusion of all structural features pertinent to the collapse-initiation. Information relevant to this issue came to light in late 2013.

The Official Account

NIST's WTC 7 report shows that girder A2001—which was in the northeast corner of the building, under the thirteenth floor and situated between column 44 and column 79—was pushed off its seat at column 79 by beams framing into it from the east due to thermal expansion of the beams caused by the raging fires produced by burning office materials.

This failure caused the large area supported by girder A2001 to collapse down eight stories, to the fifth floor, leaving column 79 laterally unsupported for nine stories, which caused it to buckle.

This single-column failure then caused a complete north-to-south interior collapse, which in turn precipitated a complete east-to-west interior collapse, ultimately leaving the exterior columns laterally unsupported and causing all of them to buckle nearly simultaneously.

The Best Evidence

When NIST issued its WTC 7 report in November 2008, the structural drawings for the building were inexplicably missing. Accordingly, the report could not be scrutinized from a structural standpoint.

A Freedom of Information Act (FOIA) request was successful in obtaining the release of a large number of the drawings in late 2011.[161] Review of the released WTC 7 drawings showed that there were two serious structural-feature omissions from the NIST analyses relevant to the NIST "collapse initiation" theory. They were:

1. Steel plate stiffeners that provided critical support for girder A2001.[162]

2. Floor beams S3007, G3007, and K3007, which provided lateral support for beam G3005.[163]

Analyses performed by independent engineers show that when the stiffeners and lateral support beams are included, NIST's probable collapse sequence is impossible, because:

1. The girder flange for column 79 could not bend or fail with the stiffeners present.[164]

2. Beam G3005—which NIST claimed buckled from thermal expansion and led to the collapse of WTC 7—could not have buckled if G3005's omitted lateral support floor beams S3007, G3007, and K3007 were present.[165]

In December 2013, well-known attorney William F. Pepper,[166] serving as legal counsel for Architects and Engineers for 9/11 Truth, sent a letter to the US Commerce Department's inspector general, reporting these omissions. "It is the unanimous opinion of the structural engineers who have carefully studied this matter," said Pepper, "that an independent engineering enquiry would swiftly reach the same conclusion."[167]

Pepper added that his clients, after being ignored by NIST for nearly two years, finally got a response from a NIST public relations officer, who acknowledged that the stiffeners had been omitted. However, besides ignoring the omission of the lateral support beams, this PR officer said that the stiffeners did not need to be considered. Pepper said that his clients were in "disbelief and aghast" that NIST would omit these material features and, when the omissions were brought to NIST's attention, completely dismiss their critical importance.

Conclusion

NIST's claim that the collapse of WTC 7 was initiated when girder A2001 was pushed off its seat at column 79 is untenable. With the alleged initiating event ruled out, all of NIST's claims about subsequent structural failures must be considered baseless and invalid.

15

The Claim That No Steel Was Recovered from WTC 7

Introduction

The mysterious collapse of World Trade Center 7—a forty-seven-story steel-framed skyscraper adjacent to the Twin Towers that fell suddenly into its own footprint at 5:21 PM on September 11—was officially claimed to have resulted from fire alone.

Given the fact that all previous collapses of steel-framed buildings involved controlled demolitions using explosives, the unprecedented sudden collapse of WTC 7 should have precipitated an intensive investigation to determine exactly what happened, so that, if the collapse was indeed brought about by fire alone, such a disaster could be prevented from happening again.

A crucial element in such an investigation would be an examination of recovered steel from the collapse, to see if the quality of the steel had been inadequate, or whether, as some suspected, WTC 7 had been brought down with the use of explosives. It would also be crucial for the report of the investigation to be peer-reviewed.

The Official Account

No steel from WTC 7 was recovered from the collapse site, as NIST reports have repeatedly pointed out.[168] Just as there was no reference to recovered WTC 7 steel in NIST's *Final Report on the Collapse of World Trade Center Building 7* (2008),[169] no reference to recovered steel appears in *The 9/11 Commission Report* (2004).[170]

Because no steel from WTC 7 was recovered, it was impossible to carry out any metallography.[171] Accordingly, it was impossible for NIST to make any statements about the quality of WTC 7's steel in its investigations.[172] NIST has been able to describe the steel only on the basis of construction-related documents.[173]

The Best Evidence

I. There is ample physical evidence refuting NIST's claim that no steel was recovered from WTC 7:

1. Early evidence of WTC 7 steel recovery was reported in a 2001 letter to *JOM*[174] written by three professors from the Worcester Polytechnic Institute, titled "An Initial Microstructural Analysis of A36 Steel WTC Building 7."[175]

2. In 2002, FEMA (the Federal Emergency Management Agency) published a report by the same professors describing the strange thinning and corrosion of World Trade Center steel. Sample 1 was a beam that "appeared to be from WTC7," although "the exact location of this beam in the building was not known."[176] When asked about this, a senior communications officer for NIST said, "It was not possible to conclusively link" that steel sample to WTC 7.[177] But a statement like this from a communications officer cannot effectively cast doubt on the evaluation of three scientists.

3. That the steel appeared to have come from WTC 7 was confirmed by Professor Jonathan Barnett, lead author of the FEMA study, in a 2008 BBC documentary.[178]

4. Appendix D of the same FEMA report notes that "pieces that were searched for and inspected include...burnt pieces from WTC 7" and a photo of a "WTC 7 W14 column tree with beams attached to two floors." Another photo showed a "seat connection in fire-damaged W 14 column."[179]

5. It is clear from a 2005 damage study that NIST knew about the FEMA report, for it referred to "the steel from WTC7 (Sample 1 of Appendix C, FEMA/BPAT study)."[180]

6. In 2012, a Freedom of Information Act (FOIA) request by researcher David Cole produced several photographs of John Gross examining the WTC 7 steel in a scrapyard. Gross was the co-project leader on NIST's Structural Fire Response and Collapse Analysis.[181]

FIG 1: *John Gross examining Swiss cheese–appearing steel from WTC 7* [182]

He had responsibility to "determine and analyze the mechanical and metallurgical properties and quality of
steel, weldments, and connections from steel recovered
from WTC 1, 2, and 7."[183]

II. The examination of steel from WTC 7 was also covered in various news stories, including two from the *New York Times* and one
from Worcester Polytechnic Institute:

1. A *New York Times* article of November 2001 cited Dr.
   Jonathan Barnett of Worcester Polytechnic Institute as
   speaking about "steel members in the [WTC7] debris
   pile that appear to have been partly evaporated in
   extraordinarily high temperatures."[184] (The presence of
   inexplicably intense heat is corroborated in Chapter 6,
   "The Claim That There Was No Molten Steel or Iron in
   the WTC Debris.")

2. A 2002 *New York Times* story noted: "Perhaps the deepest
   mystery uncovered in the investigation involves extremely thin bits of steel collected from the trade towers and

from 7 World Trade Center, a 47-story high-rise that also collapsed for unknown reasons. The steel apparently melted away, but no fire in any of the buildings was believed to be hot enough to melt steel outright."[185]

3. A story in the official publication of the Worcester Polytechnic Institute stated: "A one inch [steel] column has been reduced to half-inch thickness. Its edges— which are curled like a paper scroll—have been thinned to almost razor sharpness. Gaping holes—some larger than a silver dollar—let light shine through a formerly solid steel flange. This Swiss cheese appearance shocked all of the fire-wise professors, who expected to see distortion and bending—but not holes."[186]

Conclusion

An abundance of evidence shows that NIST's claim—that no steel from WTC 7 was found—is false. By denying this evidence (which was even cited in one of NIST's own reports[187]), NIST could claim that there was no evidence that the building had been brought down by explosives.

By denying the availability of WTC 7 steel, moreover, NIST positioned itself to explain the collapse by resorting to a computer simulation into which variables could be inserted at will—given the fact that there was to be no peer review[188]—and which has been shown to be false.[189]

16

The Claim That Foreknowledge of WTC 7's Fall Was Based on Witness Observations

Introduction

On September 11, 2001, many people knew well before World Trade Center 7 collapsed that this forty-seven-story high-rise building was going to come down.[190] There were even two premature announcements of the collapse by major television networks. How can this foreknowledge be explained?

Advocates of the official narrative of the collapse of WTC 7 have proposed, at different times, two differing explanations—here called Account 1 and Account 2—which can both be called official accounts.

Account 1, the earlier explanation, was widely disseminated on the Internet and at one time received some support from the National Institute of Standards and Technology (NIST), thus making it a de facto official account.[191]

Account 2 is the current official account of the collapse, having been put forth in NIST's final (2008) report.[192]

The Official Accounts

Account 1: WTC 7 was critically damaged by flying debris from the collapsing WTC 1, which caused structural damage and fires in WTC 7. These fires were especially large and hot, being fed by diesel fuel stored in the building.[193] Seeing the structural damage and fires, fire chiefs and engineers concluded that WTC 7 was in danger of collapse. Concerns were therefore expressed and appropriate actions taken: firefighters were withdrawn from the building, and firefighters and others were told the building might come down. Accordingly, collapse predictions were rational responses to direct observation by witnesses.[194]

Account 2: The earlier explanation of WTC 7's collapse (Account 1) is incorrect. Impact damage from flying debris caused by WTC 1's collapse was insufficient to put WTC 7 at risk and did not play a significant role in its collapse.[195] And the fires were not intensified by diesel fuel stored in the building.[196]

WTC 7 came down primarily due to fire. This was the first time in history that a steel-framed high-rise had collapsed due to fire.[197] The fire triggered this collapse by means of a unique and unobserved sequence of events inside the building, including thermal expansion of floor systems, an unseated girder, and floor collapses, resulting in a cascade of column buckling.[198]

A single column failure had caused a complete north-to-south interior collapse, which in turn precipitated a complete east-to-west interior collapse, ultimately leaving the exterior columns laterally unsupported and causing all of them to buckle in a nearly simultaneous way.

Although the fires in WTC 7 were affecting the steel components of the building over a period of hours, the building did not actually become unstable, nor was its fate sealed, until minutes, or even seconds, before it began to come down.[199]

The Best Evidence

Neither Account 1 nor Account 2 fits the evidence.

Contrary to what is often implied by supporters of the official 9/11 narrative, witnesses who expected WTC 7 to come down evidently did not reach this conclusion because of anything they personally perceived but because of what they were *told*.[200]

What witnesses personally perceived most obviously cannot explain Account 2, which posits a sequence of last-minute events inside the building that was unprecedented, unpredictable, and invisible to witnesses.

But both accounts are contradicted by the facts that (1) some people were certain that the building was going to come down, that (2) some of them had this certainty early, and that (3) some of the major media gave premature announcements of the collapse of WTC 7.

1. On the issue of *certainty*, MSNBC reporter Ashleigh Banfield

said early in the afternoon: "I've heard several reports from several different officers now that that is the building that is going to go down next," with one of them saying "they're just waiting for that to come down at this point."[201] In fact, many members of the Fire Department of New York are on record as having been confidently waiting for the building to come down.[202] For example:

- Firefighter Thomas Donato said: "We were standing, waiting for seven to come down. We were there for quite a while, a couple hours."[203]

- Firefighter James Wallace said: "They were saying building seven was going to collapse, so we regrouped and went back to our rig. We went to building four or three; I don't know. We were going to set up our tower ladder there. They said no good because building seven is coming down. We waited for building seven to come down."[204]

- Assistant Commissioner James Drury said: "I must have lingered there. There were hundreds of firefighters waiting to—they were waiting for 7 World Trade Center to come down."[205]

- Chief Thomas McCarthy said: "So when I get to the command post, they just had a flood of guys standing there. They were just waiting for seven to come down."[206]

- Paramedic Steven Pilla said: "We walked back. We didn't do [sic] any further because building number seven was coming down. That was another problem, to wait for building seven to come down."[207]

The evidence that many witnesses were certain of collapse, which is solid,[208] cannot be explained either by Account 1 or by Account 2.

2. The existence of *early* knowledge is also well supported:

- Firefighter Vincent Massa, speaking of the firefighters waiting for WTC 7 to come down, has said: "The whole time while we were waiting—there were hours that went by."[209]

- Massa's estimate is confirmed by a wider study of the FDNY oral histories. The study found that of 60 firefighters who mention predictions about the collapse of WTC 7, the times of these predictions can be determined in 33 cases: in 17 cases the predictions occurred within the two hours before collapse, while in the other 16 cases the predictions were made more than two hours before collapse. In six cases the predictions were apparently made more than four hours before collapse.[210]

- Some reports indicate that the FDNY had been cleared from WTC 7 as early as 2 p.m. and had been told to abandon the building because it was doomed.[211] This forecast appears to have come from Mayor Giuliani's Office of Emergency Management.[212]

How could confident and valid collapse predictions have been made so far in advance? Account 2, the current official explanation, is especially incapable of answering this question, since the unique and fatal internal collapse sequence central to this explanation was not witnessed by anyone and took place right before collapse. In any case, since no steel-framed building had ever collapsed before without being imploded, there would have been no basis for such predictions.

3. The official accounts are also contradicted by *premature announcements* of the collapse of WTC 7 by CNN and the BBC.

- CNN announced the impending collapse of WTC 7 a full seventy minutes before it collapsed.[213] Directly after its premature announcement, and intermittently for the following hour, CNN displayed the caption, "Building 7 at World Trade Center on fire, may collapse." Then, four and a half minutes prior to the collapse, a new caption appeared: "Building #7 ablaze, poised to collapse." Finally, three minutes later there was another caption: "Building 7 at World Trade Center on fire, on verge of collapse." At no time during these seventy minutes could viewers see evidence of any alteration in WTC 7, such as increased fire, partial collapse, or even leaning.[214]

- BBC announced the collapse of WTC 7 twenty-three minutes prematurely, and even gave a version of Account 1 to explain why it collapsed.[215] This premature announcement, along with the explanation, was especially peculiar, given the fact that a steel-framed building had never before collapsed because of fire.

Conclusion

Neither Account 1 nor Account 2 of the collapse of WTC 7 can account for the certainty of many people on the scene that the building was going to collapse, the fact that some of them had this foreknowledge long in advance, and that two of the TV networks announced that the building had come down before the event took place. It would seem difficult to explain these facts unless one supposes that the information came from the people who intended to bring the building down.

This foreknowledge corroborates, therefore, the evidence and conclusions presented in previous chapters (see chapters 6, 10, 11, 12, 13, 14, and 15) that WTC 7 was brought down through a process of controlled demolition.

17

The Claim That a Massive Explosion in WTC 7 Reported by Michael Hess and Barry Jennings Was Caused by the North Tower Collapse

Introduction

The importance of this chapter is that two men occupying senior positions within the New York City administration reported a massive explosion deep inside WTC 7 on the morning of 9/11, which trapped them in a stairwell for ninety minutes. On September 11, 2001, Barry Jennings was the Deputy Director of the Emergency Services Department for the New York City Housing Authority. Michael Hess was the New York City Corporation Counsel.

After a plane hit the North Tower (WTC 1) at 8:46 AM, Jennings and Hess had each been summoned to a meeting in the Mayor's Office of Emergency Management (OEM) operations center on the twenty-third floor of WTC 7. They arrived at the OEM to find the office abandoned and left the building using the stairs. Both were trapped on the way down by a massive explosion that seemed to come from the basement.

Serious questions about the destruction of WTC 7 have been raised by the account of Barry Jennings.[216] If corroborated, it would challenge the official story of the WTC 7 collapse, according to which it was caused by fire and fire alone.

This account by Jennings and Hess would support evidence presented in the other chapters on WTC 7, suggesting that WTC 7 did not fall from fire alone but was brought down through demolition.

Background

While en route to work on 9/11, reported Jennings, he received an urgent phone call right after the North Tower was hit at 8:46 AM, telling him to report to the OEM. He arrived at WTC 7 about the time the South Tower (WTC 2) was hit at 9:03 AM, to find police in the lobby. Along with Michael Hess, who was looking for Mayor Giuliani, Jennings took the elevator to the twenty-third floor. Arriving, they found the OEM locked. They returned to the lobby, and were then escorted by a security guard to a freight elevator, which conveyed them back up to the OEM.

Jennings was amazed to find no one there. He saw half-eaten sandwiches and steaming coffee on the table. He then placed several phone calls to ask what he should do and was told by a superior to "get out of there; get out of there now."[217]

The elevators had stopped working, so he and Hess started down the stairs. When they reached the sixth floor there was a powerful explosion from below, which caused the landing on which they stood to give way. In darkness they were forced to climb back up to the eighth floor, where Jennings broke a window with a fire extinguisher. Hess called down through the window for help, and after a ninety-minute wait they were rescued by NYC firefighters.

At the time of the explosion, Jennings said, both towers were still standing. If true, this would place the explosion before 9:59 AM, when the South Tower began to collapse. Later, as Jennings was escorted out through the WTC 7 lobby, he found it destroyed beyond recognition.

In four key respects, Jennings's account of an explosion within WTC 7 contradicts NIST's account, according to which the seeming explosion was simply an effect of the North Tower collapsing at 10:28 AM.

1. *Jennings's time of arrival and the WTC 7 evacuation:*
    Although Jennings reported that he arrived at the empty OEM around the time that the second plane hit at 9:03 AM, the official account says that the men did not arrive at the OEM until just before the South Tower fell at 9:59 AM. (Hess made no public statement about the time they arrived.)

2. *Hess's report of an explosion:* Jennings's report of an explosion from below while they were in the stairwell was initially also reported by Hess, although he later changed his report.

3. *The destroyed WTC 7 lobby*: The destruction of the lobby reported by Jennings was omitted by NIST.

4. *Jennings's time of departure* from WTC 7 is important to confirming his arrival time, given that he and Hess said that they were trapped for about ninety minutes.[218]

Although the NIST investigation reported interviews with both men, FOIA requests for these interviews have been denied.[219] Evidence supporting Jennings's account must, therefore, be found elsewhere.

The Official Account

The 2005 NIST account related to Jennings and Hess, which was written in two paragraphs,[220] can be broken down into its series of claims:

1. When the first aircraft struck WTC 1 [8:46 AM], the electrical power went out for several seconds inside WTC 7.[221]

2. Many people immediately began leaving the building, and the OEM operations center began receiving calls related to the emergency.[222]

3. As the second aircraft struck WTC 2 [9:03 AM], a decision was made to evacuate WTC 7.[223] By the time WTC 2 was struck by the second aircraft at 9:03 AM many WTC 7 occupants had already left the building and others had begun a self-evacuation of the building.[224]

4. At 9:59 AM, WTC 2 collapsed, and debris from the collapse struck the south face of WTC 7.[225]

5. At 10:28 AM, WTC 1 collapsed, and a significant amount of damage was done to WTC 7.[226] A large amount of debris crashed through the front center of the building from approximately the tenth floor down to ground level, and debris ripped a part of the southwest corner off from approximately the eighth floor up to the eighteenth floor.[227]

6. The collapse of WTC 1 also appears to be responsible for starting fires inside of WTC 7.[228]

7. With the collapse of the two towers, a New York City employee and a WTC 7 building staff person became trapped inside.[229]

8. The two had gone to the OEM center on the twenty-third floor and found no one there. As they went to get into an elevator to go downstairs, the lights inside of WTC 7 flickered as WTC 2 collapsed. At this point, the elevator they were attempting to catch no longer worked, so they started down the staircase. When they got to the sixth floor, WTC 1 collapsed, the lights went out in the staircase, the sprinklers came on briefly, and the staircase filled with smoke and debris. The two men went back to the eighth floor, broke out a window, and called for help. Firefighters on the ground saw them and went up the stairs.[230]

9. In addition, a security officer for one of the businesses in the building was trapped on the seventh floor by the smoke in the stairway. As the firefighters went up, they vented the stairway and cleared some of the smoke. They first met the security officer on the seventh floor, and firefighters escorted him down the stairs. Other firefighters from the group continued up the stairs, shined their flashlight through the staircase smoke, and called out. The two trapped men on the eighth floor saw the flashlight beam and heard the firefighters calling and went down the stairway. The firefighters took the men outside and directed them away from the building.[231]

NIST said in another document that the two men were rescued at "12:10 to 12:15 PM."[232]

The Best Evidence

I. **The key elements of NIST's claims numbered 1–9 above are addressed below**. Some of these claims are verifiable and support the Jennings and Hess account. Others are self-contradictory.

1-3. *Re the time of the WTC 7 evacuation:* The NIST statements that many people began evacuating WTC 7 soon after the first plane hit at 8:46 AM, and that greater numbers were unofficially directed to leave after the second plane hit, are verifiable elsewhere.[233] Many people were directed not to use the elevators. (Note that the *official* order to evacuate did not come until 9:30 AM when a false report of a third plane coming in was circulated.) This means that Jennings and Hess could easily have found the lobby, the elevators, and the OEM empty soon after 9:03 AM, as Jennings claimed.

4. *Re the time that Jennings and Hess arrived:* NIST says that debris from the 9:59 collapse of the South Tower struck the *south* face of WTC 7, just as Hess and Jennings were leaving the OEM, and starting down the (northeast) stairs. However, this would place the men on the stairs a full half hour after the OEM had been officially evacuated at 9:30, which contradicts the idea that the security guard helped them to take the freight elevator to the OEM.

5&6. *Re an explosion within WTC 7:* NIST says that twenty-nine minutes later, at 10:28, the North Tower collapsed, causing extensive damage to the south and southwest faces of WTC 7.[234] This statement implies that Jennings and Hess mistook the impact to the northeast stairwell for an explosion within WTC 7. This cannot be true because:

i) it would mean that the men had taken twenty-nine minutes to descend seventeen floors from the twenty-third floor to the sixth floor, nearly two minutes per floor;

ii) both stairwells were located along the north edge of the WTC 7 core in the north half of the building, but the debris hit the south face of WTC 7, which was 355 feet from the North Tower, with WTC 6 in between the North Tower and WTC 7;

iii) as shown in the Cantor structural drawing (see footnote 8), the two stairwells inside of WTC 7 were not in the area of the south-face damage claimed by NIST;

iv) the drawing also shows that core columns 74 and 75 would have blocked the advance of any debris that might have been headed for the stairwell.[235]

8. The unreferenced NIST claim that two (unnamed) men went back up to the eighth floor is supported by a video released by NIST in 2010 following a FOIA request. The footage shows Mr. Hess calling for help through a broken window on the eighth floor, amid explosions going off around the north side of WTC 7—the side opposite from the towers. Hess can be heard to shout "an explosion." [236]

9. NIST's claim that the firefighters went up the northeast stairway to rescue Jennings and Hess was based not on firefighter testimony but on interviews with the two men, whom NIST did not name. As noted earlier, the content of these interviews has been denied to FOIA requests. This denial may have been because, as Hess told the BBC, when they arrived at the sixth floor:

> "The building began to shake, and it was as if you were in an earthquake…the whole building was shaking… *the stairway ran into a wall.* All of a sudden, as you were going down on the sixth floor, *you hit a wall.*"[237] Jennings concurred, saying that when they reached the sixth floor, "There was an explosion. And *the landing gave way.*"[238] [emphasis added]

Therefore, according to the report given by Hess and Jennings, NIST's account—that Hess and Jennings saw the firefighters' flashlight beam coming up the stairs, heard them calling up to them, and then were escorted down the stairway—would have been impossible, because the stairway was structurally blocked.

II. Evidence Addressing NIST's Omission of Jennings's Reports of Explosions

a) *Evidence from the Northeast Stairwell:* Both Jennings and Hess were interviewed after their escape. In an interview with WABC-TV reporter Jeff Rossen, Jennings stated that there was "a big explosion."[239]

A firefighter who shared this interview with Jennings said that inside WTC 7 it was "pandemonium…we couldn't get to them, we went through the building, we were lost…the back side was completely blown away, there was no way to access it, we couldn't get to them, and finally one of the fire department teams found them. But we didn't think they were going to make it."[240]

In his first account, Michael Hess echoed Jennings's account of hearing explosions, given to a reporter on 9/11:

> "I was up in the emergency management center on the twenty-third floor, and when all the power went out in the building, ah, another gentleman and I walked down to the eighth floor [sic] where there was an explosion. And we've been trapped on the eighth floor with smoke, thick smoke all around us for about an hour and a half."[241]

In a modified account given to the BBC in 2008, in which he withdrew his account of an explosion, Hess referred to his initial impression when they got down to the sixth floor: "In my mind I had assumed there had been an explosion in the basement."[242] This belief was confirmed, as we saw above, by his yelling out the window, "an explosion."

b) *Evidence of the Destroyed WTC 7 Lobby:* Jennings reported that he did not recognize the lobby on the way out: "I looked around, the lobby was gone. It looked like hell."[243] This was corroborated by CBS footage that emerged from a FOIA request in 2010.[244] All of this footage, according to NIST, was recorded between the tower collapses, at roughly 10:15 AM.

Thus the explosion itself had occurred before the footage was recorded, and certainly before the North Tower fell at 10:28. This would be consistent with the early arrival of the two men, who had been summoned to WTC 7 after the first plane hit a 8:46 AM.

III. Evidence Addressing the Time That Jennings and Hess Departed WTC 7

NIST's claim that Jennings and Hess were not rescued until 12:10 to 12:15 is objectively disproved by Hess's interview time with UPN 9 News, nearly half a mile from WTC 7. Close analysis shows the interview to have occurred either at 11:34 AM, or by 11:57 AM at the latest.[245]

Even taking the later time of 11:57 AM, and working backward by subtracting the ninety minutes that the men were trapped, plus giving a conservative estimate of thirty minutes for both their rescue and for Hess to get to the interview location, the latest the men could have arrived in the stairwell would have been just before 10:00 AM, the time of the South Tower collapse.

Conclusion

Again, the importance of this chapter is that both Jennings and Hess felt a massive explosion below them in the northeast stairwell of WTC 7, and reported that the sixth floor landing "gave way," with its stairs "running into a wall."

The time of their experience is consistent with the pre-10:15 AM obliteration of the enormous WTC 7 lobby, as shown in the FOIA-released CBS footage of 2010.

These near ground-level phenomena could not have been caused by the collapses of the Twin Towers, because WTC 6 stood between these towers and WTC 7. Instead, the obliteration of the entire lobby points to a massive internal explosion—yet NIST omitted the word "explosion" from its account.

Given the evidence for explosions in the North and South Towers that has been reviewed in the section on the Twin Towers, the question arises whether WTC 7 had been planned for demolition shortly after the collapse of the South Tower (at which time its dust and debris would have concealed the nature and speed of the collapse of WTC 7), but for some reason had to be delayed until later in the day.

III.

The Attack on the Pentagon

Introduction

Although the "9/11 attacks" include an attack on the Pentagon as well as on the World Trade Center, far less attention has been devoted to the Pentagon. As with the WTC attacks, the first investigation of the Pentagon attack was supervised by FEMA. In 2003, it published a report, called the *Pentagon Building Performance Report*, which was written in 2002 by volunteers from the American Society of Civil Engineers. However, this preliminary report was not followed up by a more extensive report on the building written by NIST or any other official organization. So the 2003 FEMA report on the Pentagon building remained the only official account of the attack on the Pentagon.

Among people who have seriously studied the evidence about the destruction of the World Trade Center, there is almost complete consensus. The same cannot be said about the attack on the Pentagon. In particular, the main issue on which there has been a lack of consensus is whether American Flight 77, or any other large airliner, struck the Pentagon. Accordingly, this book has fewer chapters contradicting the official story about the Pentagon than those about the WTC.

Nevertheless, the panelists were agreed (85 percent or higher) on the central issue: that the official account of the Pentagon attack is not true.

The central chapter in this section involves the claim that the Pentagon was damaged from a surprise attack by an airplane piloted by an al-Qaeda hijacker, Hani Hanjour. The other three chapters provide evidence concerning official foreknowledge of the Pentagon attack, and why it was not prevented.

18

The Claim That Hani Hanjour Piloted AA 77 into the Pentagon

Introduction

One of the central elements in the 9/11 story, as told by the government, the press, and the 9/11 Commission, is that American Flight 77, which allegedly hit the Pentagon, was piloted by a young Saudi named Hani Hanjour. But numerous reports in the press, some of which are even reflected in *The 9/11 Commission Report*, imply that Hanjour would have been incapable of flying a Boeing 757 through the trajectory reportedly taken by American 77.

The Official Account

The 911 Commission Report reported that American Flight 77, a Boeing 757, was flown by al-Qaeda pilot Hani Hanjour into the Pentagon. After disengaging the autopilot, he executed a 330-degree downward spiral through 7,000 feet in about three minutes, then flew into Wedge 1 of the Pentagon between the first and second floors at 530 mph.[246]

Several stories in the press pointed out that a pilot flying AA 77's trajectory would have required considerable skill. On September 12, for example, the *Washington Post* carried a story saying:

> [J]ust as the plane seemed to be on a suicide mission into the White House, the unidentified pilot executed a pivot so tight that it reminded observers of a fighter jet maneuver.... Aviation sources said the plane was flown with extraordinary skill, making it highly likely that a trained pilot was at the helm.[247]

The following day, a *Detroit News* story said:

> Whoever flew at least three of the death planes seemed very skilled. . . . Investigators are particularly impressed with the

pilot who slammed into the Pentagon and, just before impact, performed a tightly banked 270-degree turn at low altitude with almost military precision.[248]

A week later, a CBS report said that the "difficult high-speed descending turn" was "so smooth" that the hijackers' "flying skills" must have been very good.[249] And the following month, an air traffic controller at Dulles International Airport, who had been in the radar room on the morning of 9/11, recounted how she had seen "an unidentified plane to the southwest of Dulles, moving at a very high rate of speed" toward the protected airspace over Washington. She said:

> The speed, the maneuverability, the way that he turned, we all thought in the radar room, all of us experienced air traffic controllers, that that was a military plane.[250]

The Best Evidence
Two kinds of evidence refute the official account: media evidence about Hanjour's flying skills and statements by commercial pilots.

Media Evidence About Hanjour's Flying Skills
Shortly after 9/11, news stories started appearing indicating that Hani Hanjour was anything but a highly skilled pilot. For example, a story about an airfield in Maryland called Freeway Airport said:

> Freeway Airport evaluated suspected hijacker Hani Hanjour when he attempted to rent a plane. He took three flights with the instructors in the second week of August, but flew so poorly he was rejected for the rental.[251]

In October, the *Washington Post* lifted up the problem even further in a story titled "Hanjour: A Study in Paradox." After mentioning several incidents in which instructors had "questioned his competence," this story said: "[H]ow and where [Hanjour obtained a commercial pilot's license] remains a lingering question that FAA officials refuse to discuss."[252]

In 2002, reports of Hanjour's incompetence received even greater national exposure. In a *New York Times* story titled "A Trainee Noted for Incompetence," Jim Yardley wrote:

Hani Hanjour . . . was reported to aviation agency in February 2001 after instructors at his flight school in Phoenix had found his piloting skills so shoddy and his grasp of English so inadequate that they questioned whether his pilot's license was genuine.

Yardley's story ended with a quotation from a former employee of the flight school who was, he said, "amazed that [Hanjour] could have flown into the Pentagon," because "he could not fly at all."[253]

Statements by Commercial Pilots

In addition to these stories in the press, several former airline pilots have stated that Hanjour could not possibly have maneuvered a large airliner through the trajectory allegedly taken by Flight AA 77 and then hit the Pentagon as described in the official account. For example:

- Russ Wittenberg, who flew large commercial airliners for thirty-five years after serving in Vietnam as a fighter pilot, says it would have been "totally impossible for an amateur who couldn't even fly a Cessna" to have flown that downward spiral and then "crash[ed] into the Pentagon's first floor wall without touching the lawn."[254]

- Ralph Omholt, a former 757 pilot, said, "The idea that an unskilled pilot could have flown this trajectory is simply too ridiculous to consider."[255]

Conclusion

Although there have been many interpretations of the evidence regarding the attack on the Pentagon, one thing is certain: the official account that Hani Hanjour piloted an aircraft that hit the Pentagon is untrue. This suffices to bring the entire official claim about the Pentagon into question.

19

The Claim That the Attack on the Pentagon Could Not Have Been Prevented: First Version

The Official Account

The attack on the Pentagon by American 77 (under the control of al-Qaeda) could not have been prevented for four reasons.

- First, although the FAA had received multiple signs before 9:00 AM that this plane was suffering an in-flight emergency,[256] the FAA did not notify the military about this flight until 9:24—at which time it reported that the flight, which may have been hijacked, appeared to be heading back toward Washington.[257]

- Second, although Andrews Air Force Base was only a few miles away, it had no fighters on alert.[258]

- Third, the only fighters on alert in the Eastern United States were two at Otis Air Force Base, which were already occupied protecting New York City against further attacks, and two fighters 130 miles away at Langley Air Force Base.[259]

- Fourth, the Langley fighters, which did not get airborne until 9:30,[260] were still 105 miles away when the Pentagon was struck at 9:38.[261]

The Best Evidence

Discrepancies in both timelines and aircraft availability challenge the given reasons for the claim that the attack at the Pentagon could not have been prevented:

- First, an FAA memorandum of May 21, 2003, to the 9/11 Commission said: "Within minutes after the first aircraft hit the World Trade Center, the FAA immediately established . . . phone bridges [with the military]. . . . [T]he FAA made formal notification about American Flight 77 at 9:24 AM, but information about the flight was conveyed continuously during the phone bridges before the formal notification."[262] This statement was read into the 9/11 Commission's record.[263] Loss of communication with American 77 was reported by the FAA Indianapolis Center "[s]hortly after 9:00."[264]

- Second, Colin Scoggins,[265] the military specialist at the FAA's Boston Center, stated that although DCANG [District of Columbia National Guard] did not "have an intercept mission," it did "fly every morning" and that under the circumstances NEADS [Northeast Air Defense Sector] "could have grabbed . . . those aircraft."[266]

- Third, Scoggins said that fighters at Atlantic City, Burlington, Selfridge, Syracuse, and Toledo would have also been ready to go.[267] With regard to Syracuse in particular, an ANG commander told NORAD on 9/11, "Give me ten minutes and I can give you hot guns."[268] If this request had been made at 9:10, this statement indicates, these fighters could have been in the air in time to protect the Pentagon.

- Fourth, even if fighters had to be sent from Langley Air Force Base (as the Official Account claimed in the third and fourth bullet points, above), they should have been airborne long before 9:30 (see the first bullet point under the Official Account, above).

Conclusion

The first official attempt to show that the Pentagon attack could not have been prevented was a failure.

20

The Claim That the Attack on the Pentagon Could Not Have Been Prevented: Second Version

The Official Account

The military could not have intercepted American 77, the 9/11 Commission reported, because it "never received notice that American 77 was hijacked."[269]

Some military leaders, including General Larry Arnold, the head of NORAD's US Continental region, had told the 9/11 Commission that the military had been notified about this flight at 9:24.[270] However this statement, which "made it appear that the military was notified in time to respond," was "incorrect," the 9/11 Commission pointed out in 2004.[271]

The Best Evidence

The truth of the 9/11 Commission's second account may be questioned on two grounds:

First, the charge that the testimony of General Arnold and other military leaders was "incorrect" amounts to the charge that they lied.[272] But if the commission's new story were true, military leaders would not have invented the original story—which implies that the military was guilty of standing down, or at least of incompetence. This would have been an irrational fabrication.

Second, the commission's revised account contradicted several facts:

- The FAA's memo of May 22, 2003, said that the military was notified earlier than 9:24, not later.

- The FAA memo was supported by a *New York Times* story published four days after 9/11, which said, "During the hour or so that American Airlines Flight 77 was under the control of hijackers, up to the moment it struck the west side of the Pentagon, military officials in a command center on the east side of the building were urgently talking to law enforcement and air traffic control officials about what to do."[273]

- The commission claimed that, although the FAA's Air Traffic Control System Command Center had known about American 77's troubles since 9:20 AM, this knowledge did not get passed to the military. However, Ben Sliney, the operations manager at the facility, said that the command center had a "military cell, which was our liaison with the military services. They were present at all of the events that occurred on 9/11. . . . [E]veryone who needed to be notified about the events transpiring was notified, including the military."[274]

Conclusion

The second official attempt to show that the Pentagon attack could not have been prevented was no more successful than the first attempt.

21

The Claim That a Domestic Airplane Attack on the Pentagon Was Not Expected

The Official Account

Critical to the success of the 9/11 attacks was the element of surprise, which was emphasized by key White House and Pentagon officials.

- President George Bush said, "They [al-Qaeda] struck in a way that was unimaginable."[275]

- Secretary of Defense Donald Rumsfeld said, "Never would have crossed anyone's mind."[276]

- General Richard Myers, Deputy Commander of the Joint Chiefs of Staff, said, "You hate to admit it, but we hadn't thought about this."[277]

- White House Press Secretary Ari Fleischer said, "Never did we imagine what would take place on September 11th, where people used those airplanes as missiles and weapons."[278]

- National Security Advisor Condoleezza Rice said, "I don't think anybody could have predicted that these people would take an airplane and slam it into the World Trade Center, take another one and slam it into the Pentagon; that they would try to use an airplane as a missile, a hijacked airplane as a missile."[279]

- Air Force Lieutenant Colonel Vic Warzinski, a Pentagon spokesman, said: "The Pentagon was simply not aware that this aircraft was coming our way, and I doubt prior to Tuesday's event, anyone would have expected anything like that here. There was no foreshadowing, no particular warning that would have led anyone with any reasonable view of the world to think this was a threat we faced."[280]

The Best Evidence

The following evidence suggests that an attack on the Pentagon was not at all unexpected:[281]

I. **Pre-9/11 Military Exercises Involving Planes Flown into the Pentagon**

- In 1999, NORAD conducted hijacking exercises where planes were flown into the Pentagon and the World Trade Center.[282]

- The US military held an exercise rehearsing a response to an airliner crash at the Pentagon on October 24–26, 2000. Emergency responders from the Pentagon and Arlington County assembled in a conference room in the Office of the Secretary of Defense for a mass casualty exercise that involved a commercial airliner crashing into the Pentagon and killing 341 people.[283]

- Department of Defense medical personnel trained for the scenario of a "guided missile in the form of a hijacked 757 airliner" being flown into the Pentagon in May 2001.[284]

II. **Government Officials and Others Told Not to Fly**
Several warnings from security sources to Pentagon and other officials about flying on September 11 were reported in the news:

- In a story about warnings, *Newsweek* reported: "On Sept. 10, *Newsweek* has learned, a group of top Pentagon officials suddenly canceled travel plans for the next morning, apparently because of security concerns."[285]

- San Francisco Mayor Willie Brown received a warning from what he described as his airport security people late Monday evening.[286]

- Salman Rushdie was prevented, by an emergency

resolution from the FAA, from flying the week of
Tuesday, September 11, 2001.[287]

III. Secretary of Defense Donald Rumsfeld Twice Predicts Imminent Pentagon Attacks

1. On the morning of September 11, Secretary of Defense
    Donald Rumsfeld, seeking approval for enhanced missile
    defense, held a well-attended 8:00–8:50 AM Pentagon
    breakfast meeting with House supporters. The meeting
    was winding down just about the time the first tower was
    hit at 8:46 AM.

During the course of the meeting, Rumsfeld reportedly said
that "sometime in the next two, four, six, eight, ten, twelve months
there would be an event that would occur in the world that would
be sufficiently shocking that it would remind people again how
important it is to have a strong healthy defense department."[288]

2. Later, in a meeting in Rumsfeld's office, Christopher Cox,
    the defense policy committee chairman of the House of
    Representatives, reported Rumsfeld to have been more
    specific. Cox said: "Just moments before the Department
    of Defense was hit by a suicide hijacker, Secretary
    Rumsfeld was describing to me why America needs to
    . . . focus on the real threat facing us in the twenty-first
    century: terrorism, and the unexpected":

    > "If we remain vulnerable to missile attack, a terrorist
    > group or rogue state that demonstrates the capacity to
    > strike the US or its allies from long range could have the
    > power to hold our entire country hostage to nuclear or
    > other blackmail.

    > "And let me tell you. . . there will be another event. . . .
    > There will be another event."[289]

    > According to *The Telegraph*, Donald Rumsfeld, the
    > secretary of defense, was in his office on the eastern
    > side of the building, in a meeting with Christopher
    > Cox. Rumsfeld, recalls Cox, watched the TV coverage
    > from New York and said: "Believe me, this isn't over yet.

There's going to be another attack, and it could be us."[290]
Moments later, the plane hit [the Pentagon]. (When the
attack did occur, it did not threaten Rumsfeld, as the
attack was on the opposite side of the building.)

IV. NBC's Pentagon Correspondent Jim Miklaszewski Was Warned of Pentagon Attack by Intelligence Officer

Sometime between 9:03 and 9:37 AM, NBC's Pentagon correspondent Jim Miklaszewski said:

> The first time I heard the word "terrorism" out of any
> US official came shortly after the second plane hit,
> and I bumped into a US military intelligence official,
> and I said, "Look, what have you got?" And he said,
> "Obviously this is clearly an act of terrorism." And then
> he got very close to me, and, almost silent for a few
> seconds, he leaned in and said, "This attack was so well
> coordinated that if I were you, I would stay off the E
> Ring—where our NBC office was—the outer ring of the
> Pentagon for the rest of the day, because we're next."[291]

The intelligence official's apparent foreknowledge was unac-
countably specific:

a) How did he know the Pentagon would be hit next?

b) Even if he had just guessed that the Pentagon would be
    hit next, how could he have guessed that the outermost E
    Ring would be the specific target?

c) Of course, if an airplane attack had been aimed at one
    of the walls, the E Ring would have been struck. But
    why would he have guessed that the attack would have
    targeted one of the walls, which are only eighty feet high,
    when it would have been have been easier for a plane to
    dive into the Pentagon's roof, where it might have killed
    the secretary of defense and some top brass.

V. FBI Confiscates Security Camera Videotapes Within Minutes of Pentagon Attack

On the morning of 9/11, the Pentagon was surrounded by
rush-hour traffic jams.[292] A Department of Justice after-action

report describes the difficulty the FBI had in getting to the scene following the official attack time of 9:37 AM:

> The FBI Evidence Recovery Team began arriving before 10:00 a.m. and set up in a grassy area a short distance from the heliport. Because of the extremely congested traffic conditions, it took several hours for the entire FBI contingent to negotiate the route from the District of Columbia to the Pentagon.[293]

The first priority of the Evidence Recovery Team was "to find and collect all the airplane parts and other bits of evidence from the lawn on the west side of the building, before fire-fighters and other rescue workers completely trampled it."[294] In spite of these conditions and priorities, FBI agents identified at least two private businesses whose security cameras may have captured the attack. The FBI agents then confiscated their vid-eotapes *within minutes after the Pentagon was hit:*

a) José Velasquez, the Citgo gas station supervisor, was interviewed by the *Richmond Times-Dispatch*: "Velasquez says the gas station's security cameras are close enough to the Pentagon to have recorded the moment of impact. 'I've never seen what the pictures looked like. The FBI was here within minutes and took the film.'"[295]

b) A *Washington Times* story reported: "A security camera atop a hotel close to the Pentagon may have captured dramatic footage of the hijacked Boeing 757 airliner as it slammed into the western wall of the Pentagon. Hotel employees sat watching the film in shock and horror several times before the FBI confiscated the video."[296]

The FBI agents who arrived so promptly to seize the business videotapes appeared to be operating separately from the traffic-delayed FBI Evidence Recovery Team.

Conclusion

This compelling array of evidence suggests that various officials had foreknowledge of the Pentagon attack. The strike on the Pentagon—whatever its nature—requires a full, impartial investigation with subpoena power. (The topic of 9/11 foreknowledge is also covered in chapters 16, 31, 32, 38, 45, and 50.)

IV.

THE 9/11 FLIGHTS

Introduction

Nothing is more central to the official account of the 9/11 attacks than the claim that the Twin Towers and the Pentagon were struck by airplanes that had been hijacked by al-Qaeda operatives. Also, United Flight 93 was said to have crashed in Pennsylvania after some passengers stormed hijackers who had taken over the plane.

However, there are at least four very good reasons to reject the claim that the 9/11 airliners were hijacked by al-Qaeda terrorists

22

The Claim That the Four 9/11 Flights Were Hijacked

The Official Account

The *9/11 Commission Report* said that four airplanes (American Airlines flights 11 and 77, and United Airlines flights 93 and 175) were hijacked on 9/11.[297]

The Best Evidence

Pilots are trained to "squawk" the universal hijack code (7500) on a transponder if they receive evidence of an attempted hijacking, thereby notifying FAA controllers on the ground.[298] But leading newspapers and the 9/11 Commission pointed out that FAA controllers were not notified.[299]

A CNN story said that pilots are trained to send the hijack code "if possible."[300] But entering the code takes only two or three seconds, whereas it took hijackers, according to the official story, more than thirty seconds to break into the pilots' cabin of UA 93.[301]

Conclusion

The fact that not one of the eight pilots (each flight had a copilot) performed this required action casts serious doubt on the hijacker story.[302]

23

The Claim That United Flight 93 Crashed in Pennsylvania

The Official Account

The 9/11 Commission reported that United Flight 93, having been taken over by an al-Qaeda pilot, was flown at a high speed and steep angle into a field near Shanksville, Pennsylvania.[303]

In response to claims that United Airlines Flight 93 was shot down, the US military and the FBI said that United 93 was *not* shot down.

The Best Evidence

Residents, the mayor, and journalists near Shanksville reported that no airliner was visible at the designated crash site;[304] that contents were found as far as eight miles from the designated crash site;[305] and that parts—including a thousand-pound engine piece—were found over a mile away.[306]

Conclusion

The widely dispersed airplane parts, along with the absence of a visible plane at the alleged crash site, are not consistent with the 9/11 Commission's claim that the plane crashed at that site.

24

The Claim That Hijackers Were Responsible for Changes to 9/11 Flight Transponders

Introduction

The 9/11 Commission and the media have accepted the idea that the four 9/11 flights were difficult to track because hijackers had turned off or changed the transponder signals.

The official account held that radar information was lost for three of the four September 11 aircraft because hijackers had, after seizing control of the three flight decks, manually turned off these transponders in order to evade detection and interception by the US air defense system.

This conclusion appears to be based only on circumstantial information—the simple loss of flight data to air traffic control.

However, to this day, manual deactivations of transponders still cannot be verified by air traffic control.

The Official Account

On the morning of September 11, 2001, flights American 11, American 77, United 93, and United 175 were taken over by on-board hijackers, who from within the cockpits turned off the transponders for the first three aircraft and changed the code transmitted by UA 175's transponder.[307] The 9/11 Commission explained:

- On 9/11, the terrorists turned off the transponders on three of the four hijacked aircraft. With its transponder off, it is possible, though more difficult, to track an aircraft by its primary radar returns. But unlike transponder data, primary radar returns do not show the aircraft's identity and altitude. Controllers at centers rely so heavily on transponder signals that they usually do not display primary radar returns on their radar scopes. But they can change the configuration of their scopes so they can see primary radar returns. They did this on 9/11 when the transponder signals for three of the aircraft disappeared.[308]

- At 8:21, American 11 turned off its transponder, immediately degrading the information available about the aircraft. The controller told his supervisor that he thought something was seriously wrong with the plane, although neither suspected a hijacking. The supervisor instructed the controller to follow standard procedures for handling a 'no radio' aircraft.[309]

- Because the hijackers had turned off the plane's transponder, NEADS personnel spent the next minutes searching their radar scopes for the primary radar return. American 11 struck the North Tower at 8:46.[310]

- At 8:51, the controller noticed the transponder change from United 175 and tried to contact the aircraft. There was no response.[311]

- At 8:54, the aircraft [American 77] deviated from its assigned course, turning south. Two minutes later the transponder was turned off and even primary radar contact with the aircraft was lost.[312]

- The failure to find a primary radar return for American 77 led us to investigate this issue further. Radar reconstructions performed after 9/11 reveal that FAA radar equipment tracked the flight from the moment its transponder was turned off at 8:56.[313]

- On American 11, the transponder signal was turned off at 8:21; on United 175, the code was changed at 8:47; on American 77, the signal was turned off at 8:56; and on United 93, the signal was turned off at 9:41.[314]

The Best Evidence

The evidence below shows that changes to the transponder data broadcast by the four aircraft on 9/11 were not necessarily caused by hijackers:

- *The 9/11 Commission Report* provides no evidence to show that hijackers manually deactivated three transponders to cause the loss of air traffic control data.

- Flight studies by the National Transportation Safety Board (NTSB) and Federal Aviation Authority (FAA) omit any mention of why the transponder signals for these flights were lost.

- Transponder activity is not listed among the Flight Data Recorder mandatory parameters and therefore cannot be established through FDR recordings.[315]

- A 2001 *Christian Science Monitor* story reporting how Flight 11's transponder was turned off was speculative:

  > Flight 11's transponder had stopped working. It was no longer sending a radar pulse....Still, the controllers hoped that the plane simply had an electrical problem.... The controller speculates that the hijacker may have deliberately deactivated the plane's transponder.[316]

- In the 2014 disappearance of Malaysia Airlines Flight MH370, news stories overlooked the issue of whether proof of manual deactivation is available or not. For example, CNN reported, "Kit Darby, a longtime pilot, said Tuesday it was not clear whether the transponder was turned off intentionally."[317]

Conclusion

No good evidence has been provided to support the official claims that hijackers manually deactivated or altered the operation of the transponders aboard the 9/11 flights. Instead, a spectrum of evidence exists to call into question whether hijackers were on the planes at all.[318]

Accordingly, the transponder claims should not serve as supporting evidence for the alleged takeovers of the 9/11 flights by the accused, or even as evidence of these men's presence aboard the flight decks of these aircraft.

25

The Claim That No Information Could Be Obtained from the Black Boxes of Any of the Four 9/11 Planes

Introduction

All commercial airliners carry two virtually indestructible "black boxes" containing devices to record physical data and pilot communications—a Flight Data Recorder (FDR) and a Cockpit Voice Recorder (CVR).

The FDR records many parameters, including the plane's speed, altitude, and course, while the CVR records conversation both inside the cockpit and throughout the plane's external communications.[319]

These devices are highly durable and are installed in a plane's tail section, where they are least likely to be damaged on impact. They are designed to withstand intense heat and violent crashes.[320]

The Official Account

The 9/11 Commission dealt with two sets of aircraft: those involved in the World Trade Center and those that were not:

- The black boxes for the two planes that struck the Twin Towers—AA Flight 11 and UA Flight 175—were never found.[321]

- The black boxes for UA Flight 93 and AA Flight 77 were found,[322] but the CVR for AA 77 was badly burned and the information recorded on it was not recoverable.[323]

- A transcript from UA 93's CVR was released by the FBI in the 2006 trial of Zacarias Moussaoui.[324]

- According to the American Society of Engineers' 2003 *Pentagon Building Performance Report*, the AA 77 data recorder was "found nearly 300 ft. into the structure."[325]

The Best Evidence

The official claims above are contradicted by a substantial amount of evidence to the contrary:

- Contrary to the official claim about AA 11 and UA 175, two men—a FDNY fireman who worked in the cleanup of Ground Zero, Nicholas DeMasi, and volunteer Mike Bellone—described their discovery in October 2001 of three of the four black boxes in the rubble of the Twin Towers.[326]

- A memorandum dated September 18, 2001, to Governor George Pataki from New York State Emergency Management Office Director Edward F. Jacoby, Jr., reported that "[i]nvestigators have identified the signal from one of the black boxes in the WTC debris."[327]

- General Paul Kern, the commanding general of the US Army Materiel Command, reported in 2002 that, "Radio frequency detectors developed at CECOM [Communications Electronics Command] were used to find 'black box' flight recorders from the airliners that crashed into the two towers."[328]

- Although the four virtually indestructible black boxes were reportedly never found, the passport of alleged AA 11 hijacker Satam al Suqami was reportedly found near Ground Zero,[329] and life jackets and portions of seats from AA 11 were reportedly found on the roof the Bankers Trust building. How could they survive when the black boxes could not?[330]

- Except for the two WTC flights, only one flight over land has ever resulted in the loss of a black box, and it crashed extremely high in the Andes. (As for flights over water, the only ones that have not been recovered have been in crashes over very deep water.)[331] Given those facts, it seems extremely unlikely that the black boxes from the two WTC airplanes would not have been found.

- With regard to AA 77, which reportedly hit the Pentagon, the 2003 *Pentagon Building Performance Report* said that the flight data recorder "was found almost 300 feet inside the building."[332] However, this claim contradicts what was publicly reported. A *Newsweek* story in 2001 reported that before 4:00 AM three days after the attack, two firefighters, Burkhammer and Moravitz, discovered them "near the impact site." According to *Newsweek*:

> [They] were combing through debris near the impact site. Peering at the wreckage with their helmet lights, the two spotted . . . two odd-shaped dark boxes, about 1.5 by 2 feet long. They'd been told the plane's "black boxes" would in fact be bright orange, but these were charred black. . . . They cordoned off the area and called for an FBI agent, who in turn called for someone from the National Transportation Safety Board (NTSB) who confirmed the find: the black boxes from AA Flight 77.[333]

- Likewise, Arlington County spokesman Dick Bridges said that members of the FBI's evidence response team found the two recorders "right where the plane came into the building."[334]

- According to a file released by the NTSB in response to a FOIA request from Aidan Monaghan, the flight data file for American Flight 77, which was based on this FDR, was created at 11:45 PM on Thursday, September 13. This is a serious contradiction within the official story: According to the Pentagon, the FBI, and even the NTSB, the FDR was found early on the morning of Friday September 14, and authorities later in the day were hoping that information on it could be recovered. And yet, according to the NTSB file released only after there was a FOIA request for it, the file based on flight data for AA 77 had already been created the previous day. How could the file based on the AA flight data have been created a day before the FDR itself was found?[335]

- According to an NTSB investigation handbook, accident investigators are required to list the manufacturer/ model, serial number, and maintenance readout of the

Flight Data Recorder.[336] However, there have been no serial numbers published for any of the recovered black boxes from the four flights.[337] George Nelson, a retired Air Force colonel and a specialist in aircraft accidents, reports that every plane has many "time-change parts" that must be changed periodically because they are crucial for flight safety. Each time-change part has a distinct serial number. These parts are virtually indestructible, so an ordinary fire resulting from an airplane crash, Nelson says, could not possibly "destroy or obliterate all of those critical time-change parts or their serial numbers."[338] That the serial numbers on the AA 77 black boxes were not reported is another serious problem with the official account.

Conclusion

In light of the above-reported facts—that the flight data file for AA 77 was evidently made before the FDR itself was reportedly found; that a firefighter and a volunteer reportedly found three of the black boxes from the Twin Towers (contrary to the claim that none of them were found); that *Newsweek* reported that the black boxes at the Pentagon were found at the entrance site (rather than 300 feet inside, as the *Pentagon Building Performance Report* said); and that none of the serial numbers for the allegedly retrieved black boxes were reported—it is clear that the official account cannot be trusted.

V.

THE US MILITARY EXERCISES ON AND BEFORE 9/11

Introduction

Chapters 26 and 27 deal with strange anomalies in the major military exercises held on and before September 11, 2001:

1) Critical to the success of the 9/11 attacks was the element of surprise, according to key White House and Pentagon officials. However, contrary to claims made in *The 9/11 Commission Report*, US military exercises prior to 9/11 involved hijackings in which planes were used as weapons, both within and outside US airspace.

2) Until September 11, 2001, the North American Aerospace Defense Command (NORAD) conducted four major annual war exercises, which included simulated war situations. Although these exercises were traditionally held in October or November, they were all running on September 11, 2001.

26

The Claim That the Military Was Not Prepared for Hijacked Domestic Planes Used as Weapons

The Official Account

Critical to the success of the 9/11 attacks was the element of surprise, a point emphasized by key White House and Pentagon officials.[339] According to the 9/11 Commission, the element of surprise rested on two factors:

- Hijacked planes were used as weapons—a departure from predictable, traditional hijackings.[340]

- The attacks originated, unpredictably, from within the country, rather than from outside.[341]

The Best Evidence

The military had trained for the possibility of hijacked planes used as weapons, including hijacked planes originating within the country. John Arquilla, a special operations expert at the Naval Postgraduate School, stated in 2002 that "the idea of such an attack [using hijacked airliners for suicide attacks against major buildings] was well known, had been wargamed as a possibility in exercises before Sept. 11, 2001, and previous airline attacks had been attempted."[342]

Multiple training drills using planes as weapons had taken place before September 11, 2001.

- In October 2000, a military exercise had created a scenario of a simulated passenger plane crashing into the Pentagon. The exercise was coordinated by the Defense Protective Service and the Pentagon's Command Emergency Response Team.[343]

- *US Medicine* reported that two health clinics housed

within the Pentagon trained for a hijacked airplane to hit the Pentagon in May 2001. "Though the Department of Defense had no capability in place to protect the Pentagon from an ersatz guided missile in the form of a hijacked 757 airliner, DoD medical personnel trained for exactly that scenario in May."[344]

- The Department of Transportation in Washington held an exercise on August 31, 2001, which Ellen Engleman, the administrator of the department's Research and Special Projects Administration, described thus:

  > Ironically, fortuitously, take your choice, 12 days prior to the incident on September 11th, we were going though a tabletop exercise. It was actually much more than a tabletop...in preparation for the Olympic...which was a full intermodal exercise....Part of the scenario, interestingly enough, involved a potentially highjacked plane and someone calling on a cell phone, among other aspects of the scenario that were very strange when twelve days later, as you know, we had the actual event.[345]

- One such operation involved planes originating from inside the United States. According to *USA Today*:

  > In the two years before the Sept. 11 attacks, the North American Aerospace Defense Command conducted exercises simulating...hijacked airliners used as weapons to crash into targets and cause mass casualties....[O]ne operation, planned in July 2001 and conducted later, involved planes from airports in Utah and Washington state that were hijacked.[346]

- The operation involving multiple hijacking drills using planes from inside the United States was Amalgam Virgo 2002, planned for 1,500 people in July 2001 and scheduled for operation in June 2002.[347]

Conclusion

Contrary to claims by *The 9/11 Commission Report*, US military exercises prior to 9/11 involved hijackings—within as well as outside US airspace—in which planes were used as weapons.

Any new investigation should ask why the highest responsible officials denied that such preparation had preceded the attacks on 9/11, and why, given that preparation, no actions were taken to stop the hijacked planes from reaching their targets.

27

The Claim That the Military Exercises Did Not Delay the Response to the 9/11 Attacks

Introduction

Until September 11, 2001, the North American Aerospace Defense Command (NORAD) conducted four major annual war exercises a year.[348] These aerial practice drills, run cooperatively with the US Strategic Command and the US Space Command, simulated war situations for a period of one or two weeks.

The two largest, Global Guardian and Vigilant Guardian, were command-level (high-level) exercises that ran together, involved all levels of command, and were designed to exercise most aspects of the NORAD mission. Global Guardian also linked with other exercises sponsored by the chairman of the Joint Chiefs of Staff and the unified commands, which included Amalgam Warrior, Apollo Warrior, and Crown Vigilance.[349]

These exercises, traditionally held in October or November, were all running on September 11, 2001.

The Official Account

The 9/11 Commission Report states that when Boston FAA Flight Center called NEADS (NORAD's Northeast Air Defense Sector) to report the hijacking of Flight 11, NEADS asked, "Is this real world or exercise?"[350]

The commission's footnote to this question reported that the large-scale exercise Vigilant Guardian, which postulated a bomber attack from the former Soviet Union, had not compromised the military response.[351] This statement reflected the claims of several military officers:

- According to General Ralph Eberhart, Commander of NORAD at Peterson Air Force Base, "it took about thirty seconds" to make the adjustment to the real-world situation.[352]

- According to Colonel Robert Marr, the head of NEADS, "we found that the response was, if anything, expedited by the increased number of staff at the sectors and at NORAD because of the scheduled exercise."[353]

- General Richard Myers, chairman of the Joint Chiefs of Staff, concurred, saying in 2005 that the exercises "actually enhanced the response."[354]

The Best Evidence

I. Although the 9/11 Commission mentioned only one military exercise—Vigilant Guardian—that was scheduled for 9/11, evidence shows that at least twelve exercises had been scheduled for that day:

1. Vigilant Guardian: An annual NORAD exercise traditionally held in October,[355] often in conjunction with Global Guardian.[356] On 9/11, all levels of command at NORAD headquarters, including NEADS, were participating in this command-post exercise (CPX),[357] 24/7.[358]

2. Global Guardian: A massive annual Command Post-Exercise (CPX) and Field Training Exercise (FTX),[359] which was sponsored jointly by the US Strategic Command, US Space Command, and NORAD, and was linked to Vigilant Guardian and Amalgam Warrior.[360] Global Guardian is traditionally held in October or November each year.[361] According to a military newspaper dated March 23, 2001, the overarching Global Guardian exercise had indeed been originally scheduled for October,[362] but was subsequently moved to early September.

3. Crown Vigilance was sponsored by Air Combat Command and was linked to Global Guardian.[363]

4. Also running was Amalgam Warrior, a large-scale live-fly exercise involving two or more NORAD regions, traditionally held in April and October.[364]

5. Amalgam Virgo: NORAD officers told the 9/11 Commission Team 8, "On 9/11 there were two FTX exercises planned: Amalgam Virgo and Amalgam Warrior."[365]

6. Northern Vigilance: A large annual real-world NORAD operation that on 9/11 diverted much of the US air defense fleet to Canada and Alaska to counteract a Russian drill.[366] This operation involved NORAD's Cheyenne Mountain Operations Center (CMOC) in Colorado.[367]

7. Apollo Guardian, linked to Global Guardian and run by the US Space Command, was also running on September 11, 2001. "Hijacks were included in these exercises to exercise transition in Rules of Engagement (ROE)."[368]

8. Whiskey 105 at Otis Air Force Base: Six F-15s from Otis (out of a contingent of eighteen) took off on a routine Atlantic Ocean exercise at 9:00 AM, eight minutes after two "alert" F-15s on the same runway were scrambled in response to the first WTC attack. The six training jets were recalled at 9:25 AM to be armed and to join the response.[369]

9. Andrews Air Force Base (outside Washington, DC): There were only seven pilots available in the AAFB 121st Fighter Squadron on 9/11 because many had not returned from the large-scale training exercise Red Flag, in Las Vegas.[370] Three F-16 fighter jets took off on a training exercise at 8:36 AM from Andrews AFB and did not return until 2:35 PM. Flight strips indicated that Andrews-based fighters were not scrambled in response to the hijackings until 11:12 AM.[371]

10. New Jersey Air National Guard: When the World Trade Center was hit, two F-16 fighters from the 177th Fighter Wing based in Atlantic City were on a routine training mission, eight minutes flying time away from

New York, but the pilots were not informed of the hijackings until after the second tower was hit at 9:03 AM. Two other bombers from this group were also on a routine training exercise. No jets took off from Atlantic City in response to the attacks until after the Pentagon was hit at approximately 9:37.[372]

11. Washington DC Army Aviation Support Unit: Members of this unit were attending annual weapons training, a ninety-minute drive away.[373] The unit's mission was to maintain "a readiness posture in support of contingency plans," to exercise "operational control" of the Washington area airspace, and to provide "aviation support for the White House, US government officials, Department of Defense, Department of the Army, and other government agencies,"[374] including the Pentagon.

12. National Reconnaissance Office: NRO, a large intelligence agency of the Department of Defense, had planned a 9:32 AM simulation of a small plane crashing into one of its own towers near Washington's Dulles Airport.[375]

The rescheduling from October to early September of seven aerial drills—the two largest having been Global Guardian and Vigilant Guardian, and the five related aerial drills that accompanied them—resulted in an unprecedented number of simultaneous drills that morning. This was an enormous departure from other years.

These drills included at least two hijackings (a Boeing 747 flying from Tokyo to Anchorage, and a Korean Airlines Boeing 747 flight from Seoul to Anchorage),[376] and one drill in which a plane was planned to simulate hitting a building (the National Reconnaissance Office).

II. One would expect that having so many exercises would have caused some confusion, which might have slowed down the military response. Indeed, statements to this effect have been made:

- According to a summary of a 9/11 Commission interview with Canadian Lt. General Rick Findley, who was at NORAD as the Battle Staff Director at Cheyenne Mountain Operations Center on September 11, 2001, there was, following the second attack on the Twin Towers, "confusion as to how many, and which aircraft, were hijacked. There was no situational awareness that was directly credible, and CMOC was relying on the communications over the phone lines with its operations sectors. Findley opined that AA 11 was reported still airborne and headed towards Washington, DC, because of the added confusion of many hijack reports."[377]

- At Andrews Air Force Base outside Washington, DC, FAA air traffic controller James Ampey, stationed at Andrews Tower, reported in a 9/11 Commission interview that an unusually high number of aircraft were taking off and landing at Andrews that morning because previously scheduled military exercises were underway. The radar screens were showing "emergencies all over the place."[378]

- General Larry Arnold, commander of the Continental U.S. NORAD Region, said, "By the end of the day, we had twenty-one aircraft identified as possible hijackings."[379]

- Pentagon spokeswoman Victoria Clarke: "There were lots of false signals out there. There were false hijack squawks, and a great part of the challenge was sorting through what was a legitimate threat and what wasn't."[380]

- FAA Deputy Administrator, Monte Belger, said, "Between 9:20 and 9:45 there were many confusing reports about various aircraft being unaccounted for."[381]

- An independent study in 2011 gave detailed accounts of nine falsely reported hijackings on 9/11, plus nine other reported aircraft emergencies.[382]

Conclusion

Because of the rescheduling of military exercises normally scheduled for different times, an extraordinary number of exercises were underway the morning of September 11, 2001.

The Department of Defense and the 9/11 Commission failed to report all but one of the exercises that occurred that morning. They also denied that such exercises slowed down military responses to the attacks.

Had the 9/11 Commission reported the full extent of the exceptional number of exercises it knew were operating that morning, the above-quoted statements by military officers such as Eberhart, Marr, and Myers—that the exercises did not, by causing confusion, slow down the military response—would have seemed implausible.

Any new investigation should probe the collective evidence, which points to the following scenario:

(1) The Pentagon, after creating conditions that confused the military response to the attacks, sought to cover up its creation of these conditions.

(2) The 9/11 Commission facilitated this cover-up by not making public the information held in its records cited above.

VI

CLAIMS ABOUT MILITARY AND POLITICAL LEADERS

Introduction

This section deals with eight political and military leaders who had major roles on 9/11: four political leaders and four generals. Assuming the official account of 9/11 to be basically correct, we would not expect the official accounts of the way these eight men acted on that day to contain serious inconsistencies—either within themselves or with well-supported facts. We certainly would not expect the accounts of all eight men to be marred by such inconsistencies. But a close examination of these accounts shows this to be the case.

This section of the book contains ten chapters about these eight men, and it is especially lengthy and complex. Therefore, we offer an overview chapter, which summarizes the main points of the other ten chapters.

28

Overview

Introduction

The official accounts of the activities of eight political and military leaders with central roles on 9/11—roles that put them in position to affect the outcome of crucial events of that day—comprise one of the most remarkable features of 9/11. In all eight cases, facts suggest that each story is false or at best dubious.

President George W. Bush

On the morning of 9/11, President Bush was visiting a grade school in Sarasota, Florida. When it appeared that hijackers were going after high-value targets, the head of the Secret Service detail allowed President Bush to remain at the school for 30 minutes and to make a television address to the nation, thereby letting any terrorists know that the president was still there. (Note: References supporting this chapter are included in Chapters 29–38.)

The Secret Service is charged with protecting the president. One of the unanswered questions, wrote the *St. Petersburg Times*, is "why the Secret Service did not immediately hustle Bush to a secure location." The 9/11 Family Steering Committee asked, "Why was President Bush permitted by the Secret Service to remain in the Sarasota elementary school?"

The 9/11 Commission Report merely said, "The Secret Service told us they were anxious to move the President to a safer location, but did not think it imperative for him to run out the door." (Chapter 29) This break in protocol suggests—even if it does not prove—that the Secret Service, at some level, knew that the president was not in danger.

In addition, the White House, during the week of the first anniversary of the 9/11 attacks, described Bush's visit to the school room in a false way, which later had to be corrected after a videotape of the event emerged. (Chapter 30)

Vice President Dick Cheney

According to *The 9/11 Commission Report*, Vice President Cheney did not enter the PEOC (Presidential Emergency Operations Center), where he took charge of the government's response to the attacks, until "shortly before 10:00," hence after the Pentagon attack.

However, a number of witnesses—including Secretary of Transportation Norman Mineta, White House photographer David Bohrer, and Cheney himself (on *Meet the Press*)—reported that Cheney was in the PEOC *before* the Pentagon attack. Most important was Mineta, who reported that Cheney had given responses to questions from a young officer, as a plane approached the Pentagon, about whether the "orders still stand." Cheney's reply that they did stand can best be understood as Cheney's confirmation of a stand-down order. (Chapter 31)

Another dispute about Cheney involves the time that he gave the military permission—allegedly authorized by President Bush—to shoot down any hostile passenger airplanes. This issue is important in relation to United 93, which allegedly crashed in Pennsylvania. Although there were many reports that the flight was shot down by the US military, the military and the 9/11 Commission maintained that Cheney's shoot-down authorization was not given until after United 93 had already crashed. (Chapter 32)

Secretary of Defense Donald Rumsfeld

According to Donald Rumsfeld and *The 9/11 Commission Report*, Rumsfeld was in his office and oblivious to the attacks until he felt the attack on the Pentagon. Also he did not know about the hijacking of United 93 until after it had crashed.

However, counterterrorism coordinator Richard Clarke's book *Against All Enemies*, which appeared in 2004 several months before the publication of *The 9/11 Commission Report*, portrayed Rumsfeld as being in the Pentagon's video center in the Executive Support Center from shortly after the second WTC attack until after the attack on the Pentagon. Also, Robert Andrews, a deputy assistant secretary of defense, stated independently that, after the second WTC attack, Rumsfeld went across the hall to the Executive Support Center to join Clarke's video conference. It appears that the accounts given by Secretary Rumsfeld and the 9/11 Commission were false. (Chapter 33)

General Richard Myers, acting chairman of the Joint Chiefs of Staff

According to *The 9/11 Commission Report* and General Myers, Myers was on Capitol Hill during the attacks, not returning to the Pentagon until after it had been attacked. However, this account is contradicted by several witnesses:

- The 2004 book *Against All Enemies*, by counterterrorism coordinator Richard Clarke, portrayed Myers as having, along with Secretary of Defense Rumsfeld, gone to the Pentagon's video center at roughly 9:10 AM—shortly after the second (9:03) attack on the World Trade Center—which would mean that Myers could not have been on Capitol Hill at that time.

- Thomas White, the Secretary of the Army, indicated that Myers was in a breakfast meeting with Rumsfeld from 8:00 until 8:46 AM (when the first plane hit the WTC).

- The 2009 book by General Hugh Shelton, for whom Myers was substituting as chairman of the Joint Chiefs of Staff on that morning, portrayed Myers as being in the Pentagon when it was hit.

It thus appears that the account given by Myers and the 9/11 Commission was false. (Chapter 34)

General Hugh Shelton, chairman of the Joint Chiefs of Staff

General Shelton reported that, on the morning of 9/11, he was on a plane—the Speckled Trout—to Europe.

After learning of the second WTC attack, he said, he ordered his flight crew to return to the Pentagon. According to Shelton, he was almost immediately given permission to return to the US, returned to Andrews Air Force Base by roughly noon, and reached the Pentagon shortly thereafter. However, the claim that Shelton's plane returned to the Pentagon shortly after noon is contradicted by several facts:

- The Speckled Trout flight navigator reportedly said that the plane, having not quickly received clearance, had to go into a holding pattern over Greenland (for two hours) and again over Canada.

- The flight-tracking strip indicated that the Speckled Trout did not land at Andrews until 4:40 PM.

- A military assistant traveling with Shelton stated that they drove from Andrews to the Pentagon in the "late afternoon."

- General Myers stated that Shelton had arrived at the Pentagon at 5:40 PM, having "just returned from an aborted European flight."

It appears that at least part of General Shelton's story is not true. (Chapter 35)

Brigadier General Montague Winfield

For two years it was both assumed and reported on television that Brigadier General Winfield, the Deputy Director of Operations (DDO) at the National Military Command Center (NMCC), was in charge the morning of 9/11.

But in July 2003, the 9/11 Commission was told that between 8:30 AM and roughly 10:00 AM, Winfield had been replaced—at his own request to attend a meeting to discuss the ratings of Air Force officers—by Charles Joseph "Joe" Leidig, a high-ranking official who two months earlier had been made the Deputy for Command Center Operations and in August had qualified to stand watch in Winfield's place. However, this account raises several puzzling questions, including these:

- Why did Brigadier General Winfield present himself, on CNN and ABC programs in 2002, as the DDO during the attacks?

- Why was Brigadier General Winfield not called back to the NMCC after the second attack on the Twin Towers (which made clear that America was being attacked)?

- Why did General Myers, who at the time was the acting chairman of the Joint Chiefs of Staff, describe Winfield—in a memoir published in 2009—as the "duty officer in charge" of the NMCC on the morning of 9/11?

These unanswered questions suggest the untruth of the claim of the Pentagon and the 9/11 Commission that Leidig, rather than Winfield, served as the DDO during the 9/11 attacks, even though it is not clear why, if this claim is untrue, the Pentagon and the 9/11 Commission made the claim. (Chapter 36)

General Ralph Eberhart, commander in chief of NORAD

Being ultimately responsible for the defense of America on 9/11, Eberhart was a complete failure: His interceptor pilots did not prevent any of the attacks; he made himself incommunicado from 9:30 to 10:15; he made several implausible and contradictory statements about his activities; and he caused delays in responding, partly because of the many military exercises he had scheduled for that day. Although he has been hailed as a "9/11 hero," considerable evidence suggests that Eberhart was actually derelict in his duty that day. (Chapter 37)

New York City Mayor Rudolph Giuliani

After the attacks on the Twin Towers, Mayor Giuliani and his emergency management team set up temporary headquarters in a building at 75 Barclay Street. While there, he told Peter Jennings of ABC News that he had been warned "that the World Trade Center was going to collapse." But while testifying to the 9/11 Commission in 2004, he did not mention this warning. He instead claimed that he had become afraid that the Barclay Street building might collapse. In 2007, a group of people with a video camera asked Giuliani why the people in the towers had not been warned. Giuliani replied, "I didn't know the towers were going to collapse. . . . No one that I know of had any idea they would implode. That was a complete surprise." (Chapter 38)

Conclusion

Two of these accounts are about men—Bush and Shelton—who

were out of town, whereas the others are about men who were in Washington or New York. But they all have two things in common:

- All eight men were officials who were in position to affect the outcome of the 9/11 attacks.

- The 9/11 Commission's account of each man's activities is contradicted by considerable evidence.

These accounts provide, therefore, a remarkable conclusion: that the 9/11 Commission gave false accounts of the behavior of eight key decision-making officials on 9/11.

29

The Claim That It Was Not Imperative for President Bush to Be Hustled Away from the Florida School

Introduction

On the morning of September 11, 2001, President Bush was in Sarasota, Florida, scheduled to read with grade school students for a photo op.[383]

The Official Account

- When the president arrived, he was told at 8:55 AM that a small plane had hit the World Trade Center. Bush responded that "a commercial plane has hit the World Trade Center and we're going to . . . do the reading thing anyway."[384]

- While Bush was seated in the classroom, his chief of staff, Andrew Card, came in (at about 9:05[385]) and reportedly whispered in the president's ear: "A second plane hit the second tower. America is under attack."[386]

- Bush remained in the classroom another five to seven minutes,[387] then made a statement to the nation from the school, after which he left the school at about 9:35.[388]

- The *St. Petersburg Times* asked "why the Secret Service did not immediately hustle Bush to a secure location."[389] Likewise, the Family Steering Committee—which was instrumental in getting the 9/11 Commission created— asked, "Why was President Bush permitted by the Secret Service to remain in the Sarasota elementary school where he was reading to children?"[390]

- The 9/11 Commission explained, "The Secret Service told us they were anxious to move the President to a safer location, but did not think it imperative for him to run out the door."[391]

The Best Evidence

- The Secret Service is charged with the protection of the president. In a book about the Secret Service, Philip Melanson wrote, "With an unfolding terrorist attack, the procedure should have been to get the president to the closest secure location as quickly as possible."[392]

- The presidential visit had been highly publicized, and one journalist had written, in fact, that "Bush's presence made...the planned reading event a perceived target," because "the well-publicized event at the school assured Bush's location that day was no secret."[393]

- Given this fact, combined with evidence that many planes had been hijacked and that terrorists were going after high-value targets,[394] the Secret Service should have assumed that a hijacked airliner may have been bearing down on the school at that very moment, so the president should have been removed immediately. Indeed, as soon as the second strike on the World Trade Center was seen on television, the Marine carrying the president's phone said to Sarasota County Sheriff Bill Balkwill: "We're out of here. Can you get everybody ready?"[395]

- However, this Marine's instructions were evidently overridden: The head of the Secret Service detail allowed Bush to remain at the school thirty minutes longer to make his previously scheduled television address to the nation at 9:29, thereby letting any terrorists know that he was still at the school.[396]

Conclusion

This break in protocol suggests that the Secret Service, at some level, knew that the president was not in danger.

30

The Claim That Bush Left the Florida Classroom Quickly

Introduction

After President Bush entered the classroom in Sarasota, Florida, his chief of staff, Andrew Card, whispered in his ear, reportedly saying: "A second plane hit the second Tower. America is under attack."[397]

The Official Account

After getting this message from Card, President Bush, while doing nothing to frighten the children, left the room quickly.

- The president remained seated "only a matter of seconds," Card told the *San Francisco Chronicle,* and then "excused himself very politely to the teacher and to the students and he left."[398]

- The president "didn't want to alarm the children," Karl Rove told NBC. Knowing that "the drill was coming to a close . . . he waited for a few moments . . . —not very long at all . . . and he came into the staff room."[399]

- Sandra Kay Daniels, the teacher of the second-grade class that Bush visited, told the *Los Angeles Times*: "I knew something was up when President Bush didn't pick up the book and participate in the lesson. . . . He said, 'Mrs. Daniels, I have to leave now. I am going to leave Lt. Gov. Frank Brogan here to do the speech for me.' Looking at his face, you knew something was wrong. . . . He shook my hand and left."[400]

The Best Evidence

Whereas all the stories quoted above were published in 2002, on or near the first anniversary of 9/11, stories from earlier that year gave a very different account.

- In a *Tampa Tribune* article published September 1, 2002, Jennifer Barrs wrote that after Card whispered in the president's ear, Bush remained silent for about thirty seconds and then picked up his book and read with the children "for eight or nine minutes."[401]

- The *Tampa Tribune* article, which came out ten days before the aforementioned article by Sandra Kay Daniels, had indicated that Daniels herself had read with the students "for eight or nine minutes." It added that Daniels, having observed that Bush was so "lost in thought" that he "forgot about the book in his lap," had been confronted with a difficult problem: "I couldn't gently kick him. . . . I couldn't say, 'OK, Mr. President. Pick up your book, sir. The whole world is watching.'"[402]

- Various reports indicated that after the reading lesson was over, Bush continued to talk.[403] Bush was "openly stretching out the moment" and even "lingered until the press was gone," wrote Bill Sammon, the White House correspondent for the *Washington Times*, who referred to Bush as "the dawdler in chief."[404]

The fact that Bush had not left the room quickly was confirmed by a videotape of the classroom visit, which had been shot by the local cable-TV director and which became available online in June 2003.[405]

- The *Wall Street Journal* reported in March 2004 that this videotape showed that Bush "followed along for five minutes as children read aloud a story about a pet goat."[406]

- This tape became more widely known when it was included in Michael Moore's film *Fahrenheit 9/11*, released in June 2004.

- When the *Wall Street Journal* contacted the White House for its March 2004 article, spokesman Dan Bartlett admitted that the president had remained in the class-room for at least seven minutes, explaining that Bush had not left immediately because his "instinct was not to frighten the children by rushing out of the room."[407]

- Even if this explanation were valid, the real question, which the *Wall Street Journal* article did not ask, was why, on the first anniversary of 9/11, the Bush White House started telling a lie about how long Bush had remained in the classroom.

The foregoing raises two questions: Was this because the White House, having successfully portrayed Bush as a strong leader in response to the 9/11 attacks, wanted to conceal the fact that he had continued listening to children reading a story rather than taking immediate action as president and commander in chief? Was it because the Secret Service knew (as suggested in the chapter about the president's not being hustled away) that the country was not really "under attack" by foreign terrorists?

Conclusion

Whatever the motive, the Bush White House used the national media on the first anniversary of 9/11 to circulate a false story about the president's actions on that day.

31

The Claim That Vice President Cheney Did Not Enter the PEOC Until Shortly Before 10:00 AM

The Official Account

Vice President Dick Cheney took charge of the government's response to the 9/11 attacks after he entered the PEOC (the Presidential Emergency Operations Center), aka "the bunker." According to the *9/11 Commission Report*, Cheney did not enter the PEOC until almost 10:00 AM,[408] which was at least twenty minutes after the Pentagon attack.

The Best Evidence

Secretary of Transportation Norman Mineta told the 9/11 Commission that after he joined Cheney and others in the bunker at approximately 9:20 AM, he listened to an ongoing conversation between Cheney and a young man, which took place when "the airplane was coming into the Pentagon."[409]

The young man, having reported for the third time that the plane was coming closer, asked whether "the orders still stand." Cheney said emphatically that they did. *The 9/11 Commission Report*, by claiming that Cheney did not enter the PEOC until long after the Pentagon was damaged, implied that this exchange between Cheney and the young man—which can most naturally be understood as Cheney's confirmation of a stand-down order—could not have occurred.

However, testimony that Cheney was in the PEOC by 9:20 was reported not only by Mineta but also by Richard Clarke[410] and White House photographer David Bohrer.[411] Cheney himself, speaking on *Meet the Press* five days after 9/11, reported that he had entered the PEOC before the Pentagon was damaged.[412] Final proof was provided by official reports indicating that Secret Service agents reported that Cheney had entered the PEOC before 9:30 AM.[413]

Conclusion

The 9/11 Commission's attempt to bury the exchange between Cheney and the young man confirms the importance of Mineta's report of this conversation, which indicated that Cheney entered the PEOC much earlier than the 9/11 Commission claimed, and also suggested that Cheney gave a stand-down order.

32

The Claim That Cheney Could Not Have Authorized Shooting Down United 93.

Introduction

At 9:26 AM on 9/11, the Bush administration ordered a national ground stop, meaning that no more civil planes were allowed to take off; at 9:45, all planes already in the air were ordered to land.[414] Those orders provided the background for the possibility of an order to shoot down civilian airplanes that violated this order. Controversy remains about whether United 93, which, the 9/11 Commission claimed, crashed in Shanksville, Pennsylvania, was shot down.

The Official Account

Vice President Cheney reached the Presidential Emergency Operations Center "shortly before 10:00."[415] At 10:02, he "began receiving reports from the Secret Service of an inbound aircraft—presumably hijacked—heading toward Washington."[416] Although this aircraft was United 93, the commission said, this was not known at the time, because the military did not learn about the hijacking of this flight until after it had crashed.[417]

Through a military aide, Cheney gave authorization to shoot civilian airplanes down at "some time between 10:10 and 10:15," again "probably some time between 10:12 and 10:18," and then obtained confirmation from President Bush by 10:20.[418] Reporting that Richard Clarke had "ask[ed] the President for authority to shoot down aircraft," the 9/11 Commission wrote, "Confirmation of that authority came at 10:25."[419]

Shoot-down authorization came, therefore, far too late to affect the fate of United 93, which crashed at 10:03.[420]

The Best Evidence

Considerable evidence indicates that the shoot-down authorization came not at some time after 10:10 but closer to 9:50, and therefore early enough for the military to have shot down United 93, which reportedly crashed at 10:03:

1. The fullest evidence appeared in counterterrorism coordinator Richard Clarke's 2004 book, *Against All Enemies*.[421]

- Just before the Pentagon attack, Clarke wrote, he told Major Michael Fenzel, his liaison to Cheney, that he wanted authorization for "the Air Force to shoot down any aircraft—including a hijacked passenger flight—that looks like it is threatening to attack and cause large-scale death on the ground."[422]

- Fenzel called back rather quickly. (Clarke said, "I was amazed at the speed of the decisions coming from Cheney and, through him, from Bush.") Fenzel's call came after the Pentagon attack but before Air Force One took off from Florida's Sarasota Bradenton International Airport, which would mean between 9:38 and 9:55.[423]

- Fenzel said: "Tell the Pentagon they have authority from the President to shoot down hostile aircraft, repeat, they have authority to shoot down hostile aircraft." Clarke reported that he then said, "DOD, DOD, . . . the President has ordered the use of force against aircraft deemed to be hostile."[424]

2. A 2003 article in *U.S. News and World Report*, discussing "President Bush's unprecedented order to shoot down any hijacked civilian airplane," stated, "Pentagon sources say Bush communicated the order to Cheney almost immediately after Flight 77 hit the Pentagon and the FAA, for the first time ever, ordered all domestic flights grounded."[425] This report, reinforced by the previous and following points, would put the shoot-down authorization shortly after 9:45.

3. Barbara Starr, CNN's Pentagon correspondent, said in a 2002

program reviewing the events of 9/11: "It is now 9:40, and one very big problem is out there: United Airlines Flight 93 has turned off its transponder. Officials believe it is headed for Washington, D.C. . . . On a secure phone line, Vice President Cheney tells the military it has permission to shoot down any airliners threatening Washington."[426]

4. In 2002 and 2003, a number of military leaders stated that they received the shoot-down authorization while United 93 was still aloft.

- Colonel Robert Marr, the head of NEADS, said, "[W]e received the clearance to kill if need be."[427]

- General Larry Arnold, the commander of NORAD within the Continental United States, said, "I had every intention of shooting down United 93 if it continued to progress toward Washington, DC."[428]

- Brigadier General Montague Winfield, the deputy director of the National Military Command Center in the Pentagon, reportedly said: "The decision was made to try to go intercept Flight 93. . . . The Vice President [said] that the President had given us permission to shoot down innocent civilian aircraft that threatened Washington, DC."[429]

In spite of all of this evidence, *The 9/11 Commission Report*, published in July 2004, declared, "By the time the military learned about [United 93], it had crashed."[430] On the basis of this claim, the 9/11 Commission declared that the above-cited statements by Marr, Arnold, and Winfield were all "incorrect."[431]

However, besides contradicting these statements, the 9/11 Commission's claim conflicts with an FAA memo to the commission of May 23, 2003.

- This memo said that in an FAA teleconference with the military that had begun "minutes after the first aircraft hit the World Trade Center"—hence shortly after 8:46 AM—the FAA had "shared real-time information . . . about . . . all the flights of interest,"[432] which would have included United Flight 93.[433]

- 9/11 Commissioner Richard Ben-Veniste, putting the FAA memo in the commission's record, said that it provided evidence that the "FAA was providing information as it received it, immediately after the first crash into the Towers."[434] But the 9/11 Commission dealt with this memo by simply omitting any reference to it in *The 9/11 Commission Report*.

Conclusion

The 9/11 Commission claimed that Cheney did not issue a shoot-down authorization until 10:10 or later, whereas the evidence shows that Cheney gave the authorization by 9:50—at least twenty minutes earlier than the commission claimed. This twenty-minute discrepancy means no less than the difference between whether military pilots could, or could not, have been ordered to shoot down United Flight 93 (which reportedly crashed at 10:03).

The commission's claim about the time of the shoot-down authorization was not the only part of the official account of the shoot-down authorization that was problematic: The press focused on the Bush administration's claim that Cheney had transmitted authorization received from the president (rather than declaring it on his own, which would have been illegal), about which even the 9/11 Commission was skeptical.[435]

More important to the truth about 9/11, however, was the 9/11 Commission's claim that the shoot-down authorization was not given by Cheney until 10:10 or later, hence after United 93 had crashed. This claim is contradicted by reports from Richard Clarke, *U.S. News and World Report*, Pentagon correspondent Barbara Starr, the FAA, and three military officers: Colonel Marr, General Arnold, and Brigadier General Winfield.

Moreover, the 9/11 Commission's 10:10-or-later claim pre-supposed the commission's claim that Cheney did not enter the PEOC, where he took charge, until almost 10:00, and this claim is contradicted by abundant evidence, as shown in Chapter 31.[436] Any new investigation needs to ask why the 9/11 Commission made a claim about the time of Cheney's shoot-down authorization that contradicted a great deal of evidence.

33

The Claim That Secretary of Defense Rumsfeld Was Not in a Position to Do Anything About the Attacks or the Crash of United 93

Introduction

Questions have been raised about whether Secretary of Defense Donald Rumsfeld could have had responsibility for one or more of the 9/11 attacks, and whether he was partially responsible for the crash of United Airlines Flight 93, which, according to the 9/11 Commission, occurred in Shanksville, Pennsylvania.

The Official Account

The activities of Secretary Rumsfeld on the morning of the 9/11 attacks show that he could not have had any responsibility for any of the attacks, even in the sense of having been able to prevent them, or anything to do with the crash of United 93.

- On the morning of 9/11, Secretary Rumsfeld held a breakfast meeting with members of Congress at the Pentagon, which lasted until about 9:00.[437] As the meeting was breaking up, they learned that "the first plane had hit the World Trade tower."[438] Authorities believed this crash to have resulted from pilot error.[439]

- "He [Rumsfeld] returned to his office for his daily intelligence briefing." After he was "informed of the second strike in New York . . . he resumed the briefing while awaiting more information." After the Pentagon was struck, Secretary Rumsfeld went to the parking lot to assist with rescue efforts.[440]

- "Secretary Rumsfeld was not in the NMCC [National Military Command Center] when the shoot-down order was first conveyed," reported *The 9/11 Commission Report*. He went from the parking lot to his office, where he spoke to the President [shortly after 10:00], then to the Executive Support Center, where he participated in the White House video teleconference. He moved to the NMCC shortly before 10:30, in order to join Vice Chairman Myers."[441]

As that summary shows, Rumsfeld was in meetings when the attacks on the WTC and the Pentagon occurred.

With regard to the Pentagon in particular, the military, as *The 9/11 Commission Report* pointed out, "never received notice that American 77 was hijacked":[442]

- The military might have learned that American 77 (which was to crash into the Pentagon) was in trouble, possibly hijacked, if any of the people dealing with the crisis had been involved in the White House video teleconference, which was conducted from the Situation Room by counterterrorism coordinator Richard Clarke. However, the 9/11 Commission reported, "We do not know who from Defense participated, but we know that in the first hour, none of the personnel involved in managing the crisis did."[443]

- Rumsfeld in particular, as the summary shows, was not involved in Clarke's video conference until a few minutes after 10:00.

Moreover, Rumsfeld also could not have had anything to do with the crash of United 93, which occurred at 10:03, for two reasons:

- Rumsfeld, as the summary shows, did not enter the NMCC until 10:30.

- "By the time the military learned about [United 93's hijacking], it had crashed."[444]

The Best Evidence

Claims made about Rumsfeld in *The 9/11 Commission Report*, which reflect claims made by Rumsfeld himself in 2004, have been contradicted by several authoritative sources:

1. Richard Clarke, the national counterterrorism coordinator, wrote a best-selling book, *Against All Enemies*[445]—which came out in March 2004, several months earlier than *The 9/11 Commission Report*. Clarke's book contradicted in advance claims that the 9/11 Commission would make in its report about Rumsfeld's activities on 9/11 between 9:00 and 10:00 AM.

- Reporting about his video conference, which evidently began at roughly 9:10,[446] Clarke wrote: "As I entered the Video Center … I could see people rushing into studios around the city: Donald Rumsfeld at Defense and George Tenet at CIA."[447] So, whereas Rumsfeld and the commission say that Rumsfeld went from his breakfast meeting to his office for a CIA briefing, where he remained until the Pentagon attack, Clarke said that, shortly after the second WTC attack, Rumsfeld went to the Pentagon's teleconferencing studio.

- Clarke indicated, moreover, that Rumsfeld continued to participate in the videoconference: After the Pentagon attack, Clarke could "still see Rumsfeld on the screen."[448] A little later, Clarke wrote, "smoke was getting into the Pentagon secure teleconferencing studio," and "Franklin Miller urged him [Rumsfeld] to helicopter to DOD's alternate site," but Rumsfeld replied, "I am too goddam old to go to an alternate site." So, "Rumsfeld moved to another studio in the Pentagon."[449]

Clarke's account of Rumsfeld's location from 9:10 to 9:45 seems more plausible than the account provided by Rumsfeld and *The 9/11 Commission Report*, because:

- Clarke's account, if false, could have been proven wrong by the videoconference tape.

- It is not plausible that, after being told of the second attack on the World Trade Center, the secretary of defense would have continued listening to a CIA briefing.

- It is not plausible that the 9/11 Commission would have failed to contradict Clarke's account of Rumsfeld had it been able to do so. Instead, it simply did not mention it.[450]

2. Robert Andrews, the Principal Deputy Assistant Secretary of Defense for Special Operations and Low Intensity Conflict, gave a lecture in 2007 that contradicted the Rumsfeld-9/11 Commission account of Rumsfeld's movements:[451]

- Knowing that Rumsfeld had gone to the Executive Support Center (ESC) to join Clarke's video conference after the second WTC attack, Andrews stated, he rushed to the counterterrorism center [CTC] to get materials that Rumsfeld would need.[452]

- Then, after feeling and hearing an explosive event in the Pentagon, Andrews rushed back to the ESC, where he served as Rumsfeld's advisor during the White House videoconference. "I was there in the Support Center with the Secretary when he was talking to Clarke on the White House video-teleconference, and to the President," Andrews said.[453]

3. A third authoritative source contradicting the official account of Rumsfeld's activities was Paul Wolfowitz, the deputy secretary of defense, in an early April 2002 interview with military historian Alfred Goldberg,[454] who would later be the first author of *Pentagon 9/11*.[455] Wolfowitz gave a report inconsistent with the 9/11 Commission's claim that Rumsfeld had not gone into the NMCC until after United 93 had crashed:

- Wolfowitz stated that after the Pentagon attack, he and others were told to go outside the building, but that they were allowed to go back in within "less than ten minutes"—which means, if the Pentagon was attacked at 9:38, he was referring to going back in at roughly 9:50.

- Wolfowitz reported, "We went into the NMCC, where the Secretary was, and General Myers. General Shelton was in Europe."

- He next said: "We proceeded with discussions by secure video conference. One issue was what to do about the plane over Pennsylvania, getting orders to get fighters up to intercept it, and the Secretary getting approval from the President to shoot it down."[456]

This report by Wolfowitz contradicted two central elements in the account of Rumsfeld's locations provided in *The 9/11 Commission Report*:

- Whereas the 9/11 Commission claimed that Rumsfeld did not go into the NMCC until 10:30, Wolfowitz reported talking with Rumsfeld there before 10:00.

- Whereas the 9/11 Commission claimed that the military did not learn about UA 93's troubles until after it crashed, Wolfowitz reported that he and Rumsfeld, along with General Myers, had discussed "what to do about the plane over Pennsylvania."

Conclusion

The 9/11 Commission absolved Donald Rumsfeld of any responsibility for what happened after 9:03 that morning by claiming that, in the first hour of the White House video teleconference, "none of the [Defense] personnel involved in managing the crisis [participated]."[457] Reports by both Richard Clarke and Robert Andrews, however, show that Rumsfeld participated in this videoconference during this crucial hour.

The 9/11 Commission also absolved Rumsfeld from any involvement in the crash of UA 93 by claiming that the military did not know anything about UA 93 until after it had crashed, and that Rumsfeld was not in the NMCC prior to 10:30. Paul Wolfowitz, however, indicated that he discussed what to do about UA 93 with Rumsfeld and Myers before 10:00.

Testimony by Richard Clarke, Robert Andrews, and Paul Wolfowitz, accordingly, provided very strong evidence that the 9/11 Commission made false claims relevant to Rumsfeld's behavior. Further investigation of Rumsfeld's actual behavior on the morning of 9/11, therefore, is needed.

34

The Claim That General Myers Was Not at the Pentagon During the Attacks

Introduction

On September 11, 2001, General Richard B. Myers, vice chairman of the Joint Chiefs of Staff (JCS), became the acting chairman, because the chairman of the JCS, General Hugh H. Shelton, was flying to a NATO meeting in Budapest.[458] Myers's account of his activities during the morning of 9/11 is reflected in the 9/11 Commission's report. But some features of this account raise questions.

The Official Account

General Myers was not at the Pentagon during the attacks. He was on Capitol Hill with Senator Max Cleland to discuss the upcoming hearing to confirm Myers as the new chairman of the Joint Chiefs of Staff.[459] Senator Cleland verified that this meeting did occur.[460]

While Myers was waiting in Cleland's outer office, a television report gave him the impression that the World Trade Center had been hit by "a small plane or something like that," so he and Cleland went ahead with their meeting.[461] Soon, having learned from a staffer that the second tower had been hit, they ended their meeting. Returning to the exterior office, they learned from TV that flames had erupted in the WTC.[462]

While watching the TV coverage, Myers received a call on his military aide's cell phone from General Ralph Eberhart, the commander of NORAD, saying that he was working with the FAA to get all planes grounded. Myers then got a call from his executive assistant, who said that a major hijacking seemed to be underway and recommended that Myers "return to the Pentagon as soon as possible."[463] "As we raced away from Capitol Hill,"[464] Myers wrote, "the Pentagon was hit . . . [b]efore we even got to the 14th Street Bridge."[465]

At 9:46, NORAD staff "reported that they were still trying to locate Secretary Rumsfeld and Vice Chairman Myers." General Myers returned to the National Military Command Center "shortly before 10:00," at which time he joined the NMCC's air threat conference call[466]—which had begun without him at 9:37.[467]

General Myers, accordingly, was not in the Pentagon during the attacks on the WTC and the Pentagon. With regard to the hijacking of United Flight 93 (which, the 9/11 Commission reported, crashed in Shanksville, Pennsylvania), Myers could not have ordered fighter jets to bring it down, because "[b]y the time the military learned about the flight, it had crashed."[468]

The Best Evidence

The accuracy of the accounts provided both by Myers and *The 9/11 Commission Report* are called into question by the following:

- Contradictions with accounts provided by counterterrorism coordinator Richard Clarke, Deputy Secretary of Defense Paul Wolfowitz, Navy Captain Charles Joseph Leidig, General Hugh Shelton, and Army Secretary Thomas White

- Inconsistencies with accounts Myers had provided in 2001

- Implausibilities

Contradictions

1. The official account of General Myers's activities during the attacks contradicts the account that had been provided in counterterrorism coordinator Richard Clarke's 2004 book, *Against All Enemies*,[469] which had appeared several months before the publication of *The 9/11 Commission Report* and which described Myers as being in the Pentagon during the attacks:

- Describing the beginning of the White House videoconference, which his account suggests began at approximately 9:10,[470] Clarke wrote:

    As I entered the Video Center . . . I could see people rushing into studios around the city: Donald Rumsfeld at Defense and George Tenet at CIA. . . .

Air force four-star General Dick Myers was filling in for the Chairman of the Joint Chiefs, Hugh Shelton, who was over the Atlantic.[471]

- Shortly before 9:28, Clarke reported, he had this exchange with Myers:

  [Clarke] "JCS [Joint Chiefs of Staff], JCS. I assume NORAD has scrambled fighters and AWACS. How many? Where?"

  [Myers]: "Not a pretty picture, Dick. . . . We are in the midst of Vigilant Warrior, a NORAD exercise, but . . . Otis has launched two birds toward New York. Langley is trying to get two up now . . . . "

  [Clarke] "Okay, how long to CAP[472] over DC? . . . . "

  [Myers] "Fast as we can. Fifteen minutes?" Myers asked, looking at the generals and colonels around him. It was now 9:28.[473]

- Accordingly, Clarke's account in his *Against All Enemies*—which was not mentioned in either *The 9/11 Commission Report* or in Myers's 2009 book, *Eyes on the Horizon*—contradicts the account given by Myers and the 9/11 Commission.

2. The official account of Myers's activities was also contradicted by statements made in 2002 by Paul Wolfowitz, the deputy secretary of defense, with regard to two points: (A) In an interview conducted by Alfred Goldberg (who would later become the first author of *Pentagon 9/11*, a major study published in 2007[474]), Wolfowitz gave a report that contradicted the claim, made by Myers and *The 9/11 Commission Report*, that Myers had been away from the Pentagon until he returned "shortly before 10:00."

- Wolfowitz stated that after the Pentagon attack, he and others were told to go outside the building, but that they were allowed to go back in within "less than ten minutes"—which means, if the Pentagon was attacked at

9:38, he was referring to going back in at roughly 9:50.

- Wolfowitz reported: "We went into the NMCC, where the Secretary was, and General Myers. General Shelton was in Europe."

- Wolfowitz next said: "We proceeded with discussions by secure video conference. One issue was what to do about the plane over Pennsylvania, getting orders to get fighters up to intercept it, and the Secretary getting approval from the President to shoot it down."[475]

This report by Wolfowitz, therefore, contradicted the claims by *The 9/11 Commission Report* that Myers was not in the Pentagon when the building was attacked and that the military, led by General Myers, had not been informed about United Flight 93's troubles before it crashed.

(B) In 2001, Wolfowitz—and even Myers himself—contradicted the claim about United 93 that *The 9/11 Commission Report* would make: that the military knew nothing was wrong with it until it crashed.

- Wolfowitz, answering a question on the *PBS NewsHour with Jim Lehrer*, said: "We responded awfully quickly . . . and, in fact, we were already tracking in on that plane that crashed in Pennsylvania. I think it was the heroism of the passengers on board that brought it down. But the Air Force was in a position to do so if we had had to."[476]

- In 2001, Myers said at his confirmation hearing: "[I]f my memory serves me, . . . we had launched on the [airliner] that eventually crashed in Pennsylvania. . . . [W]e had gotten somebody close to it, as I recall."[477]

3. One of the claims by Myers and *The 9/11 Commission Report* that was contradicted in the interview of Wolfowitz—that Myers was not in the Pentagon during the attacks—was also contradicted in a 9/11 Commission document labeled "Secret Memorandum for the Record."[478] This memorandum, which was dated a year earlier than *The 9/11 Commission Report*, quoted statements that

were made in 2003 by Admiral Charles Joseph "Joe" Leidig, a naval officer who had assumed duties in the NMCC as Deputy for Command Center Operations about two months before 9/11.[479] According to this document:

- On the morning of 9/11, Leidig said, he served as the NMCC's Deputy Director of Operations (DDO) in place of Brigadier General Montague Winfield from 8:30 until Winfield relieved him some time after 10:00.

- During a discussion of Delta Flight 1989, which occurred between 9:23 and 9:26,[480] Leidig was "certain that the Vice Chairman [of the Joint Chiefs of Staff] was in the room at the time. He [Leidig] recalled looking at him and saying there is a recommendation to evacuate the Sears tower in Chicago. He remembered General Meyers [sic] saying that was a good idea."[481]

According to this memorandum, therefore, Captain Leidig supported Wolfowitz's report that Myers was in the Pentagon, not somewhere else, shortly before the Pentagon attack.

4. The claim by the 9/11 Commission and Myers that he was not in the NMCC until "shortly before 10:00," and hence was not there immediately after the Pentagon attack, was contradicted by the officer he was replacing that day, General Hugh Shelton:

- In Shelton's 2009 book, describing what happened on the plane that had been taking him to Europe—but which he, after learning about the attack on the Pentagon, turned around—he wrote: "Meanwhile, Dick [Myers] was on the phone, and the first report was that a *hand grenade* had just gone off in the Pentagon parking lot. . . . Since our connection was encrypted, he was able to give me a complete status report from the NMCC."[482]

- Continuing his discussion with Myers, Shelton added: "I need you to call Ed Eberhart . . . at NORAD and let him know that we're coming back on *Speckled Trout,* and that I would consider it a personal favor if he would see to it

that the Chairman and his crew are not shot down on
their way back to Andrews." Myers replied: "Will do."[483]

5. Thomas White, the secretary of the army, indicated that General
Myers had been at a breakfast meeting in the Pentagon from 8:00
until 8:46, when the first plane hit the World Trade Center (not in
Senator Cleland's office on Capitol Hill).[484]

- White told *Frontline*: "Don Rumsfeld had a breakfast,
  and virtually every one of the senior officials of the
  Department of Defense—-service chiefs, secretary,
  deputy, everybody, chairman of the Joint Chiefs of Staff.
  And as that breakfast was breaking up, the first plane had
  hit the World Trade tower."[485]

- By "chairman of the Joint Chiefs of Staff," White had
  to mean Myers, the acting and soon-to-be-confirmed
  chairman, because General Hugh Shelton, the outgoing
  chairman, was on his way to Europe.[486]

Inconsistencies

1. The official story about Myers, which was based on *The 9/11
Commission Report* and Myers's statements in 2004 and later, contradicted assertions Myers had made in 2001:

- Official story, 2004: Myers learned of the Pentagon attack
  while being driven back to the Pentagon.[487]

September 13, 2001: Myers learned of the attack while still in
Senator Cleland's office.[488]

- Official story, 2004: While Myers was being driven back
  to the Pentagon, he was called by General Eberhart.[489]

October 2001: Myers received the Eberhart call while still in
Senator Cleland's office.[490]

- Official story, 2004: The Eberhart call to Myers came
  before the Pentagon was hit.[491]

October, 2001: The Eberhart call came *after* the Pentagon was
hit.[492]

2. Senator Cleland's stories also contained inconsistencies:

- At the confirmation hearing in 2001, Cleland said to Myers: "It's a good thing we were meeting here [on Capitol Hill] and not us meeting in the Pentagon because about the time you and I were having our visit, . . . at just about that very moment, the Pentagon was being hit."[493]

- In 2003, Cleland said that just at the moment after "Myers rushed out of [his] office, headed for the Pentagon, . . . the Pentagon was hit."[494]

Implausibilities

1. In a 2001 interview, Myers said that while he was meeting with Cleland in his office, the second tower was struck, but "[n]obody informed us of that." It was only when they finished their meeting and came out of the inner office, Myers said, that he and Cleland realized "that the second tower had been hit."[495] It was "right at that time," Myers added, that "somebody said the Pentagon has been hit"[496]—thereby indicating that the meeting had lasted until almost 9:37.

- But the idea that nobody—neither Cleland's secretary nor anyone at the Pentagon or otherwise in the military—had notified him (the acting chairman of the Joint Chiefs of Staff), so that he did not know anything about the second attack until just before the Pentagon was struck, is implausible.

- This realization likely motivated the later version of his story, according to which a staff person from the outer office told Myers and Cleland about the second WTC attack right after it occurred.[497]

2. In a 2003 speech, Senator Cleland said: "The first plane had already hit the World Trade Center and Gen. Myers bolted from his seat. We rushed into an adjoining office as we saw on TV the second plane slam into the second tower. Gen. Myers rushed out of my office, headed for the Pentagon. At that moment, the Pentagon was hit."[498]

- More than thirty minutes elapsed between these two attacks.

- Cleland's account is implausible because it suggests that there were at most ten minutes between the two attacks.

Conclusion

In light of the following:

- the contradictions between the 2004 accounts by Myers and the 9/11 Commission, on the one hand, and the accounts by Richard Clarke, Paul Wolfowitz, Captain Leidig, General Shelton, Thomas White, and even the Myers of 2001, on the other

- the inconsistencies between the earlier and later stories told by Myers

- the implausibilities in the accounts by Myers and Cleland,

the evidence suggests that the official account about Myers—according to which he was not in the Pentagon during the attacks and could not have been involved in a decision to bring down United 93—is false and should be further investigated.

35

The Claim That General Shelton Returned to the Pentagon from an Aborted Flight in the Early Afternoon

Introduction

General Hugh Shelton, chairman of the Joint Chiefs of Staff on 9/11, was scheduled to fly to Europe on September 11, 2001, to attend a NATO meeting in Hungary. He was to be accompanied by several people, including Lieutenant Commander Suzanne Giesemann, who served as an aide and would later write about this day in a book.[499] In Shelton's absence, General Richard Myers, the vice chairman of the Joint Chiefs of Staff, was to be the acting chairman of the Joint Chiefs.[500]

The Official Account

- At "around 7:30" AM,[501] General Shelton left Andrews Air Force Base (AFB) aboard a modified C-135 (the military version of a Boeing 707) nicknamed "Speckled Trout," which was usually reserved for the Air Force chief of staff.[502]

- About 100 minutes later (hence at about 9:10 AM) Shelton was informed of the second WTC attack,[503] after which he gave the order to have his plane turned around. Flights from overseas, however, were not being allowed to enter US airspace,[504] and Speckled Trout was initially denied re-entry.[505]

- Shelton next learned that the Pentagon had been hit and, being confident that his plane would not be stopped, ordered the pilot to return to Andrews AFB.[506] Shortly thereafter Shelton's plane received clearance.[507]

- On the way back to the Pentagon, Shelton's plane flew over Manhattan.[508] He wrote, "We flew directly over what had been the Twin Towers, just a few minutes after they collapsed."[509] Then the plane "vectored directly back to Andrews,"[510] and—Shelton's aide Giesemann stated—arrived there within an hour.[511]

- At Andrews, Shelton was met by an entourage of patrol cars and motorcycle cops "who escorted us, lights flashing and sirens blaring, through the eerily deserted streets of the city all the way to the Pentagon," where he went to his office and was updated by General Myers and others.[512]

- He then examined the damage to the outside of the Pentagon, after which he went to the National Military Command Center (NMCC) inside the Pentagon,[513] where he arrived—as General Myers reported—at 5:40 PM.[514]

The Best Evidence

There are four serious problems with Shelton's account of his movements that day.

First, the timeline implied by Shelton's account is implausible.

- The second WTC tower came down at 10.28 AM, so if Shelton's plane flew over the Twin Towers "just a few minutes after they collapsed," then it must have flown over New York City before 11:00.

- If, as Giesemann stated, Shelton's plane landed at Andrews "within an hour of passing New York City,"[515] it should have arrived there by roughly noon, and the escorted drive should have brought them to the Pentagon by approximately 12:30.

- Upon arriving back in the US, Shelton was again the chairman of the Joint Chiefs of Staff.[516] At 12:30 there would have been many decisions still to be made. Indeed, following the attacks on the WTC and the Pentagon, he should have, fearing further attacks, gone immediately to the NMCC. Yet, he wrote, he went first to his office and then the crash site.[517]

- He certainly should not have waited until 5:40 PM, which, according to General Myers, is when Shelton arrived at the NMCC.[518]

- The idea that Shelton spent five hours at the Pentagon before going to the NMCC is implausible. Indeed, it is contradicted by Myers's statement that at 5:40 Shelton had "just returned" from the aborted European flight.[519]

Second, Shelton's account of his return trip is also contradicted by the Andrews AFB flight-tracking strips for his flight (which were obtained through a FOIA request[520]).

- The flight-tracking strip indicates that Speckled Trout— code named "Trout 99"[521]—landed at Andrews at 4:40 PM.[522]

- Why would Shelton and Giesemann indicate that they arrived at Andrews at roughly noon—almost five hours earlier than Speckled Trout's actual arrival time?

A third problem is that the accounts by Shelton and Giesemann, which indicate that they arrived at the Pentagon by roughly 12:30, are contradicted by one of Giesemann's statements:

- Although her description of the drive from Andrews to the Pentagon parallels Shelton's, even saying that the streets were "eerily" empty,[523] Giesemann also wrote, "No one spoke as we sped across the Southeast-Southwest Freeway, usually jammed with cars at this late afternoon hour."[524]

- This "late afternoon" statement is, of course, supported by the flight-tracking strip.

A fourth problem is that Shelton's account is contradicted even more severely by a September 2011 article describing the account by the Speckled Trout flight navigator, Colonel Rob Pedersen.[525] According to Pedersen's article:

- "The first three hours [of Shelton's flight] went smoothly" until the BBC reported on the WTC strikes.

- After Shelton gave his order to turn around: "The airplane did turn, but it didn't head directly back to the United States. For the first couple of hours, the crew didn't have clearance to return—or a destination—'so we went into a holding pattern near Greenland,' Pedersen said. . . . Speckled Trout made it back to Canada, but it was initially denied entry to US airspace. The crew started holding once again."[526]

- "[I]t wasn't easy getting a security clearance, even for such a high-profile passenger. . . . '[We couldn't] say over the radio who [we were] carrying because they don't have secure communications at the FAA. . . . It took a little bit of time . . . before they let us back in,' he [Pedersen] said."[527]

- "[The] flight back to Andrews took [the crew] directly over New York City. . . . The fly-by was quick. . . . By early afternoon, they had made their way to Andrews."[528]

- Although Pedersen's account contains some obviously problematic elements—including his statement that the flight returned "by early afternoon"[529]—his story, according to which Shelton's plane was forced into a holding pattern near Greenland and again over Canada, would explain why it did not return to Andrews until 4:40.

Conclusion

The account provided by both Shelton and Giesemann, according to which they were able to return to the Pentagon without delay and reach it by roughly 12:30 PM—is contradicted by the plane's flight navigator, by the flight-tracking strip, by General Richard Myers, and by one of Giesemann's own statements. If, as it appears, Shelton and Giesemann falsely claimed that they returned almost five hours earlier than they actually did, it must be asked: Why?

And if, as appears to be the case, Shelton returned to Andrews at 4:40 PM, why was the aircraft of the top US military commander delayed for almost five hours on this critical day?

Any new investigation should ask these questions.

36

The Claim That Brigadier General Winfield Was Not the Deputy Director of Operations for the National Military Command Center During the Attacks

Introduction

The task of the National Military Command Center (NMCC), explained *The 9/11 Commission Report*, was "to gather the relevant parties and establish the chain of command between the National Command Authority—the president and the secretary of defense—and those who need to carry out their orders."[530] The person responsible for gathering these parties was the NMCC's deputy director of operations (DDO). In September 2001, the DDO was Army Brigadier General Montague Winfield. However, other people trained for this role can serve as the acting deputy director of operations.[531]

On the issue of who served as the DDO on the morning of 9/11 from 8:30 until some time after 10:00, there are two conflicting accounts. For almost two years after 9/11, it was generally assumed that the DDO's duties were carried out by Winfield himself. But on July 21, 2003, the Pentagon provided a briefing for nine members of the 9/11 Commission staff, who were told, "On 9/11, the acting-Deputy Director for Operations (DDO) was Navy Captain Charles Joseph Leidig."[532] Both accounts are supported by evidence.

This point is, accordingly, divided into two parts: Official Account #1 and Official Account #2.

Official Account #1

Brigadier General Montague Winfield carried out the tasks of the DDO on the morning of 9/11, as shown by several facts.

(1) TV specials that aired the week of the first anniversary of 9/11 portrayed Winfield as on duty in the NMCC.

- Winfield and the National Military Command Center were featured in a retrospective CNN program in which Pentagon correspondent Barbara Starr said, "Brigadier General Montague Winfield was in command of the military's worldwide nerve center that morning."

- After the attack on the Pentagon, Starr said: "Winfield and his staff never feel the impact. . . . Winfield is running a secure phone call with the White House, the FAA, and the North American Air Defense Command, NORAD."[533]

- Winfield was treated the same way in a 2002 ABC interview with Peter Jennings, in which he gave a dramatic account of the military's attempt to stop United Flight 93 (which, the 9/11 Commission reported, crashed in Shanksville, Pennsylvania).[534]

(2) General Richard Myers, who on 9/11 was the acting chairman of the Joint Chiefs of Staff, stated in his 2009 book: "Army Brig. Gen. Montague Winfield was the duty officer in charge of the center that morning . . . . General Winfield was doing a good job of managing the information flow and keeping the chain of command plugged in."[535]

(3) Winfield's biographical statement says: "Brigadier General Winfield served as the Deputy Director for Operations, J3, in the National Military Command Center. He was present as the General Officer in Charge during the terrorist attacks of 9/11."[536]

However, although the Pentagon had initially said through spokespersons, including Winfield himself, that Winfield was the DDO during the attacks, the Pentagon later said that this original story was not true.

The Rejection of Official Account #1

In spite of what the public had been previously led to believe, nine 9/11 Commission staff members—as explained in the introduction above—were told by the Pentagon on July 21, 2003, that a different officer, Captain Charles Joseph Leidig, was serving as the DDO during the attacks.[537]

On April 29, 2004, Leidig was interviewed by five members of the 9/11 Commission staff. According to the staff-written preamble to the taped interview's transcript, Winfield was in "a USAF-convened session for general officers who rated Air Force Officers," and "[s]uch meetings are not disturbed unless the reason is significant."[538] In May 2004, 9/11 Commission staff members held two interviews with Commander Patrick Gardner, who referred to Leidig as the Acting DDO on 9/11.[539]

Official Account #2

According to the Pentagon's briefing of nine members of the 9/11 staff on July 21, 2003:

- "[T]he acting-Deputy Director for Operations (DDO) was Navy Captain Charles Joseph Leidig, a trained back-up filling in for the Operations Team 2 leader, Army BG Winfield, who was at an unrelated, closed-door personnel meeting convened by the Air Force to discuss the rating of Air Force officers."

- "Captain Leidig was the primary DDO during the initial phase of the NMCC's reaction to events as they unfolded; BG Winfield transitioned into the position upon his return to the NMCC."[540]

Additional information was provided on April 29, 2004, when Miles Kara and four other members of the 9/11 Commission staff held an interview with Leidig.[541]

- The preamble, prepared by Kara, indicated: "On 9/11 Captain Leidig was the action Deputy Director for Operations (DDO). . . . He was sitting in place of the Operations Team 2 DDO, then Brigadier General Montague Winfield, USA, who was attending a meeting elsewhere in JCS spaces. The meeting was a USAF-convened session for general officers who rated Air Force officers. Such meetings are generally not disturbed unless the reason is significant."[542]

- Leidig provided information about himself: "He had been on the Joint Staff since mid-July and qualified to be a DDO about a month before 9/11. He was qualified to substitute for any of the DDO's who led the five Command Center watch teams."[543]

- About replacing Winfield, Leidig stated: "General Winfield asked him the afternoon before if he would sit in as DDO for Operations Center Team 2. By agreement, he came in at 0830, received the intelligence . . . , and assumed the duty of Deputy Director of Operations. The Assistant DDO was Commander Pat Gardner, USN. He couldn't recall the names of the other Operations Team 2 personnel on watch that day."[544]

- After describing the sequence of events that occurred while he was the acting DDO, Leidig said that General Myers, at some point, "realized the coordinator was not a General as the position called for" and his "guidance was to get General Winfield briefed up and in the chair." Finally, "General Winfield took over at some point in relation to the report of the Pennsylvania crash."[545]

In the two interviews with Commander Patrick Gardner held by 9/11 Commission staff members in May 2004, Gardner confirmed Leidig's April 29 statement that Gardner served as the Assistant DDO while he (Leidig) was the Acting DOD on 9/11.[546]

On June 17, 2004, there was a 9/11 Commission hearing, at which the public was first informed of Leidig's role as DDO on 9/11. After Chairman Thomas Kean introduced him,[547] Leidig provided to the commission a brief statement, in which he said:

- "Approximately two months prior to 11 September 2001, I assumed duties as the Deputy for Command Center Operations. . . . I qualified in August 2001 to stand watch as the Deputy Director for Operations in the NMCC."

- "On 10 September 2001, Brigadier General Winfield, U. S. Army, asked that I stand a portion of his duty as Deputy Director for Operations, NMCC, on the following day. I agreed and relieved Brigadier General Winfield at 0830 on 11 September 2001."[548]

The Best Evidence

The account of the replacement of Winfield by Leidig is problematic for a number of reasons:

(1) It would have been peculiar if Winfield, after having asked Leidig to replace him on 9/11,[549] had presented himself, in CNN and ABC programs in 2002, as the DDO during the attacks.[550]

(2) Leidig's substitution for Winfield was—according to what is presently known—never mentioned before 2003, when the 9/11 Commission was working toward its final report.

(3) A motive for a creation of this account in 2003 could have been provided by a 9/11 Commission desire to remove an embarrassing story from the official account of 9/11:

- In the 2002 ABC television program in which Winfield appeared, he said, "The decision was made to try to go intercept Flight 93."[551]

- In 2004, the 9/11 Commission claimed that the military was not notified about United Flight 93's hijacking until after it had crashed.[552] Given this claim, Winfield's continued centrality to the official story would have been an embarrassment.

(4) Leidig's responses to questions he was asked on April 29, 2004, suggest that he did not know various things that he should have known. Leidig said, for example, that aside from Commander Pat Gardner—who reportedly served as his assistant DDO—he "couldn't recall the names of the other Operations Team 2 personnel on watch that day."[553]

(5) With regard to why Winfield was not serving as the DDO that morning, the best explanation the Pentagon could provide, evidently, was that Winfield was at a "personnel meeting convened by the Air Force to discuss the rating of Air Force officers,"[554] and that "[s]uch meetings are generally not disturbed unless the reason is significant."[555] But surely two attacks on the World Trade Center

would have provided a "significant" reason to call Winfield back to the NMCC.

(6) Winfield was interviewed by the 9/11 Commission, but the notes for this interview were withdrawn from public view.[556]

(7) Although the endnotes for two paragraphs about the DDO in *The 9/11 Commission Report* cite only an interview with Leidig, thereby implying that he had been the DDO on 9/11 (whereas the report never implies that Winfield was the DDO), the report did not explicitly identify Leidig as the DDO, instead referring to the DDO simply as "a military officer."[557]

(8) Although the Pentagon said in 2003 and 2004 that Winfield had been replaced by Leidig, General Myers in his 2009 book, as reported above, stated that Winfield was "the duty officer in charge."

Conclusion

The Pentagon has not provided a credible account of Winfield's behavior during the attacks. Although initially there was reason to assume—as did the ABC and CNN programs in 2002—that Winfield performed the DDO's role, the Pentagon later contradicted this assumption by saying that Leidig had taken over the role of the DDO. The serious problems with this second account, however, suggest that the Pentagon and the 9/11 Commission have not reported the truth about the work of the DDO and Winfield's behavior during the attacks.

If so, was this an effort to minimize Winfield's role? After the Pentagon and the 9/11 Commission declared in 2004 that the military did not know about UA Flight 93's hijacking until after it had crashed, had Winfield become an embarrassment due to his statement to ABC in 2002 that the military had decided "to try to go intercept flight 93"? Any new investigation should seek to answer this question.

37

The Claim That General Ralph Eberhart Was a Hero

Introduction

NORAD is the US-Canadian military agency responsible for defending North American airspace. Its traditional operating procedures—according to which planes are to be intercepted when they deviate from their courses, turn off their transponders, or permanently lose radio contact—were not followed on 9/11.

As the commander-in-chief of NORAD on 9/11, General Ralph E. "Ed" Eberhart was ultimately responsible for all of NORAD's failures on 9/11—most importantly, the failure to intercept hijacked airliners before they could strike the Twin Towers and the Pentagon. The fourth airliner, UA 93, which was reportedly headed towards the nation's capital, may have been shot down by NORAD, but NORAD has denied this. Accordingly, the official story about 9/11 is that NORAD was four-for-four in failing to intercept hijacked airliners that day.

Nevertheless, in spite of NORAD's disastrous failures under General Eberhart's leadership, he was never held accountable or even criticized. Indeed, he was promoted shortly after 9/11 and later called a "9/11 hero."[558]

Unlike others, such as General Richard Myers and General Henry Shelton, Eberhart has not written an account of his actions on 9/11. Likewise, he was seldom discussed by the 9/11 Commission. Accordingly, we do not know much about his actions that day. But enough has been said and reported by officials and the media to add up to an official story about his actions.

The Official Account

- "On the morning of 9/11 General Eberhart was in his office at headquarter[s]—roughly 30 minutes away from

Cheyenne Mountain, where the operations center is located."[559]

- "Eberhart received a call at 6:45 AM MDT (Mountain Daylight Time, or 8:45 AM EST [sic EDT] from CMOC's [Cheyenne Mountain Operation Center's] Command Director (CD) that informed him of the ongoing circumstance of a suspected hijacking on the East Coast. He was told that this was a non-exercise. He went to his office, and saw the CNN broadcast of the World Trade Center explosion."[560]

- It seemed to Eberhart that there was "great confusion in the system" at this time. (This statement echoes the recollection of Canadian Lieutenant General Rick Findley, the Battle Staff Director at Cheyenne Mountain Operations Center, who later told the 9/11 Commission that, following the second attack on the Twin Towers, there was "confusion as to how many, and which aircraft, were hijacked."[561]) When Eberhart learned about the second WTC attack, it became obvious to him that "an ongoing and coordinated terrorist attack" was underway.[562]

- Eberhart tried to contact the chairman of the Joint Chiefs of Staff, General Henry Shelton, but could not, because Shelton was on a plane to Europe to attend a NATO meeting.[563]

- Eberhart then contacted the acting chairman of the Joint Chiefs of Staff, General Richard Myers, who was on Capitol Hill meeting with Senator Max Cleland. Eberhart called Myers sometime between 9:03 and 9:30 AM, hence before the report of the Pentagon attack, which took place at approximately 9:37 AM.[564]

- Eberhart updated Myers about the crisis, telling him that the Twin Towers had been hit, that NORAD would be launching fighter jets in response, and that he was working with the FAA to get all non-military planes in the United States grounded.[565]

- According to Myers, Eberhart told him that there were "several hijack codes in the system,"[566] which meant, said Myers, "that the transponders in the aircraft [were] talking to the ground, and they're saying . . . we're being hijacked."[567]

- Eberhart next said that he was going to remain at Building 1 of Peterson Air Force Base—the headquarters of the US Air Force Space Command (of which Eberhart was also the commander)—because "he did not want to lose communication." However, he then decided to drive to NORAD's Cheyenne Mountain Operations Center, leaving at "approximately 9:30" EDT (or 7:30 MDT), which would have been shortly after his conversation with Myers. As to why Eberhart took this trip during the crisis, he explained that things had "quieted down" and the operations center" "had communications capabilities not available at Peterson."[568]

- Although, according to the 9/11 Commission, the twelve-mile drive normally takes "roughly 30 minutes," it took Eberhart forty-five minutes. As a *Washington Post* story reported later, the trip "can be time-consuming if traffic is bad."[569] During this period, it was later reported, Eberhart "couldn't receive telephone calls as senior officials weighed how to respond,"[570] or at least could not hold them: He "lost a cell phone call with Vice President Dick Cheney."[571]

- At 9:49 AM, Eberhart, during the Pentagon's air threat conference call, ordered "all air sovereignty aircraft to battle stations, fully armed."[572]

- The 9/11 Commission asked Eberhart why he, after realizing that there was an organized attack against the country, did not implement the plan called SCATANA (Security Control of Air Traffic and Air Navigation), which would clear the sky of all nonmilitary planes, so that the military would have complete control of the US airspace. Eberhart explained that, with the radars it had, NORAD would not have been able to "control the airspace that day," so if SCATANA had been implemented suddenly, even more problems would have developed. In response to those within NORAD who had advised him to implement it immediately, Eberhart said: "I will execute SCATANA once you have a modified SCATANA that . . . doesn't cause a bad situation to become worse." Two hours after the second plane hit the WTC, Eberhart was able to execute the modified SCATANA.[573]

The Best Evidence

An examination of the evidence shows that Eberhart, rather than being a 9/11 hero, may well be the opposite. Evidence for this assertion can be divided into two categories:

1. Eberhart made several contradictory and implausible statements.

2. Eberhart caused delays by virtue of his actions and omissions.

Eberhart Made Several Contradictory and Implausible Statements:

The official story about Eberhart contains the following elements, discussed in the order they appeared in the summary of the official account above:

- Eberhart said he first tried to contact General Shelton and learned that he was on the way to Europe. However, given that Shelton's trip had been planned for some time, the claim that Eberhart did not know when his immediate superior—the chairman of the Joint Chiefs of Staff—would be absent is not credible.

- Eberhart said he called General Myers while the latter was on Capitol Hill—which, as shown in the Chapter about Myers,[574] was false.

- Although Eberhart reported that the hijacked airliners, having used the hijack code, were talking to the ground, the failure of all eight pilots to squawk the hijack code is one of the main problems with the official account, as discussed in Chapter 22.[575]

- Although Eberhart justified driving to the operations center by saying that things had "quieted down," two hijacked airliners were reportedly still in the air. His statements about "several hijack codes" imply that he was aware of this.

- If Eberhart had a good reason to get to the operations center, he could have reached it quickly by helicopter, rather than wasting forty-five minutes or longer driving the distance.[576]

- Although Eberhart claimed that he was unable to communicate by cell phone during the trip, at 9:49 AM (7:49 MDT) he reportedly ordered— during an air threat conference call—interceptor pilots to get to their battle stations.[577]

- Although "battle stations" sounds like an effective action, it actually means that pilots wait in their jets with the engines off, unprepared to scramble immediately.[578]

- Eberhart's claim that he could not implement SCATANA immediately, without making a bad situation worse, is not credible, given that SCATANA was a procedure set up for emergencies, and the modified SCATANA would have surely been already worked out, especially given the fact that NORAD was doing exercises at the time that included a plane crashing into a Manhattan skyscraper. Also, the NORAD officers who were urging Eberhart to order SCATANA evidently saw no problem with Eberhart's doing so.

Accordingly, the official account about Eberhart contains inaccuracies, extraordinary claims, and actions and omissions that would have delayed the interception of the hijacked airliners.

Eberhart Caused Delays Through Further Actions and Omissions

There were additional irregularities regarding Eberhart's actions, omissions, and statements.

- It is standard operating procedure for NORAD to intercept a flight if it has lost radio contact, turned off its transponder, and gone off course. This was true of all four 9/11 flights and yet NORAD, under Eberhart, did not intercept any of them.[579]

- As to why NORAD failed to intercept, it gave out a timeline in 2001, claiming NORAD knew about the hijackings and tried to intercept the airliners but could never get there in time.[580] NORAD told this story from 2001 until 2004. But then *The 9/11 Commission Report* gave a completely different account, according to which (1) the FAA failed to alert NORAD about American 11 until it was too late for jets to reach it and (2) the FAA failed to tell NORAD about all three of the other flights until after they had crashed.[581]

- Regarding American 77 (which reportedly hit the Pentagon), Eberhart and the 9/11 Commission said that "NEADS never received notice that American 77 was hijacked."[582] But if that were true, why did Eberhart, about six weeks after the attacks, tell the US Senate that NORAD had scrambled jets at 9:24 AM after being notified that hijacked American 77 was coming toward Washington, adding that this was a documented notification"?[583] Did the 2004 timeline mean that Eberhart's 2001 statement to the Senate was a lie? Or did it mean that the FAA was lying when it emphatically said that it had shared "real-time information" with NORAD and the Pentagon about "all the flights of interest, including Flight 77."[584]

- As to why the new story may have emerged: The 9/11 research community had shown that NORAD's first timeline did not excuse NORAD, because there would have been time to intercept the airliners before the Twin Towers and the Pentagon were hit. In June 2004, while *The 9/11 Commission Report* was being prepared, Eberhart said that this view was correct—that if NEADS had been told about the flights when the FAA claimed, his people would have been able "to shoot down all three aircraft — all four aircraft."[585]

- When Eberhart was interviewed by the 9/11 Commission in March 2004,[586] he said he had "no knowledge of the circumstances that initiated the scramble" of fighter jets at 9:24 AM from Langley. Having learned that NEADS had scrambled those fighters in response to a false report—that American 11, which had hit WTC 1, was still airborne and heading toward Washington DC—Eberhart said that he had learned about this false report only "recently."[587] It seems incredible that the head of NORAD would have been ignorant about which fighters had been scrambled until two and a half years following the attacks.

- Eberhart had the responsibility of setting the alert levels of the Infocon, which defends against attacks on the Pentagon's communications networks. Just twelve hours before the attacks, Infocon was reduced to its least protective level and then not raised until after the second WTC attack.[588]

- Eberhart was also in charge of many of NORAD's military exercises ("war games") that occurred on 9/11, such as Vigilant Guardian, which had a scenario in which terrorists hijacked an airliner with the aim of attacking New York City. The exercise was conducted "sim over live," meaning the simulated hijackings were to be inserted into the live air traffic control system. As a result, NEADS personnel for some time were uncertain whether the radar tracks were real or simulated.

- According to Eberhart's own testimony, he realized after the second WTC attack, hence shortly after 9:00 AM, that a "coordinated terrorist attack" was underway. Eberhart was the person with the primary responsibility to protect Canada and the US from attack, and yet he allowed the war games to continue until after 10:00 AM.

- Moreover, radar personnel at Cheyenne asked NEADS to "get rid of this goddamn sim." According to a 9/11

Commission interview with Canadian Lieutenant General Rick Findley, who was NORAD's battle staff director at Cheyenne Mountain Operations Center on the morning of September 11, there was, following the second attack, "confusion as to how many, and which aircraft, were hijacked."[589] Nevertheless, the sim remained until after the time of the Pentagon attack (at 9:37 AM). When asked about the impact of the military exercises by the 9/11 Commission, Eberhart falsely claimed that they had "at most cost us thirty seconds."[590]

- Researcher and reporter Michael Kane of Global Free Press, who was on the scene at a 9/11 Commission Hearing, reported: "After General Eberhart's sworn testimony, I asked him who was in charge of coordinating the multiple war games running on 9/11. He replied, 'No Comment.'"[591] However, Lieutenant Colonel Dawne Deskins of NEADS told the commission, "Exercises that are designed on the NORAD level are created at planning conferences. NORAD planning exercises are mostly held at Peterson," which is where General Eberhart was in charge.[592]

Conclusion

Eberhart made several statements that were clearly false and others that were at least highly implausible, including:

- that he decided it would be all right to drive to the operations center because things had "quieted down"

- that the airliner pilots had squawked the hijack code

- that he could not use his cell phone during his drive to the operations center

- that the military exercises would have delayed NEADS no more than thirty seconds

- that he had only recently learned that the 9:24 AM scramble was based on a false report about American 11

- that he called General Myers while the latter was on Capitol Hill.

Eberhart also caused delays through his actions and omissions:

- by turning Infocon down to the least protective level

- by taking forty-five minutes or longer to drive to the operations center with a cell phone that reportedly did not work (which meant that Eberhart—like Bush, Cheney, Rumsfeld, Myers, Shelton, and Winfield—was reportedly incommunicado during the attacks)

- by ordering interceptor pilots to "battle stations," which meant that the pilots wait in their jets with the engines off, unprepared to scramble immediately

- by delaying implementation of SCATANA until after the attacks were over

- by arranging multiple military exercises for 9/11, with at least one of them being "sim over live," then not ordering removal of these confusing "sims" until after the Pentagon attack.

Finally, in agreeing with the 9/11 Commission's statement that NORAD's 2001 timeline was false, Eberhart implied that the military (under his control) had given a false account.

In short, Eberhart did nothing effective in response to the 9/11 hijackings—despite being present in the military's teleconference as those hijackings were in progress—except to delay responses.

Considerable evidence points to Eberhart as having been derelict in his duty.[593] A formal investigation should be launched to see if there is any other conclusion that could be reached.

38

The Claim That NYC Mayor Giuliani Did Not Know WTC 7 Was Going to Collapse

Introduction

One of the most surprising events of 9/11 was that New York City Mayor Rudy Giuliani told ABC's Peter Jennings in the morning that while he and his emergency management team—who were in a building at 75 Barclay Street where they had set up tempo-rary headquarters after the Twin Towers were struck—had been warned that the World Trade Center was going to collapse, so they had decided to leave the Barclay Street building.

The account he later gave the 9/11 Commission differed con-siderably about which building was expected to collapse. The 9/11 Commission did not ask him about the apparent contradictions, so the account he gave the commission must be considered the official story.

The Official Account

On May 19, 2004, Mayor Giuliani testified before the 9/11 Commission. Volunteering to tell what he had done on the morn-ing of September 11, 2001, Giuliani said that, after finishing break-fast at a hotel some distance from the World Trade Center, he was told that a twin-engine plane had crashed into its North Tower. Then, while in a van trying to get to the World Trade Center, Giuliani and his breakfast companions learned that the South Tower had been struck by a second plane, making it clear to him that a terrorist attack was underway.

Giuliani and his companions then found that the van could get no farther than Barclay Street, at which point the police com-missioner notified him that 7 World Trade Center (which housed Giuliani's Office of Emergency Management) had been evacuated, so they would instead set up a command post at 75 Barclay Street.

Giuliani told the commission that, after going inside 75 Barclay Street and while waiting to talk to Vice President Dick Cheney on the phone:

> I heard a click, the desk started to shake, and I heard next Chief Esposito, who was the uniformed head of the police department, . . . say, "The [South] tower is down, the tower has come down." And my first thought was that one of the radio towers from the top of the World Trade Center had come down. I did not conceive of the entire tower coming down, but as he was saying that, I could see the desk shaking and . . . then all of a sudden I could see outside a tremendous amount of debris and it first felt like an earthquake, and then it looked like a nuclear cloud. So we realized very shortly that we were in danger in the [Barclay Street] building, that the building could come down. . . . So the police commissioner and I, and the deputy police commissioner, we jointly decided that we had to try to get everyone out of the building.

So Giuliani and his team left the Barclay Street building, because "if something happened and the building crashed, you'd virtually have all of city government gone."[594]

The Best Evidence

Giuliani's account to the 9/11 Commission contains two serious contradictions with what Giuliani had told Peter Jennings the morning of 9/11:

(1) He did not tell the commission that he had been warned that the World Trade Center was going to collapse.

(2) He told the commission that he and his people left the Barclay Street building for fear that this building (not the WTC) might collapse.

The Peter Jennings Interview

While being interviewed during the morning of 9/11 via telephone by Peter Jennings, who was then the anchor at ABC News, Giuliani said that after he learned about the attack on the World Trade Center:

I went down to the scene and we set up headquarters at 75 Barkley Street, which was right there with the Police Commissioner, the Fire Commissioner, the Head of Emergency Management, and we were operating out of there when we were told that the World Trade Center was going to collapse. And it [the South Tower] did collapse before we could actually get out of the [Barclay Street] building, so we were trapped in the building for 10, 15 minutes, and finally found an exit and got out.[595]

Giuliani's statement to Jennings agreed in part with the account he later gave the 9/11 Commission, but he did not tell the commission about being "told that the World Trade Center was going to collapse." Also, whereas he had told Jennings that he was concerned that the Twin Towers were going to collapse, he told the commission that he was worried that he and his people were "in danger in the [Barclay Street] building, that the building could come down."

Although the 9/11 Commission failed to ask Giuliani about these contradictions, WNBC reported that in May 2007, he was asked about the Jennings interview by a small group of people with a video camera.[596] A young woman, after reminding Giuliani of his statement to Jennings that "no steel structure in history has ever collapsed due to a fire," asked: "How come people in the buildings weren't notified? And who else knew about this? And how do you sleep at night?" Giuliani replied: "I didn't know the towers were going to collapse." A male member of the group then reminded Giuliani that he had indeed told Jennings that he had been notified in advance that the towers were going to collapse, adding, "Who told you the towers were going to collapse in advance, sir?" Giuliani replied:

I didn't realize the towers would collapse. . . . Our understanding was that over a long period of time, the way other buildings collapsed, the towers could collapse, meaning over a 7, 8, 9, 10-hour period. No one that I know of had any idea they would implode. That was a complete surprise.[597]

But this explanation contradicts Giuliani's statement to Jennings—"[W]e were told that the World Trade Center was going to collapse. And it did collapse before we could actually get out of the building." According to that statement, Giuliani had clearly expected an imminent collapse of at least one of the Twin Towers.

Giuliani's Claim About Other Building Collapses

Giuliani's alternative explanation also contradicted factual evidence: In the first place, in speaking about "the way other buildings collapsed," he implied that steel-framed high-rise buildings had previously collapsed. (Otherwise, the mention of collapsed buildings would have been irrelevant.) In fact, the young woman's statement, that "no steel structure in history has ever collapsed due to a fire," is not controversial. Two months after 9/11, for example, *New York Times* reporter James Glanz wrote that "experts said no . . . modern, steel-reinforced high-rise, had ever collapsed because of an uncontrolled fire."[598]

Also, although Giuliani claimed that he expected a tower to collapse over a seven-to-ten-hour period, steel-framed buildings had burned, some of them longer than ten hours, without collapsing:

- In 1988, the sixty-two-story First Interstate Bank Building in Los Angeles burned for three hours, with sixty-four fire companies battling the blaze. The fire gutted offices from the twelfth to the sixteenth floor, with "no damage to the main structural members."[599]

- In 1991, a huge fire in Philadelphia's One Meridian Plaza lasted for eighteen hours and gutted eight of the building's thirty-eight floors. "Beams and girders sagged and twisted . . . under severe fire exposures," said the FEMA report, but "the columns continued to support their loads without obvious damage."[600]

- During the 1990s, a series of experiments were run in Great Britain to see what kind of damage could be done to steel-framed buildings by subjecting them to extremely hot, all-consuming fires that lasted for many hours. After reviewing those experiments, FEMA said: "Despite the temperature of the steel beams reaching 800–900°C (1,500–1,700°F) in three of the tests. . . , no collapse was observed in any of the six experiments."[601]

- Finally, illustrating that the laws of physics had not changed in 2001, a fifty-story building fire in Caracas three years later raged for seventeen hours, completely gutting the building's top twenty floors, and yet this building did not collapse.[602]

However, although the implicit claim that steel-framed buildings had collapsed after burning for several hours was false, Giuliani's statement was, "*Our understanding was* that over a long period of time, the way other buildings collapsed, the towers could collapse" (emphasis added). So one might think that Giuliani was telling the truth about what he and his people believed.

However, even that statement is demonstrably false: Robert F. Shea, the acting administrator of FEMA's Federal Insurance and Mitigation Administration, said, "No one who viewed it that day, including myself, believed that those towers would fall,"[603] and this view was echoed by multiple firefighters and other experts.[604]

Accordingly, there is no basis for a revisionist account, according to which Giuliani did not tell ABC's Peter Jennings that he had been warned that "the World Trade Center was going to collapse" imminently. Given the fact that Giuliani did say this, the next question is: Who gave Giuliani this information?

Who Told Giuliani That the World Trade Center Was Going to Collapse?

A partial answer may be found in the oral histories recorded by the Fire Department of New York:

- Deputy Assistant Chief Albert Turi reported that, at a time when they had no indication of any structural instability, "Steve Mosiello, Chief Ganci's executive assistant, came over to the command post and he said we're getting reports from OEM that the buildings are not structurally sound," after which "Pete [Ganci] said, well, who are we getting these reports from? . . . Steve [Mosiello] brought an EMT person over to the command post. . . . Chief Ganci questioned him, where are we getting these reports? And his answer was . . . we're not sure, OEM is just reporting this."[605]

- Steven Mosiello's statement shows that this "EMT person" was emergency medical technician Richard Zarrillo, who said: "John [Perrugia] came to me and said you need to go find Chief Ganci and relay the following message: that the buildings have been compromised, we need to evacuate, they're going to collapse. I said okay." After he and Steve Mosiello told Ganci that the buildings were going to collapse, Ganci said "who the fuck told you that?" Mosiello told Ganci and others: "I was just at OEM. The message I was given was that the buildings are going to collapse; we need to get our people out."[606]

- John Peruggia said: "They [people in the fire operations center] advised me that the Office of Emergency Management had been activated." Later, Peruggia said, "I was in a discussion with Mr. Rotanz [the deputy director of planning and research of the OEM[607]]. . . [and some] engineer type person, and several of us were huddled talking in the lobby and it was brought to my attention, it was believed that the structural damage that was suffered to the towers was quite significant and they were very confident that the building's stability was compromised and they felt that the North Tower was in danger of a near imminent collapse. I grabbed EMT Zarrillo, I advised him of that information. I told him he was to proceed immediately to the command post where Chief Ganci was located. . . . Provide him with the information that the building integrity is severely compromised and they believe the building is in danger of imminent collapse."[608]

- Peruggia was asked whether they were talking about "just the one building or both of them," to which he said, "The information we got at that time was that they felt both buildings were significantly damaged."[609]

As these testimonies show, the message that the towers were going to collapse came from the OEM. Accordingly, if Giuliani, as he told Peter Jennings, was informed that the towers were going to collapse, the warning must have originated from the OEM.

However, the OEM was under Giuliani's control.[610] So although Giuliani said that he and others at 75 Barclay Street "were told" that the towers were going to collapse, it was his own people in his own office who were providing this warning.

The only remaining question is: How could people in the OEM have known—given the virtually universal belief that a total collapse of the towers would have been impossible—that the towers were going to collapse?

The Fire Chief Who Expected the Towers to Fall

Chief Ray Downey was reportedly an exception to the 9/11 Commission's stated belief that "none of the [fire] chiefs present believed that a total collapse of either tower was possible."[611] And this was an important exception, because, as 9/11 Commissioner Timothy Roemer said, Downey was a "very respected expert on building collapse." In fact, said a FDNY battalion chief, Downey was "the premiere collapse expert in the country."[612]

FDNY Commissioner Thomas Von Essen had told the 9/11 Commission that Downey had said to him, "Boss, I think these buildings could collapse."[613] As to why, according to Downey's nephew Tom Downey, his uncle had been "worried about secondary devices in the towers, explosive devices that could hurt the firemen."

During his Oral History interview, FDNY chaplain Father John Delendick said that after the top of the South Tower appeared to explode, he asked Downey whether jet fuel had blown up. Downey replied "at that point he thought there were bombs up there because it was too even"—meaning that it had been too even to have been produced by exploding jet fuel.[614]

Conclusion

The account Mayor Giuliani gave to the 9/11 Commission in May 2004, according to which he got out of the building at 75 Barclay Street for fear that it would come down, is contradicted by the account he had given on the morning of 9/11 to ABC's Peter Jennings.

When Giuliani was challenged to explain why he had not told people in the towers that they were going to collapse, he claimed that he "didn't realize the towers would collapse" and that "No one that [he knew] of had any idea they would implode." This is in stark contrast to Giuliani's statement to Peter Jennings that he was told that the Twin Towers were going to come down.

How Giuliani knew that WTC Buildings I and II were going to come down is a question that has not been asked publicly of Giuliani by the mainstream media or any government body. This is a question that must be asked of Giuliani, while he is under oath.

VII.

OSAMA BIN LADEN AND THE HIJACKERS

Introduction

At the heart of the official account of 9/11 is the claim that Osama bin Laden conceived the idea of the attacks, and that the attacks were carried out by nineteen members of bin Laden's al-Qaeda organization. These nineteen men were all said to be, like Bin Laden himself, devout Muslims, with Mohamed Atta, the "ringleader" of the group, described as having become extremely religious. However, evidence shows that the claim about Osama bin Laden was unsupported and that the claims about the alleged hijackers were untrue.

39

The Claim That Osama bin Laden Was Responsible for the Attacks

The Official Account

Osama bin Laden was responsible for the 9/11 attacks.[615]

The Best Evidence

The FBI did not list 9/11 as one of the terrorist acts for which Osama bin Laden was wanted.[616] When asked why, Rex Tomb, when he was the head of investigative publicity for the FBI, stated that the FBI had "no hard evidence" connecting bin Laden to 9/11.[617] There were also other statements indicating that evidence of bin Laden's guilt had not been provided.[618]

Also, although Secretary of State Colin Powell and British Prime Minister Tony Blair promised to provide evidence of bin Laden's responsibility for the 9/11 attacks,[619] neither of them did.[620]

Finally, *The 9/11 Commission Report* discussed the responsibility of bin Laden for the 9/11 attacks as if it had evidence for it. But the "evidence" consisted of statements by captured followers of bin Laden, especially KSM (Khalid Sheikh Mohammed),[621] yet the co-chairmen of the 9/11 Commission—Thomas Kean and Lee Hamilton— reported that they had been unable to question KSM or the other detainees. They were not even allowed to observe the interrogations of these men. And so, said Kean and Hamilton:

> We . . . had no way of evaluating the credibility of detainee information. How could we tell if someone such as Khalid Sheikh Mohammed . . . was telling us the truth?[622]

Accordingly, Kean and Hamilton made clear that the 9/11 Commission—like the FBI, the Bush White House, and the Blair government—provided no evidence of the responsibility of Osama bin Laden for the attacks of 9/11.

Conclusion

An investigation is needed to discover why the "war on terror" was launched with no good evidence that Osama bin Laden was responsible for the attacks.

40

The Claim That Mohamed Atta Went to Portland on September 10

The Official Account

- Mohamed Atta, accompanied by fellow al-Qaeda operative Abdul Aziz al-Omari, "boarded a 6:00 AM flight from Portland [Maine] to Boston's Logan International Airport," stated *The 9/11 Commission Report*.[623] After arriving in Boston at 6:45 AM, they boarded American Airlines Flight 11, which was scheduled to depart at 7:45 AM.[624]

- Atta and al-Omari needed to take that early morning commuter flight because, although they had already been in Boston on September 10, they then "drove to Portland, Maine, for reasons that remain unknown," and stayed overnight in a Comfort Inn in South Portland.[625]

- No theory as to why Atta and al-Omari did this seems "entirely satisfactory," wrote the *New York Times* in 2002, "given the risk . . . that, had the commuter flight been at all late, they would have missed the very flight they intended to hijack."[626] In 2004, the 9/11 Commission still considered this trip a mystery.[627]

- Nevertheless, that Atta and al-Omari made this trip was proved by an FBI chronology of their movements in Portland on September 10, complete with stops where they were videotaped,[628] plus an affidavit, signed by a judge as well as an FBI agent, stating that the blue Nissan Altima found at the Portland Jetport had been rented by Mohamed Atta, and that "American Airlines personnel at Logan discovered two bags [checked to passenger Atta] that had been bound for transfer to AA11 but had not been loaded onto the flight."[629]

- Atta's trip turned out to be helpful to the investigation, according to FBI Director Robert Mueller, who said, "Following the crash of Flight 11, authorities recovered two pieces of luggage in the name of Mohamed Atta that had not been loaded onto that flight."[630] This luggage contained Atta's will[631] and other materials that incriminated al-Qaeda.[632]

To summarize the story's main facts: (1) Atta and al-Omari drove a blue rented Nissan from Boston to Portland on September 10, then stayed overnight. (2) The next morning, they took a commuter flight back to Boston in time to board AA Flight 11. (3) After Atta had flown American 11 into the World Trade Center, authorities at Boston's Logan Airport found incriminating materials in Atta's luggage that had not been loaded onto American 11.

The Best Evidence

The official story about Atta's Portland trip contains three mysteries:
(1) Why were Atta's bags not loaded onto AA 11? In the affidavit, pointed out a *Newsday* story in 2006, "there was no explanation of why they had not been loaded."[633]

- The loading failure could not be attributed to a late flight: The commuter flight back to Boston was on time, so there was an hour until AA 11 was to depart.[634]

- This failure also could not be explained in terms of a careless ground crew, because "Atta was the only passenger among the 81 aboard American Flight 11 whose luggage didn't make the flight, American sources confirm[ed]."[635]

(2) Why would Atta have put his will in a bag that was to be loaded onto a flight he intended to crash into the World Trade Center?

(3) Why would Atta have taken the risky trip to Portland?

These three mysteries become understandable in light of news reports in the first days after 9/11.

- According to CNN reports of September 12 and the morning of the 13th, two al-Qaeda operatives, Adnan Bukhari and Ameer Bukhari, drove a rented Nissan to Portland, stayed overnight, and then flew back to Boston the next morning in time to board AA 11.[636]

- Authorities found materials that incriminated al-Qaeda in a Mitsubishi sedan that Mohamed Atta had rented and then left in the parking lot of Boston's Logan Airport.[637]

- Up to that point, this had been the official story, but later on the afternoon of September 13, CNN apologetically reported that neither of the Bukharis could have died on 9/11: Adnan Bukhari was still alive and Ameer Bukhari had died the previous year.[638]

- On September 14, although CNN continued to state that Mohamed Atta had left a rented Mitsubishi at Boston's Logan Airport,[639] the Associated Press stated that the rented Nissan had been driven to Portland by Mohamed Atta, who with his companion "spent the night at the Comfort Inn in South Portland before boarding the plane the next morning."[640]

- This story still said that authorities had found the incriminating materials left by Atta in a rental car at Boston's Logan Airport, although this part of the story was incoherent, because the new story entailed that Atta must have left his rented Nissan at the Portland Jetport.

- On September 16, a full transition to what would become the official story appeared in the *Washington Post*: Besides stating that "Atta and Alomari rented a car in Boston, drove to Portland, Maine, and took a room Monday night at the Comfort Inn," it also said that Atta's incriminating materials were "left in his luggage at Boston's Logan Airport."[641]

- By October 5, the FBI had created a chronology of the claimed movements of Atta and al-Omari in Portland on September 10, complete with videos and photographs.[642]

Internal evidence, however, shows this chronology to be a fabrication.[643]

- Internal evidence also shows that the aforementioned affidavit—which indicated that the FBI had from the outset claimed that Atta had driven the Nissan to Portland and that the incriminating materials were found in his luggage inside Boston's Logan Airport—could not have been written and dated on September 12.[644]

Summary and Conclusion

The story of the two al-Qaeda operatives flying from Portland to Boston sounded plausible at first.

But after it became clear that the Bukhari brothers could not have died on AA 11, three mysteries emerged: (1) why Mohamed Atta's luggage was not loaded onto AA 11, (2) why Atta would have put his will in a bag that was supposed to be loaded onto that doomed flight, and (3) why he would have taken the risky trip to Portland. These questions came about as by-products in the course of creating, over the course of several days, a revised version of the original story (according to which Atta and al-Omari replaced the Bukhari brothers as the al-Qaeda operatives who drove a rented Nissan to Portland).

Although this story is complex, it suggests that what became the official story was most likely based on creative imagination, not fact.

41

The Claim That Security Videos Prove Mohamed Atta Was in Portland September 10 and 11

Introduction

As explained in Chapter 40, *The 9/11 Commission Report* says that Mohamed Atta and a fellow al-Qaeda operative, Abdul Aziz al-Omari, drove a rented car from Boston to Portland, Maine, on September 10, stayed overnight, and the next morning took a commuter flight back to Boston, where they boarded American Airlines Flight 11, which they had planned to hijack and fly into the World Trade Center.

Given the ubiquity of surveillance cameras in many commercial establishments and at airport check-in counters, lounges, security checkpoints, boarding gates, and duty-free shops, we would expect that the presence of Atta and al-Omari in Portland would have been recorded by many cameras.

And indeed, according to the official account, stops made by Atta and al-Omari were videotaped at various places, including a gas station and a Wal-Mart on the evening of September 10, and the Portland Jetport (Portland International Airport), from which they allegedly departed September 11.

The Official Accounts and Best Evidence for these stops are presented in three sections below.

The Official Account #1

Nineteen Muslim hijackers boarded four domestic passenger airliners on 9/11 and crashed three of them into the World Trade Center and the Pentagon.

On the morning of September 11, two of these hijackers, Mohamed Atta and Abdul al-Omari, boarded American 11 at Boston's Logan Airport after having taken a commuter flight to Boston from Portland, Maine. Although these men had already been in Boston on September 10, they drove a rented car to Portland,[645] where they stayed overnight.[646] The next morning, they drove to the Portland Jetport, where they boarded a 6:00 AM commuter flight to Boston.[647] Several surveillance cameras caught the men on videotape.

Surveillance Camera I: Jetport Gas Station Images, Evening, September 10

An FBI press release dated October 5, 2001, reported that on the evening of September 10, 2001, "Atta and Al-Omari were at [the] Jetport Gas Station, 446 Western, Avenue, South Portland, Maine. Atta was wearing a half dark, half light colored shirt with light colored slacks."[648] The press release indicates that the FBI had seven images that were captured by a surveillance camera at the gas station.

The Best Evidence #1

Surveillance Camera I: Jetport Gas Station Images, Evening, September 10, 2001

The seven images from the Jetport gas station present two serious problems. First, an examination shows that they bear the word "MON," indicating "Monday," which is consistent with the official account—September 11 fell on a Tuesday.

However, an image discovered in the evidence presented by the FBI in 2006, for the Moussaoui trial prosecution, provides reason to question the authenticity of these videos: Exhibit FO07011 is a full-size version of an image identical to the right-hand image in the top row on the FBI press release.[649]

- The original, uncropped photo from the surveillance camera shows the date to be "11-10-01."[650]

- This date could be read as November 10, 2001 (which fell on a Saturday), or October 11, 2001 (which fell on a Thursday). Either way, this image does not support the official account, according to which Atta and al-Omari were photographed at the Jetport gas station on September 10, 2001.

The second problem is that the video was stamped "8:28 PM,"

which does not match the FBI timeline, according to which Atta and al-Omari were at the Jetport station on September 10 at 9:15 PM.[651]

- One could reply that perhaps the camera was mis-set (a not uncommon problem). However, that would be speculation.

- In any case, the material provided to the Moussaoui trial by the FBI does not support the official account.

Conclusion #1: Jetport Gas Station

Because the uncropped image supposedly originating from the Jetport Gas station bore the wrong date and its time-stamp differs by 37 minutes from the FBI's timeline, this image does nothing to support the claim that Atta and al-Omari were in Portland the evening of September 10, 2001.

The Official Account #2

Surveillance Camera II: Atta at a Wal-Mart near Portland, Maine, 9:22 PM, September 10, 2001

According to Wal-Mart security camera images, Mohamed Atta visited a Wal-Mart near Portland, Maine, for twenty minutes on the evening of September 10, 2001, at 9:22 PM.[652]

The Best Evidence #2

Surveillance Camera II: Atta at a Wal-Mart Near Portland, 9:22 PM, September 10, 2001

There are nine images allegedly provided by Wal-Mart security cameras: the first six bear no time/date stamp, showing only the word "ENTRANCE." The last three bear only the word "0/X" and a time of "21:39" (9:39 PM).[653]

Conclusion #2: Wal-Mart

Nothing in this purported visual evidence supports the FBI claim that:

- the video originated from Wal-Mart

- Atta either entered or left Wal-Mart at 9:22 PM

- Atta stayed for twenty minutes

or that he was even at Wal-Mart at all.

Official Account #3

Surveillance Camera III: Portland Airport Images,
Early Morning, September 11

The FBI Press Release of October 5, 2001, also produced four images of Atta and al-Omari going through the security check at the Portland Jetport early on the morning of September 11, along with other security camera images documenting their presence in Portland.[654]

The Best Evidence #3

Surveillance Camera III: Portland Airport Images,
Early Morning, September 11, 2001

There are two serious problems with this video evidence. First, each of the four images bears not just one time-stamp, which is standard in the industry, but *two* time-stamps: 5:45 AM and 5:53 AM. The caption below these images—published in October 2001 on the FBI website—indicates that they were created at 5:45 AM.[655]

- If this time is correct, why would the photos also contain a stamp—in the regular position for time-stamps, at the bottom of the frame—indicating that they were taken eight minutes later at 5:53:41 (a mere six minutes before the flight was to leave)?[656]

- In a newspaper article of September 20, 2001, the earlier time of 5:45 AM was stamped in the middle of the published image, but the 5:53 AM time, which in October appeared on the FBI website in the regular time-stamp position at the bottom of the image, was cropped out.[657] And yet an exhibit of the same image, presented by the FBI to the Moussaoui trial in 2006, shows the 5:53 AM time.[658]

Second, the four images show Atta and al-Omari clad in open-necked shirts and not wearing, or even visibly carrying, ties and jackets.[659] However, according to check-in agent Michael Tuohey, the men he identified as Atta and al-Omari had moments earlier been wearing jackets and ties.

- According to Tuohey, the men had arrived so late that he feared they would miss the flight.[660] Tuohey added that Atta started demanding boarding passes for the second flight (American 11), to which Tuohey replied: "Mr. Atta, if you don't go now, you will miss your plane."[661]

- If Atta was the ringleader for the hijacking operation and was to pilot AA 11 after it was taken over, the whole, long-planned operation would have needed to be canceled if he did not get to Boston on this flight. If Atta and al-Omari were so late they were in danger of missing the flight, how likely is it that, although they may have needed to take off their jackets to go through screening, they would also have taken extra time to remove their ties and place both inside their bags?

- The fact that the video images do not correspond to Tuohey's description, therefore, counts against the authenticity of these images.

Conclusion #3: Portland Airport

The four images do not provide credible evidence of the claim that Atta and al-Omari flew out of Portland, for two reasons:

- Although the Portland Jetport would have had security surveillance cameras at check-in counters,[662] security checkpoints, and boarding gates, the only purported Jetport images of Atta and al-Omari released by the FBI were at the security check point.

- These images had two different time-stamps, instead of the industry standard of one; and the attire of Atta and al-Omari did not fit the description given by the check-in agent shortly before.

Summary Conclusion

Given the weak support for the authenticity of these three sets of security camera images, so weak as to suggest that they were fabricated, they—in conjunction with Chapter 40, "The Claim That Mohamed Atta Went to Portland on September 10"—raise compelling reasons to doubt the entire story that Atta had taken a commuter flight from Portland to Boston.

42

The Claim That an Airport Video Showed Five Hijackers at Dulles Airport on September 11

Introduction

Except for the reported security video image of Mohamed Atta and Abdul al-Omari at the Portland, Maine, airport, which was released to the press soon after 9/11 (see Chapter 41), the only photographic evidence showing any of the nineteen hijackers at airports was allegedly taken at Dulles International Airport in Washington, DC—from which American Airlines 77 departed—and was presented by the Associated Press the day before *The 9/11 Commission Report* was released in July 2004.

This video, which was endorsed by the 9/11 Commission—along with the video images of Atta and al-Omari, which were endorsed by the FBI as well as the 9/11 Commission—can be considered the official photographic evidence that members of al-Qaeda were preparing to board the 9/11 planes.

The Official Account

At 8:20 AM on September 11, 2001, American Airlines Flight 77 took off from Dulles International Airport heading for Los Angeles. The flight was then hijacked by five members of al-Qaeda, who crashed it into the Pentagon at 9:37:46 AM.[663] A closed-circuit television camera, as the 9/11 Commission reported,[664] captured images of these five hijackers—Hani Hanjour, Nawaf al-Hazmi, Salem al-Hazmi, Khalid al-Mihdhar, and Majed Moqed—passing through the security checkpoint at Dulles airport before boarding AA Flight 77.[665]

The Best Evidence

Three types of evidence strongly suggest that the video images allegedly showing the five men[666] claimed to be al-Qaeda hijackers are inauthentic. First, there were over 300 security cameras at Dulles International Airport on September 11, 2001,[667] which retained their images for thirty days and which were painstakingly examined by information-systems technicians and monitored by federal agents.[668] The US government did not release a single video or any of the images from these 300 security cameras.

Second, no images supposedly showing any of the alleged hijackers of AA 77 were released until the day before *The 9/11 Commission Report* was published (in July 2004), when the Associated Press released a video allegedly portraying the five reported hijackers passing through the Dulles security checkpoint. There are serious problems with the authenticity of this video.

- Although the 9/11 Commission reported that alleged hijackers al-Mihdhar and Moqed passed the Dulles security checkpoint and were recorded on closed circuit television (CCTV) at 7:18 AM, and that Hani Hanjour was recorded on the same CCTV at 7:35 AM,[669] researchers have pointed out that "a normal security video has time and date burned into the integral video image by proprietary equipment according to an authenticated pattern, along with camera identification and the location that the camera covered. The video released in 2004 contained no such data."[670]

- An analysis from a top scientific publisher confirms that, although security videos typically record such information, neither the date, time, nor camera number was present.[671]

- Whereas most twenty-four-hour surveillance cameras use time-lapse photography with one-second intervals (in order to meet data storage limitations), the videotape with images of al-Mihdhar and Moqed was shot at thirty frames per second (30fps), the norm in continuous consumer video-camera taping (i.e., many times the normal speed of security cameras). This suggests that the videotape was not taken by a Dulles airport security camera.

Further supporting this suspicion is the fact that the video, instead of being released by the FBI, was released to the Associated

Press by a law firm "representing victims' families, who are suing airlines and the security industry for failing to avert the terror attack,"[672] and as such cannot be assumed to be impartial.

Conclusion from the First Two Types of Evidence:
The Dulles airport video—which was never officially released and shows only a few people passing an unidentified security checkpoint at an unknown time—contains no information to link its images to AA 77.

Conclusion from the third type of evidence (that Dulles airport staff made no positive identifications of the alleged hijackers):

- *The 9/11 Commission Report* stated that four of the alleged hijackers on Flight AA 77 had been selected by the automated CAPPS *(Computer Assisted Passenger Prescreening System)* for additional screening.[673] The report also said: "Hani Hanjour, Khalid al Midhar and Majed Moqed were flagged by CAPPS. The Hazmi brothers were selected for extra scrutiny by the airline's customer service representative at the check-in counter. He did so because one of the brothers did not have photo identification nor could he understand English."[674] However:

  1. None of the security screeners testified to having remembered any of the hijackers passing through security for Flight AA 77.[675]

  2. The check-in agents did not mention CAPPS flaggings—which would have been memorable events—in their FBI interviews:

     - According to an FBI interview on September 26, 2001, with Dulles check-in agent Allex Vaughn who processed the al-Hazmi brothers, Vaughn did not mention that they had been selected by the CAPPS system for additional screening.[676]

     - CAPPS is not mentioned in the September 12, 2001, FBI interview with a trainee (name redacted on the FBI report) who was working with Vaughn at the time.[677]

- ◆ Vaughn said he was shown the security system video from nearby surveillance camera #31, which allegedly showed the al-Hazmi brothers, but this footage has never been released.[678]

- *The 9/11 Commission Report* stated that Hani Hanjour and the al-Hazmi brothers were seated in first class.[679] When ticket agent Brenda Brown, who checked in first-class ticketed AA 77 passengers that morning, was interviewed by the FBI on September 17, 2001, she remembered clearly checking in several passengers on "a light travel day" but did not recall any Arab males.[680]

Conclusion

According to the 9/11 Commission, there was photographic evidence of the five alleged hijackers of AA 77 passing through the security checkpoint at Dulles International Airport. However:

- However, this claim was not supported by positive identifications of any of these men by Dulles airport staff.

- Although Dulles International Airport had over 300 surveillance cameras, the FBI did not release images from any of these.

- The only video purported to show 9/11 hijackers was provided by a law firm representing families of victims planning to sue the airlines and security industry; as such, it could not be assumed to be impartial.

- The unstamped images from this video do not provide the kinds of data normally present on security videos.

- The video was far faster than the normal speed of security camera videos.

There is, therefore, no credible photographic (or eyewitness) evidence that any of the alleged 9/11 hijackers were preparing to board AA 77, which was alleged to have crashed into the Pentagon.

43

The Claim That the Hijackers Were Devout Muslims

The Official Account

The four 9/11 planes were hijacked by devout Muslims. According to *The 9/11 Commission Report*, Mohamed Atta, the ringleader, had "adopted fundamentalism."[681] The hijackers, by virtue of their beliefs, had become a "cadre of trained operatives willing to die."[682]

The Best Evidence

The official account depends on the idea that the 9/11 planes were hijacked by devout Muslims—devout enough to die for the cause. And yet the mainstream media contained many stories contradicting the claim that the alleged hijackers were devout Muslims.

Five days after 9/11, a story in London's *Daily Mail* contained this report:

> At the Palm Beach bar Sunrise 251, [Mohamed] Atta and [Marwan] Al Shehhi spent $1,000 in 45 minutes on Krug and Perrier-Jouet champagne. . . . Atta was with a 6ft. busty brunette in her late twenties; the other man was with a shortish blonde. Both women were known locally as regular companions of high rollers.[683]

One month after 9/11, a *Boston Herald* story, titled "Terrorists Partied with Hooker at Hub-Area Hotel," reported:

> A driver for a pair of local escort services told the *Herald* yesterday that he drove a call girl to the Park Inn in Chestnut Hill on Sept. 9 around 10:30 p.m. where she bedded down with one of the mass murderers. It was her second trip to the terrorist's room that day. Two of the hijackers aboard Flight 11 that crashed into the World Trade Center—Waleed M. Alshehri and Wail Alshehri—spent Sept. 9 in the Route 9 hotel, sources said. . . .

The dirty Hub dalliances of the terrorists is just the latest link between the Koran-toting killers and America's seedy sex scene.[684]

A week earlier, a *San Francisco Chronicle* article, "Agents of Terror Leave Their Mark on Sin City," reported that at least five of the "self-styled warriors for Allah," including Mohamed Atta, had "engaged in some decidedly un-Islamic sampling of prohibited pleasures [including lap dances] in America's reputed capital of moral corrosion," Las Vegas. The group, investigators said, had "made at least six trips here." The story then quoted Osama Haikal, president of the board of directors of the Omar Haikal Islamic Academy in Nevada, as saying, "True Muslims don't drink, don't gamble, don't go to clubs."[685]

On October 10, the *Wall Street Journal* summarized these stories in an editorial titled "Terrorist Stag Parties."[686] Whereas the *Journal*'s editorial pointed to the contradiction only implicitly, by means of its ironic title, the problem had already been drawn out explicitly, five days after 9/11, in a *South Florida Sun-Sentinel* story titled "Suspects' Actions Don't Add Up."

Three guys cavorting with lap dancers at the Pink Pony Nude Theater. Two others knocking back glasses of Stolichnaya and rum and Coke at a fish joint in Hollywood the weekend before committing suicide and mass murder. . . . [This] is not a picture of devout Muslims, experts say. Let alone that of religious zealots in their final days on Earth. . . . [A] devout Muslim [cannot] drink booze or party at a strip club and expect to reach heaven, said Mahmoud Mustafa Ayoub, a professor at Temple University in Philadelphia. . . . "It is incomprehensible that a person could drink and go to a strip bar one night, then kill themselves the next day in the name of Islam. . . . Something here does not add up."[687]

The 9/11 Commission did not explain how its characterization of the hijackers as devout Muslims was consistent with these press stories. It simply ignored them. For example, referring to a trip to Las Vegas by Atta and two other hijackers roughly a month before 9/11, the commission wrote: "Beyond Las Vegas's reputation for welcoming tourists, we have seen no credible evidence explaining why, on this occasion and others, the operatives flew to or met in Las Vegas."[688]

Conclusion

The reported behavior of the men said to have hijacked the 9/11 planes cannot be reconciled with the claim that they were devout Muslims.

The 9/11 Commission made no effort to reconcile the contradiction. It simply claimed that the men were devout, with their leader having become a fundamentalist, while simply ignoring all the reports that contradict that claim.

The media had published plenty of stories demonstrating that the alleged hijackers were anything but devout Muslims, yet the same media never questioned the 9/11 Commission's claims that the attacks were carried out by fanatical Muslims, thus leaving the American public in the dark about this contradiction.

44

The Claim That Mohamed Atta Was an Extremely Religious Muslim

Introduction

As shown in the previous chapter, the alleged 9/11 hijackers did not live up to the 9/11 Commission's description of them as devout Muslims—especially Mohamed Atta, said to have become fanatically religious after going to Germany.[689] The present chapter provides an explanation of how Mohamed Atta could have been very devout while in Germany, even though Mohamed Atta's behavior in America suggested he was not.

The Official Account

The 9/11 airliners were hijacked by devout Muslims, ready to die for a cause. In the words of *The 9/11 Commission Report,* the hijackers had become a "cadre of trained operatives willing to die."[690] The *Report* also said that Mohamed Atta, called the ringleader, had by 1998 become very religious, even "fanatically so."[691]

The Best Evidence

In addition to the media stories about the hijackers in general (discussed in Chapter 43) suggesting that they were not really devout Muslims, stories abounded about Atta in particular.

For example, stories in newspapers in Venice, Florida, reported that Atta had lived there for several months. Investigative reporter Daniel Hopsicker went to Venice, where he learned that Atta and a young woman named Amanda Keller had taken a trip to Key West with a few other people, during which they drank heavily and used cocaine.[692]

Another example involves one of the best-known stories about Atta's non-Muslim behavior. This episode involved a restaurant named "Shuckums" in Hollywood, Florida. According to a Florida newspaper, two of the hijackers were "knocking back glasses of

Stolichnaya and rum and Coke at a fish joint in Hollywood the weekend before [9/11]."[693] According to the restaurant's manager, "The guy Mohamed was drunk [and] his voice was slurred."[694] According to the bartender, Atta and his companion "were wasted."[695] According to a third story:

> In Florida, several of the hijackers—including reputed ringleader Mohamed Atta—spent $200 to $300 each on lap dances in the Pink Pony strip club.[696]

At the first hearing of the 9/11 Commission in March 2003, a member of the press asked Commissioner Richard Ben-Veniste, "If Atta belonged to the fundamentalist Muslim group, why was he snorting cocaine and frequenting strip bars?" Ben-Veniste replied, "You know, that's a heck of a question."[697] But it was a question that the 9/11 Commission never addressed.

How could Atta's behavior as reported in the press be reconciled with the portrait of him as very devout? The two views of Atta could be explained if the man the world came to know as Mohamed Atta was not the original Mohamed Atta. There is good evidence, moreover, that this is the case.

Two Attas?

A young Egyptian man whose full name was Mohamed Mohamed el-Amir Awad el-Sayed Atta had studied urban planning at the Technical University of Hamburg-Harburg in the 1990s. As reported by researcher Elias Davidsson, "His friends in Hamburg knew him as Mohamed el-Amir, not as Mohamed Atta."[698]

In fact, Dittmar Machule, who was Mohamed el-Amir's tutor and thesis advisor, said: "I do not know the name Mohamed Atta" until "after the 11th of September."

Machule described this student as "very religious," someone who prayed regularly and never touched alcohol. "I would put my hand in the fire," said the professor, "that this Mohamed El-Amir I know will never taste or touch alcohol." Also, by contrast with the man known as Mohamed Atta in America, the student Machule knew as Mohamed El-Amir Atta would not even shake hands with a woman on being introduced to her.[699]

A German urban planner named Ralph Bodenstein, who

worked with Mohamed in 1995 studying traffic patterns in Cairo's historic district, said, "[H]e was a very religious person. He was growing a beard, he had just come back from a small hajj. He did pray five times a day. On the other hand, he was very full of idealism and he was a humanist. He was very much interested in social work."[700]

Volker Hauth, an architect who knew Mohamed el-Amir while he studied in Hamburg, and who went with him on trips to the Middle East, said: "The religious convictions of both of us—his Islamic and mine Protestant—were a kind of bonding for us. In Germany at that time, there were a lot of students from East Germany with no religion, and this was something difficult for Mohamed."[701]

In addition to the fact that Mohamed el-Amir was reportedly very devout, whereas the reported behavior of the man known as Mohamed Atta in America indicated that he was not, very different adjectives were commonly used to describe the two men's character traits.

According to Elias Davidsson, those who described Mohamed el-Amir often used terms such as "reserved," "introvert," "polite," "intelligent," and "very nice." For example:

- Machule described his student as "a very nice young man, polite, very religious, and with highly developed critical faculties, alert and observant."[702]

- Abdullah Bozkurt, a dealer who knew el-Amir from a car market in Hamburg, where both traded, said: "He made such a friendly impression. He easily got in contact with everybody, was always smiling and never in a bad mood."[703]

- Bechir Bejaoui, who had been a friend of el-Amir, declared under oath in a deposition made at the German Federal Criminal Agency in Hamburg that el-Amir was "friendly, pleasant, mild . . . so delicate and reasonable. . . . He was never aggressive. He was, as I said, always delicate and relaxed and friendly."[704]

On the other hand, said Davidsson, those who said anything about the character of the man known in America as Mohamed

Atta "described him as an unpleasant, arrogant and obnoxious man."

- Rudy Dekkers, president of Huffman Aviation in Venice, Florida, where Atta went to flight school, said Atta "was very arrogant. . . . [H]e had a bad attitude and we just didn't like him."[705]

- Atta, along with a man going by the name Marwan al-Shehhi, also applied to enroll at Jones Aviation in Sarasota, Florida. "According to the instructor at Jones," said *The 9/11 Commission Report*, "the two were aggressive, rude, and sometimes even fought with him to take over the controls."[706]

- Gary Jones, the vice president of Jones Aviation, said: "We told them we wouldn't teach them anymore. We told them, one, they couldn't speak English and, two, they had bad attitudes."[707]

Moreover, the contrast was not simply behavioral but also physical. The American Atta was described as 5'8" and sometimes as 5'10" tall.[708] By contrast, Professor Machule, who said of his former student that he was not a "bodyguard type" but "more a girl looking type,"[709] described him as "very small," being "one meter sixty-two" in height, which means slightly under 5'4".

Conclusion

Defenders of the official story might claim that radical transformations do occur. But it would be very unlikely that a young man who would not touch alcohol would turn into a man who would use cocaine and become drunk regularly; that a young man who would not shake hands with women would turn into one who spent time with strippers and prostitutes; and that a young man described as polite and very nice would turn into one described as arrogant, aggressive, and rude. It would especially be unlikely that a young man described by his professor as very small, being 5'4" in height, would in a few years be described as 5'8" or even 5'10".

It is much more likely—given the widely held assumption that the 9/11 planes were hijacked by Muslims—that the image of their "ringleader" was based on a truly devout young man from Egypt named Mohamed Mohamed el-Amir Awad el-Sayed Atta, who, according to the 9/11 Commission had become fanatically religious. The 9/11 Commission then simply ignored all reports of the behavior of the American Mohamed Atta that did not fit the image of a devout Muslim.

This chapter can explain why the man known to Americans as Mohamed Atta - the full name of whom was stated by Wikipedia as "Mohamed Mohamed el-Amir Awad el-Sayed Atta"—reportedly did not behave like a devout Muslim, even though the Mohamed Mohamed el-Amir Awad el-Sayed Atta who studied at Hamburg was a genuinely devout Muslim. This chapter also reinforces the conclusion of the previous one: that claims about Mohamed Atta and the other alleged hijackers should not have provided any basis for a war on Islam.

45

The Claim That "Able Danger" Failed to Identify Mohamed Atta's Probable Presence in the US in January 2000

Introduction

Able Danger was the code name for a high-level intelligence operation cofounded by generals Hugh Shelton and Peter Schoomaker, commanders in chief of the Defense Department's Special Operations Command (SOCOM).

Telling the story about Able Danger takes time, but it is important, because it strongly indicates that the man identified as "Mohamed Atta" had been in the United States in January–February 2000, about eighteen months before the 9/11 attacks, whereas according to the official story he arrived in June 2000.

Furthermore, the official story claimed that US intelligence didn't know he was in the country before 9/11, whereas an important part of US intelligence evidently knew he had been there since January–February 2000. (To understand why we speak of "the man identified as 'Mohamed Atta,'" see the endnote here, which points the reader to Chapter 44.[710])

However, government officials consistently ignored the Able Danger evidence; the 9/11 Commission failed to mention the evidence; and the Defense Department's inspector general covered it up. Louis Freeh, the former director of the FBI, called the 9/11 Commission's claim that it was not historically significant "astounding."[711]

Background

Tasked with collecting open-source Internet data on worldwide al-Qaeda networks and terrorist financing, the massive, eighty-person-strong data-mining operation Able Danger began in late 1999.

It used a link-mapping strategy to download and analyze data from thousands of websites. The terrorist network data were then presented visually on wall charts. The Able Danger leadership team included Navy Captain Scott Phillpott (the head of Able Danger); US Army Lieutenant Colonel Anthony E. Shaffer (on loan from the Defense Intelligence Agency); Erik Kleinsmith (Army Major and the chief of intelligence of the Land Information Warfare Activity); James D. Smith (a civilian defense contractor from Orion Scientific Systems); Dr. Eileen Preisser (Dual Ph.D., analytical lead, from the Land Information Warfare Activity).

During the period January–February 2000, the team had discovered the surprising probability of al-Qaeda members within a terrorist cell in Brooklyn.[712]

In mid-2000, Captain Phillpott asked Lieutenant Colonel Shaffer to open communications between the head of Able Danger and the FBI in order to collaboratively take down the cell in Brooklyn. However, SOCOM attorneys rejected this effort three times, leaving the FBI unaware of information that suggested the man identified as Atta was inside the US in early 2000.[713]

Soon after 9/11, when photos of the suspected terrorists were released, Phillpott, Shaffer, Preisser, and Smith were shocked to recognize alleged lead hijacker Mohamed Atta and two other alleged hijackers from an Able Danger chart.

Two weeks later, Dr. Preisser, along with three Republican congressmen—Curt Weldon, Chris Shays, and Dan Burton—showed the "Atta chart" to Deputy National Security Advisor Stephen Hadley in the White House, who said he would show it to President Bush.[714]

In October 2003, Lieutenant Colonel Shaffer contacted 9/11 Commission Executive Director Philip Zelikow, while both were in Afghanistan, to report that Able Danger had identified Atta more than a year before the attacks.

In March 2004, Shaffer's Defense Intelligence Agency security clearance was suspended, preventing him from further accessing the documents.[715]

In June 2005, Congressman Curt Weldon (vice chairman of the House Armed Services and Homeland Security Committees) talked about Able Danger in an interview with the *Norristown*

Times Herald,[716] and in a subsequent speech on the floor of the House he called for an investigation.[717]

Thomas Kean and Lee Hamilton, the co-chairs of the 9/11 Commission, which had not mentioned Able Danger in its July 2004 final report, stated in August 2005 that Able Danger was not "historically significant."[718]

One day before a 2005 US Senate hearing on the matter, key Able Danger witnesses Shaffer, Phillpott, and Smith were placed under a gag order by Secretary of Defense Donald Rumsfeld.[719]

At the same Senate hearing, Able Danger team member Erik Kleinsmith testified that he was ordered, under Army oversight regulations, to destroy all 2.5 terabytes of the Able Danger material, which he did in May or June of 2000.[720]

In October 2005, Congressman Weldon called for "a full independent investigation by the Inspector General [IG] of the Pentagon."[721] The IG investigation concluded that the five Able Danger witness "recollections were not accurate."[722]

The Official Story

I. As *The 9/11 Commission Report* informed us, Mohamed Atta was the "tactical leader of the 9/11 plot."[723] He first arrived in the United States on a tourist visa, June 3, 2000.[724] The 9/11 Commission also said that "American intelligence agencies were unaware of Mr. Atta until the day of the attacks."[725]

II. In August 2005, a year after the 9/11 Commission had closed, commissioners Kean and Hamilton explained to the media why Able Danger had not been included in *The 9/11 Commission Report*:

a) They had been informed about Able Danger in 2003, but were "never told that it had identified Mr. Atta and the others as threats."[726] Although the project leader Captain Phillpott was interviewed by the commission about Atta in July 2004, his "knowledge and credibility" were not "sufficiently reliable" to warrant further investigation of Able Danger, so they concluded that the project was not "historically significant."[727]

b) When the commission asked the Pentagon for all its documents related to Able Danger, "none of the documents turned over to the Commission mention Mohamed Atta or any of the other future hijackers."[728]

According to an *Associated Press* story reported in mid-September 2005:

> The commission's former chairman, Thomas Kean, said there was no evidence anyone in the government knew about Atta before Sept. 11, 2001.... Kean said the recollections of the intelligence officers cannot be verified by any document. "Bluntly, it just didn't happen and that's the conclusion of all 10 of us," said a commissioner, Senator Slade Gorton.[729]

III. Although several of the Able Danger team officers and intelligence analysts had been scheduled to testify at a hearing of the Senate Judiciary Committee September 21, 2005, the Defense Department said that open testimony "would not be appropriate [because of] security concerns."[730]

IV. In a September 2006 investigative report, the DOD Office of the Inspector General (IG) wrote:

> We concluded that prior to September 11, 2001, Able Danger team members did not identify Mohammed [sic] Atta or any other 9/11 hijacker. While we interviewed four witnesses who claimed to have seen a chart depicting Mohammed Atta and possibly other terrorists or "cells" involved in 9/11, we determined that their recollections were not accurate.[731]

The Best Evidence

I. Regarding Mohamed Atta's date of arrival in the United States:

1. Three senior staff from the Able Danger project gave written testimony to a September 2005 Senate hearing that Mohamed Atta was identified as a potential member of a terrorist cell in New York in January–February 2000,

four months earlier than the June 2000 date stated by the official account. A fourth member of the project, Mr. Kleinsmith, was asked during the same hearing:

> Are you in a position to evaluate the credibility of Captain Philpott, Colonel Shaffer, Mr. Westphal, Ms. Preisser, or Mr. J.D. Smith, when they say they saw Mohammed [sic] Atta on the chart?
>
> Mr. Kleinsmith. Yes, sir. I believe them implicitly from the time that I had worked with all of them.[732]

2. After 9/11, civilian sightings of Atta during the spring of 2000 were reported in the news:

- Johnelle Bryant of the US Department of Agriculture, "in defiance of direct orders from the USDA's Washington headquarters," told Brian Ross of ABC News that Atta came into her office "sometime between the end of April and the middle of May 2000," asking for a loan to buy a small airplane (which she refused to give). Bryant reported that when she wrote down his name, she spelled it A-T-T-A-H, leading him to respond, "No, A-T-T-A, as in Atta boy!"[733]

- In April 2000 and into the summer, Atta was, according to the head of security and a reference librarian, seen repeatedly using the computers in the Portland Maine Public Library.[734]

- A federal investigator reported to the *Associated Press* on condition of anonymity that Atta and another hijacker rented rooms in Brooklyn and the Bronx in the spring of 2000. A senior Justice Department official reported that Atta's trail in Brooklyn began with a parking ticket issued to a rental car he was driving.[735]

II. Regarding the reasons given in the Kean-Hamilton 2005 statement for excluding Able Danger from *The 9/11 Commission Report:*

a) The 9/11 Commission staff members were briefed twice by Able Danger project members:

- The first briefing was by Lieutenant Colonel Anthony Shaffer on October 23, 2003. Although he was no longer with the Able Danger project, he was given clearance to meet with 9/11 Commission Executive Director Philip Zelikow and some commission staff members who were visiting Bagram Airfield, Afghanistan, where Shaffer was stationed.

  In an hour-long meeting, Shaffer told commission staff about the Able Danger project and how it had identified Atta in early 2000. In 2005, answering the Kean-Hamilton claim that he had not mentioned Atta to the commission, Shaffer insisted that he had named Atta, saying: "I kept my talking points (from the meeting). And I'm confident about what I said."[736]

- The second briefing was by Captain Scott Phillpott (who had held four US naval commands) on July 13, 2004. Phillpott, the leader of Able Danger, was interviewed by commission staff member Dieter Snell.[737] Although Phillpott's statement clearly reinforced Shaffer's October 2013 statement, The 9/11 Commission Report had included neither on the grounds that, as mentioned above, Captain Phillpott's "knowledge and credibility" were not "sufficiently reliable" to warrant further investigation of Able Danger.[738]

b) Kean and Hamilton also rejected Able Danger's Atta claim on grounds that the Pentagon records contained no documentary evidence. They thus disregarded the consistent briefings and testimony from four members of the project's senior management team.

A clue to why may be provided by Anthony Shaffer's report (backed up by Curt Weldon; see IV-a below) that when Christopher Kojm, deputy executive director of the 9/11 Commission, was asked by Congressman Curt

Weldon's chief of staff why the commission had not included Able Danger in its report, Kojm replied, "It did not fit with the story we wanted to tell."[739]

c) With regard to the commission's claim that Able Danger was not historically significant, former FBI director Louis Freeh said, "The Able Danger intelligence, if confirmed, is undoubtedly the most relevant fact of the entire post-9/11 inquiry," and called the commission's claim "astounding."[740]

III. Regarding the Pentagon concern that "it is simply not possible to discuss Able Danger in any great detail in an open public forum" such as the Senate Judiciary Committee:

• Phillpott, Shaffer, and Smith had already made their written submissions when testifying before the September 21, 2005, Senate hearing on Able Danger.

• Senate Judiciary Committee Chairman Arlen Specter said he was surprised by the Pentagon's decision because "so much of this is already in the public domain."[741] "That looks to me like it may be obstruction of the committee's activities."[742]

IV. Regarding the inspector general's 2006 conclusion that the Able Danger team's recollection of an Atta chart was not accurate:

a) In late June 2005, Congressman Curt Weldon, during an address to the House, had presented an enlarged version of the chart that he had received from Dr. Eileen Preisser and had then given to Stephen Hadley in the White House. Pointing out Mohamed Atta's name in the center of the chart, Weldon had asked:

> Why is there no mention, Mr. Speaker, of a recommendation in September of 2000 to take out Mohammed Atta's cell which would have detained three of the terrorists who struck us?
>
> We have to ask the question, why have these issues not been brought forth before this day? I had my Chief

of Staff call the 9/11 Commission staff and ask the question: Why did you not mention Able Danger in your report? The Deputy Chief of Staff [Christopher Kojm] said, well, we looked at it, but we did not want to go down that direction.

So the question, Mr. Speaker, is why did they not want to go down that direction? Where will that lead us? Who made the decision to tell our military not to pursue Mohamed Atta?[743]

b) In late August, 2005, three members of the Able Danger team had gone public, confirming the Atta chart: defense intelligence analyst Lieutenant Colonel Anthony Shaffer,[744] project leader Scott Phillpott,[745] and defense contractor James D. Smith, who said he was "absolutely positive that Atta was on our chart."[746]

Important testimony from Smith came in a hearing of the House Armed Services Committee on February 15, 2006. Explaining that he had used Arab intermediaries in Los Angeles to buy a photograph of Atta, Smith added that it was one of some forty photos of al-Qaeda members on a chart that he had given to Pentagon officials in 2000.[747] Smith also said:

> I have recollection of a visual chart that identified associations of known terrorist Omar Abdul-Rahman within the New York City geographic area. . . . Mohamed Atta's picture. . . was on the chart. . . . The particular Atta chart is no longer available, as it was destroyed in an office move that I had in 2004.

Smith later, explaining to the Pentagon's inspector general how his Atta chart was destroyed, said:

> [I]t had been up there so long I had quite a lot of tape up there because it had been rolled up. In the process the tape was tearing the chart. . . . It shredded itself as I was trying to pull it off the wall carefully . . . so I just threw it away.[748]

During questioning by Weldon, the following exchange had occurred:

James Smith: "I have direct recollection of the chart because I had a copy up until 2004. . . . At the time, after 9/11 when the pictures were released in newspapers and I did the compare on the chart, when I saw [Atta's] picture there, I was extremely elated and, to anyone that would listen to me, I showed them the chart that was in my possession."

Weldon: "How sure are you that it was Mohammed Atta's name and picture [on the chart]?"

Smith: "I'm absolutely certain. I used to look at it every morning. . . ."

Weldon: "And was that the chart you think that was given to me that I gave to the White House?"

Smith: "Yes, sir. It was."

Weldon: "And you're aware that when I gave that chart to the White House, Dan Burton, the chairman of the Government Ops Committee, was with me and stated to the *New York Times*, that he actually showed the chart to Steve Hadley and explained the linkages?"

Smith: "Yes, sir."[749]

c) Confirming the public statements released in August 2005 by Phillpott, Shaffer, and Smith, two more people reported having seen a chart with Atta's name on it when the Pentagon interviewed eighty Able Danger employees in early September 2005. Dr. Eileen Preisser and a Mr. (probably Christopher) Westphal brought the number of people who had seen the chart up to five, four of whom remembered Atta's picture.[750]

d) A purported image of one of Able Danger's charts, shown in FIG 2, is available online,[751] supporting the existence of the charts and what they looked like:

e) Regarding the Pentagon's inspector general's 2006 ninety-page summary claiming that the team's recollections were not accurate, David Ray Griffin's *New Pearl Harbor*

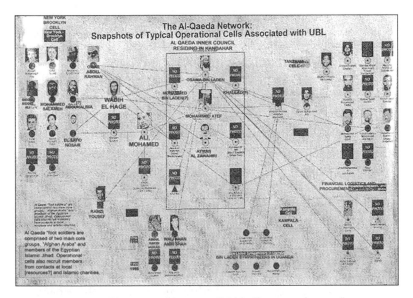

FIG 2: *Purported image of Able Danger chart of al-Qaeda network*

Revisited has a detailed analysis showing its lack of transcripts, circular reasoning, and prejudicial treatment of witnesses.[752]

f) In an unusual departure from government and military investigation procedures, the inspector general's 2006 report refers only to the positions of its witnesses and does not identify them by name, thus offering witness protection through anonymity, although it was not a criminal investigation.[753]

Congressman Weldon declared, "The report trashes the reputations of military officers who had the courage to step forward and put their necks on the line to describe important work they were doing to track al-Qaeda prior to 9/11.... I am appalled that the DOD IG would expect the American people to actually consider this a full and thorough investigation."[754]

Conclusion

The official 9/11 account is discredited by the evidence in this chapter. To summarize:

1) Having described Mohamed Atta as the "tactical leader of the 9/11 plot," *The 9/11 Commission Report* claimed that he entered the US in June 2000, but in fact he had come months earlier (January–February 2000).

2) According to the official story, US intelligence didn't know he was in the country before 9/11, whereas a major research agency co-founded by two commanders-in-chief of the Defense Department's Special Operations Command (SOCOM) produced evidence showing that the man being called Mohamed Atta was probably in the United States from January 2000 onward.

3) This evidence was blocked from the FBI on three occasions by SOCOM attorneys.

4) The commission was notified of the Atta evidence in October 2003 and July 2004, yet failed to include the evidence in its July 2004 report and later described it as having no "historical significance."

5) The five witnesses to the evidence were later claimed to have been unreliable or deficient in memory.

Given this evidence, the 9/11 official account is, at best, discredited, and the public is apparently faced with lies and cover-up. At worst, the man called Mohamed Atta was protected by elements within the Pentagon and allowed to act and travel freely until 9/11.

VIII.

THE PHONE CALLS FROM
THE 9/11 FLIGHTS

Introduction

The claim that passengers and crew made phone calls from the 9/11 flights was essential to the official account of 9/11. According to this account:

- Officials first learned of the hijacking of one of the flights from solicitor general Ted Olson, who reported that he had received two phone calls from his wife, Barbara Olson.[755]

- Phone calls from the planes were the source of information about how the hijackings occurred and what was going on inside the planes.[756]

- For example, one of Barbara Olson's calls was the only source of the report that the alleged hijackers had box cutters.[757]

According to the early press stories, some of the calls were made from onboard phones, and some of them—about fifteen of them—were made from cell phones.[758] However, studies showed that most of the reported cell phone calls would have been impossible, and by 2006, the FBI declared that only two of the calls were indeed from cell phones.[759] Further research that is documented in these chapters show the whole idea of phone calls from the planes to be unsupportable.

46

The Assumption That the Todd Beamer "Let's Roll" Call from United 93 Was Authentic: Part I

The Official Account

Todd Beamer was one of the passengers on UA 93 who heroically prevented the hijackers from hitting their target in Washington DC. He became the most celebrated of these heroes for saying, as a group of passengers were preparing to make their move, "Are you guys ready? Okay, let's roll."[760]

This now-famous utterance was made known by GTE supervisor Lisa Jefferson, with whom Beamer had a thirteen-minute telephone conversation before the plane crashed, and who was later mentioned in *The 9/11 Commission Report*.[761]

Beamer ended up talking to Jefferson because, having tried to make a credit card call to his wife, Lisa Beamer, his call was routed to a GTE (Verizon) customer-service operator named Phyllis Johnson, who then forwarded the call to Jefferson. Beamer continued talking to Jefferson, rather than having her transfer him to Lisa Beamer, because his wife was pregnant and he did not want to upset her.[762]

The telephone records show that Beamer initiated four telephone calls, only the fourth of which was connected. This call lasted for 3,925 seconds (slightly over 65 minutes),[763] although Beamer was on the phone talking to the two GTE representatives (Johnson and Jefferson) for only about 20 of those minutes.[764] "Mr. Beamer told the operator," said the FBI's summary of its interview with Jefferson, "that the plane had been hijacked and that he saw two hijackers with knives and someone else enter the cockpit."[765]

In November 2001, President Bush used "Let's roll" in a speech that served as a call to war for America to hunt down the terrorists.[766] In 2002, the *Washington Post* wrote, "Embraced and promoted by President Bush as a patriotic battle cry," the phrase "Let's Roll" was "emblazoned on Air Force fighter planes."[767]

The Best Evidence

There are eight reasons to doubt the authenticity of the reported call to Lisa Jefferson from the man who identified himself as Todd Beamer.

1. It is very unlikely that a passenger on UA 93 could have been able to talk to Jefferson continuously for thirteen minutes by telephone.[768] According to Lisa Beamer's 2002 book, Jefferson herself was amazed, saying that "it was a miracle that Todd's call hadn't been disconnected." As to why Jefferson considered it a miracle: "Because of the enormous number of calls that day, the GTE systems over-loaded and lines were being disconnected all around her . . . She kept thinking, *This call is going to get dropped!*"[769]

2. The man self-identified as Todd Beamer talked to GTE operators Johnson and Jefferson for approximately fifteen minutes rather than talking to his wife, Lisa Beamer. Jefferson asked him, "Would you like me to try to reach your wife and patch her call through?" He replied: "No, no. I don't want to upset her unnecessarily. She's expecting our third child in January, and if I don't have to upset her with any bad news, then I'd rather not."[770] This explanation is inconsistent with the FBI report that he had first tried to reach his residence at 9:43:48 AM.[771]

It is implausible that Beamer would have later decided not to call his wife, for three reasons:

- According to Jefferson's account, Beamer was con-vinced he was going to die, yet was passing up a last chance to talk to his wife.

- He supposedly did not ask to talk with her because he did "not want to upset her," although learning of his death would presumably upset her.

- The self-identified Todd Beamer said to Lisa Jefferson: "I just want to talk to somebody and just let someone know that this is happening."[772] However, he did not ask to be connected to any of his relatives or friends.

3. In spite of the situation he was in, the alleged Todd
   Beamer remained remarkably calm during most of the
   call. Jefferson recalled: "Todd, when he came to me,
   he was calm. . . . [H]e stayed calm through the entire
   conversation."[773] Jefferson also wrote: "[H]is voice was
   devoid of any stress. In fact, he sounded so tranquil it
   made me begin to doubt the authenticity and urgency
   of his call."[774] She later told Beamer's wife, "If I hadn't
   known it was a real hijacking, I'd have thought it was a
   crank call, because Todd was so rational and methodical
   about what he was doing."[775]

4. There was no way to confirm that the man who talked
   to Phyllis Johnson and Lisa Jefferson was really Todd
   Beamer.

   • Neither of these women knew him, so they would
     not have recognized his voice.

   • Because the caller did not want to be connected to
     Lisa Beamer, she also could not say whether the voice
     was really that of her husband.

   • According to Jefferson, she did not have the call
     recorded,[776] nor did the adjacent Airfone Operations
     Surveillance Center (AOSC), to whom Jefferson
     immediately reported the call.[777]

   • There was no reported FBI interview with Phyllis
     Johnson, the GTE operator who allegedly first took
     the call.[778]

5. According to the FBI's telephone report on UA 93, which
   was provided for the Moussaoui trial in 2006, four calls
   were attributed to Todd Beamer. The first lasted "0 seconds" (meaning it was not connected). The second, which
   also lasted "0 seconds," reportedly occurred at exactly the
   same time as the first one (9:42:44). The third call also
   lasted "0 seconds" and was dialed to the Beamer's home.
   The fourth call—which allegedly reached a GTE operator
   and lasted 3,925 seconds (about 65 minutes)—was placed

at exactly the same time (9:48:48) as the third one.[779] Thus two sets of numbers were evidently connected in the identical second, and no official explanation was given as to how this could have occurred.

6. According to Jefferson, the phone of the man to whom she was speaking remained connected long after UA 93 crashed. Reporting that he had left the phone after saying "Let's roll," she wrote that the line "just went silent." Although she held on for "probably fifteen minutes" (the early evidence had indicated it was thirteen minutes), she "never heard a crash." She added: "I can't explain it. We didn't lose a connection because there's a different sound that you use. It's a squealing sound when you lose a connection. I never lost connection, but it just went silent."[780]

7. On September 29, 2001, the FBI received detailed records from Verizon's wireless subscriber office in Bedminster, New Jersey, indicating that Todd Beamer's cell phone made nineteen outgoing calls after the alleged 10:03 AM crash time of Flight UA 93.[781] This fact, along with the sixth one, indicates either that the man self-identified as Todd Beamer was not on UA 93, or else Todd Beamer's cell phone was not on the flight or this flight did not crash.

8. Todd Beamer was celebrated for having said: "Are you guys ready?" Let's roll!" But this expression was not contained in the FBI's summary of its interview with Lisa Jefferson on the day of the phone call. Instead, according to the FBI summary: "At approximately 9:00 AM Central time, Beamer said the passengers were about to attack the hijackers. . . . [H]e asked Jefferson to call [redacted] to tell them that he loved them. . . . Next, Jefferson heard another passenger give the go-ahead to make their move. After that point, she heard nothing."[782]

The first time Todd Beamer's alleged "battle cry" was quoted in print was evidently in an article by Jim McKinnon of the *Pittsburgh Post-Gazette* five days later, on September 16. McKinnon had apparently learned this phrase from Todd Beamer's wife, Lisa

Beamer, whom McKinnon had interviewed. Having stated that Todd Beamer had (reportedly) dropped his phone after asking Lisa Jefferson to call his wife, McKinnon wrote: "That's when Jefferson heard what Lisa Beamer believes were her husband's last words: Let's roll."[783]

In any case, the FBI summary of its interview with Lisa Jefferson did not merely fail to contain the phrase "Let's roll!" (which could have simply been an omission on the part of an FBI agent). It also explicitly attributed the go-ahead signal "Let's Roll" to another passenger, not to Todd Beamer.

Conclusion

The true nature of the reported conversation between GTE employee Lisa Jefferson and the man identifying himself as Todd Beamer is in serious question.

There are eight problems with the official account of this call. The first three problems cast doubt on the possibility that the call could have even taken place. The fourth one shows that there is no way to confirm the authenticity of the call. The next three raise very serious questions about the connection of the call.

Finally, attributing "Let's roll" to Todd Beamer contradicts what Lisa Jefferson told the FBI on 9/11, the day she received the call.

Given the pivotal importance of this call in starting the "war on terror," these problems, like the problems in the Barbara Olson story, show the evidentiary basis for this "war" to have been as weak as the evidence for the "weapons of mass destruction" in starting the Iraq "war."[784]

47

The Assumption That the Todd Beamer "Let's Roll" Call from United 93 Was Authentic: Part II

Introduction

As explained in the previous chapter, the famous "Let's roll" story of how Todd Beamer led a passenger revolt aboard UA Flight 93, thereby preventing the plane from reaching the Capitol,[785] was based on an alleged telephone call from Mr. Beamer to GTE telephone supervisor Lisa Jefferson.[786]

As also stated in the previous chapter, President Bush in November 2001 used "Let's roll" to call America to arms in a rallying speech to hunt down the terrorists.[787] And in 2002, the *Washington Post* wrote: "Embraced and promoted by President Bush as a patriotic battle cry," the phrase "Let's Roll" was "emblazoned on Air Force fighter planes, city fire-trucks, school athletic jerseys, and countless T-shirts, baseball caps and souvenir buttons."[788]

The previous chapter raised eight serious questions about the authenticity of the Beamer calls. The present chapter highlights another problem: a fatal contradiction between three official reports, on the one hand, and the telephone records concerning the start time of the hour-long Beamer airphone call to GTE supervisor Lisa Jefferson, on the other.

The Official Account

1. According to *The 9/11 Commission Report* of 2004, the hijacking of UA Flight 93 began at 9:28 AM (Eastern):

> The hijackers attacked at 9:28. While traveling 35,000 feet above eastern Ohio, United 93 suddenly dropped 700 feet. Eleven seconds into the descent, the FAA's air traffic control center in Cleveland received the first of two radio transmissions from the aircraft. During the first broadcast, the captain or first officer could be heard

declaring "MayDay" amid the sounds of physical struggle in the cockpit. The second radio transmission, 35 seconds later, indicated that the fight was continuing. The captain or first officer could be heard shouting: "Hey get out of here—get out of here—get out of here."[789]

The 9/11 Commission Report cited several studies from the National Transportation Safety Board (NTSB), the Federal Aviation Authority (FAA), and the Aircraft Communication and Reporting System (ACARS) to substantiate the time of the beginning of Flight 93's hijacking as 9:28 AM.[790]

2. The evidence presented by the FBI under oath during the Moussaoui trial in 2006, and backed by telephone records, shows that the Beamer call reached GTE supervisor Lisa Jefferson at 9:48:48 and lasted 3,925 seconds (or 65.4 minutes).[791]

The Best Evidence

The two timelines presented above in the official accounts are glaringly at odds with one another.

In addition, GTE supervisor Lisa Jefferson reported in her interview with the FBI on September 11, 2001, that at *approximately* 8:45 AM (Central Time, 9:45 AM Eastern):

Beamer called to state that the airplane was about to be hijacked. He stated that three individuals, two wielding knives, the third with a bomb strapped to his waist with a red belt, were preparing to take control of the flight. Jefferson estimated that she spoke to Beamer for seven minutes before the two armed hijackers entered the cockpit, securing the door behind them.[792]

Serious Problems with the Beamer Call:

1. There is an insurmountable conflict between:

a) the NTSB, FAA, and ACARS reports of 9:28 AM (Eastern time) as the start time of the Flight 93 hijacking, and

b) the telephone records presented at the Moussaoui trial showing that the call to Jefferson was placed by Beamer at 8:48 AM Central time (9:48 AM Eastern), which would have been, according to Jefferson's estimate, seven minutes before the hijacking began.

2. Jefferson's estimate that she spoke with Beamer for seven minutes "before the two hijackers armed with knives entered the cockpit" places the Beamer account of the hijacking at approximately 9:52 AM, more than twenty minutes after the 9:28 AM time shown in the various NTSB, FAA, and ACARS flight data reports.

3. Although *The 9/11 Commission Report* stated that the plane dropped abruptly[793] from 35,000 feet at 9:28 AM, Jefferson reported in her FBI interview that during his call at approximately 9:45 AM, "Beamer stated that after a short period, the aircraft maneuvered erratically and continued to do so."[794]

4. Although *The 9/11 Commission Report* stated that there were struggles and shouts of "MayDay" and "Get out of here" from the cockpit during the hijacking,[795] Jefferson noted in her FBI interview "that there was an unusually low amount of background noise."[796]

5. The problem about the time of the start of the Beamer call reinforces the sixth problem, discussed in the previous chapter: that Beamer, according to Jefferson, had left the phone after saying "Let's roll." Although she held on for "probably 15 minutes," she said, she "never heard a crash." She added: "I can't explain it. We didn't lose a connection because there's a different sound that you use. It's a squealing sound when you lose a connection. I never lost connection, but it just went silent." Thus, according to Jefferson's report, the call remained open ten to fifteen minutes after the official crash time of 10:03 AM.[797]

Conclusion

The two conflicting timelines differ by more than twenty minutes. Given the problems with the Beamer call outlined in the preceding chapter, three questions arise:

1) Why was Beamer describing an event that had, according

to three official sources, occurred twenty minutes earlier, as if it were unfolding in the present moment?

2) Why do the telephone records presented by the FBI at the Moussaoui trial in 2006 place the Beamer hijacking call at 9:48 AM, although three official sources place the hijacking twenty minutes earlier?

3) Given that airphones are powered by the airplane's electrical system, how could the Beamer line have remained open for forty-five minutes after the plane had crashed and disintegrated?

Hence, these questions about the beginning of the alleged Beamer call complement the time-related questions about the end of the alleged call raised in Chapter 46, thereby reinforcing the doubts about the authenticity of the Todd Beamer call to Lisa Jefferson—upon which was founded the entire "Let's roll" campaign glorifying the heroism of the passengers of UA Flight 93.

48

The Assumption That the Reported Phone Calls from Barbara Olson Were Authentic

Introduction

Americans were first told that terrorists had hijacked an airliner when CNN gave a report about US Solicitor General Theodore "Ted" Olson, who said that his wife, well-known TV commentator Barbara Olson, had called him twice from American Airlines Flight 77 (AA 77), stating that terrorists had taken over this flight. This would have been roughly a half hour before this plane, according to the official story, crashed into the Pentagon.

The Official Account

Ted Olson reported, according to CNN, that his wife had "called him twice on a cell phone from American Airlines Flight 77," saying that "all passengers and flight personnel, including the pilots, were herded to the back of the plane by armed hijackers," who had "knives and cardboard cutters."[798]

Although Olson had originally told CNN that his wife had used a cell phone, the FBI's September 11th summary of its interview of him said: "[Mr. Olson] doesn't know if the calls were made from [Barbara Olson's] cell phone or the telephone on the plane."[799] But during a September 14 interview on *Hannity & Colmes,* Olson suggested that his wife had reached him at the Department of Justice by using the "airplane phone."[800] Ted Olson continued to go back and forth between the two alternatives.[801]

In any case, the first call from his wife, Olson told the FBI, lasted "about one minute."[802] The second call, he told Larry King, lasted "two or three or four minutes."[803] *The 9/11 Commission Report* stated (in 2004) that the FBI and the Department of Justice believed that there had actually been four calls from Barbara Olson.[804]

The Best Evidence

The story about Barbara Olson's report of the hijacking of AA 77 was foundational for the official account of 9/11. This foundational role is illustrated by the fact that, although it has been widely held that the hijackers had box cutters, this idea was provided only by Ted Olson's report of his wife's phone calls. In any case, in spite of the foundational role of the Olson story, there are three serious problems with its credibility:

1. One problem is that, although Ted Olson went back and forth on whether his wife had used an onboard phone or a cell phone, she evidently could not have used either:

- With regard to the possibility that Barbara Olson had used a cell phone, the FBI ruled this out in 2004, saying, "All of the calls from Flight 77 were made via the on-board airphone system."[805]

- There is also evidence that Barbara Olson could not have made the calls attributed to her in *The 9/11 Commission Report:* This is the evidence, cited in the Burnett section of Chapter 50, indicating that the cell phone technology available in 2001 would not have allowed cell phone calls from this airliner.[806]

- Further evidence that Barbara Olson could not have used an onboard phone to call from AA 77 is provided by a page in the Boeing 757 Aircraft Maintenance Manual (757 AMM), dated January 28, 2001. The first sentence of this page states, "The passenger telephone system was deactivated by ECO FO878." (ECO F1463 and F1532 were later orders to remove the phones.) This page indicates, in other words, that by January 28, 2001, the passenger phone system for the AA 757 fleet had been deactivated.[807]

- The impossibility of Olson's having used an onboard phone is further supported by a pilot and a flight attendant.

  - After serving as a fighter pilot and attending the

US Navy Fighter Weapons School, Captain Ralph Kolstad served as an airline pilot for twenty-seven years, during thirteen of which he flew Boeing 757s and 767s for American Airlines. He wrote: "[T]he 'air phones,' as they were called, were . . . deactivated in early or mid 2001. They had been deactivated for quite some time prior to Sep 2001."[808]

◆ Flight attendant Ginger Gainer, after reporting that the Boeing 757s prepared for international flights had stickers on the seatback phones "indicating that they were inoperative," added: "I asked several current and former Flight Attendants for American, . . . who flew domestic . . . , and they all said that they recalled the phones as having been disabled at the time, or gone."[809]

• There is one more reason to be skeptical about the claim that Barbara and Ted Olson talked that morning by telephone: Neither the telephone company records, nor the Department of Justice phone call records, nor Barbara Olson's cell phone call records have ever been made public, in spite of the robust discussion surrounding the authenticity of her reported phone calls.[810]

2. A second, more serious, problem is that the Olson story was contradicted in the FBI's 2006 report presented at the trial of Zacarias Moussaoui. In its report about phone calls from AA 77, the FBI stated that there was one call from Barbara Olson (not two), and that this call was "unconnected," so that it lasted "0 seconds."[811] This report thereby contradicted Ted Olson's report that his wife had made two calls to him, one that lasted "about one minute" and another that lasted "two or three or four minutes."[812]

3. A third problem is that Barbara Olson's story as told by her husband is simply implausible. According to this story, sixty passengers—including pilot Charles Frank "Chic" Burlingame III, a former Navy pilot who was a weightlifter and a boxer[813]—were held at bay in the back of the plane by

three or four hijackers (one or two would have been in the pilot's cabin). And yet these alleged hijackers were, as a 9/11 Commission staff document mentioned, "not physically imposing, as the majority of them were between 5'5" and 5'7" in height and slender in build."[814] If these small men were armed only with knives and box cutters, the pilots and the male passengers could have easily overpowered them.

Conclusion

Although Ted Olson reported two calls from his wife, and the 9/11 Commission attributed four calls to her, the best evidence shows three problems in the official account. These problems, taken in reverse order, lead to this threefold conclusion:

1. Barbara Olson's account of what occurred on AA 77, as told by her husband, is *implausible*.

2. The FBI's report on phone calls from AA 77 indicates that she *did not* reach her husband from that flight.

3. Various accounts indicate that she *could not* have called her husband from AA 77.[815]

49

The Treatment of the Reported Cell Phone Calls as Authentic: First Version

Introduction

Although the public's understanding about the 9/11 attacks depended heavily, from the beginning, on alleged "cell phone calls from the planes," for several years—from September 2001 until July 2004, when *The 9/11 Commission Report* was issued—there was no official statement about the reported calls. But ideas about such cell phone calls were conveyed to the public in this period by America's mainstream media,[816] and these ideas were never challenged by the FBI or (later) by the 9/11 Commission. This set of ideas, by default, can be called the *first* official account of the reported cell phone calls.

This first official account is of interest because in 2006 it was contradicted by the FBI, and *The 9/11 Commission Report* can be seen, when read in light of this later FBI report, to have explicitly endorsed only two of the reported cell phone calls, both of which came from low elevations (as reported in the following chapter).

The Official Account

Passengers and flight attendants on the 9/11 flights were able, reported the media, to use cell phones (as well as onboard phones) to let people on the ground know what was happening on their planes:

- The day after 9/11, a BBC story said: "A senior US intelligence official told MSNBC.com that mobile phone communications [cell phone calls] from [UA] Flight 93 indicate that three passengers overpowered the hijackers but were unable to maintain control of the plane."[817]

- The next day (September 13, 2001) a *Washington Post* story said, "[Passenger Jeremy] Glick's cell phone call from Flight 93 and others like it provide the most dramatic accounts so far of events aboard the four hijacked aircraft."[818]

- The same *Post* story about this flight said, "The plane was at once a lonesome vessel, the people aboard facing their singular fate, and yet somehow already attached to the larger drama, connected again by cell phones."[819]

The media also gave accounts of particular passengers and flight attendants on the planes who used cell phones to communicate with people on the ground. (Wherever possible, the FBI interview of the recipient of the cell phone call, usually conducted the morning of 9/11, is sourced in the note.)

- On the afternoon of 9/11, CNN reported that US Solicitor General Theodore "Ted" Olson told CNN that his wife, well-known CNN commentator Barbara Olson, had "called him twice on a cell phone from American Airlines Flight 77," stating that the plane had been taken over by hijackers armed with "knives and cardboard cutters."[820] When interviewed by the FBI, Olson said that he did not know if her calls were made from her cell phone or the telephone on the plane.[821] In subsequent media interviews, Olson went back and forth on whether his wife used her cell phone or a seat-back phone, but her call was almost unanimously reported in the media, in line with the initial CNN story, as a cell phone call.

- Later on 9/11, an Associated Press story reported that businessman Peter Hanson called his father—Lee Hanson of Connecticut—from United 175. The AP stated that "a minister confirmed the cell phone call to Lee Hanson."[822]

- According to the *Washington Post* on September 13, Kathy Hoglan talked about her nephew, Mark Bingham. In "his cell phone call to her" from UA 93, she reportedly said, he "managed only to tell his aunt and mother, Alice Hoglan, that the plane had been hijacked and that he loved them."[823]

- On September 16, a *Washington Post* writer, David Maraniss, discussing UA 175, said: "Brian Sweeney called his wife Julie: 'Hi, Jules,' Brian Sweeney was saying into his cell phone. 'It's Brian. We've been hijacked, and it doesn't look too good.'"[824] According to the FBI's interview with Julie Sweeney on October 2, 2001, she had been out when her husband called. She "returned home to find that her husband had left a message, made from his cell phone aboard the plane, on their answering machine. The answering machine recorded that the message was left at approximately 8:58 AM."[825] At that time, US 175 was reportedly at about 25,000 feet. (It is important to note that the message was on Julie Sweeney's answering machine, which would make it difficult to argue that her report—that her husband had called on his cell phone—was based on faulty hearing or memory.)

- Maraniss also, saying that people aboard UA 93 were "connected [to the larger drama] by cell phones," added, "Thomas E. Burnett Jr., a California businessman, called his wife, Deena, four times." In an AP story on September 12, Martha Raffaele wrote, "In a series of four cellular phone calls, Burnett had his wife, Deena, conference in the FBI." The FBI's report of its interview with Deena, carried out on 9/11 itself, indicated that she had spoken of "three to five cellular phone calls."[826] A year later, McClatchy reporter Greg Gordon wrote that Deena Burnett had been "strangely calmed by her husband's steady voice over his cell phone."[827] A segment about Deena Burnett on CBS's *Early Show* said, "Tom Burnett made four cell phone calls from Flight 93 to Deena Burnett at home, telling her he and some other passengers were going to 'do something.'"[828]

- On September 22, a story in the *Pittsburgh Post-Gazette* about UA 93 passenger Marion Britton began, "She called longtime friend Fred Fiumano, from whom she had borrowed a cell phone."[829]

Responses by the 9/11 Commission and the FBI: Summary

The 9/11 Commission Report supported the truth of the picture provided in the media—that there had been several cell phone calls from the 9/11 planes—by virtue of referring to FBI interviews reporting cell phone calls.

- With regard to the aforementioned report about business-man Peter Hanson—according to which he had called his father—the FBI, which had interviewed the father (Lee Hanson), wrote, "He believed his son was calling from his cellular telephone."[830]

- With regard to the aforementioned stories that Deena Burnett had received several calls from her husband, Thomas Burnett, the FBI, which interviewed her on 9/11 itself, wrote, "Burnett was able to determine that her husband was using his own cellular telephone."[831]

- In discussing UA 93 (which was the source of most of the reported cell phone calls), the commission wrote: "Shortly [after 9:32 AM], the passengers and flight crew began a series of calls from GTE airphones and cellular phones. . . . At least ten passengers and two crew members shared vital information with family, friends, colleagues, or others on the ground."[832]

Accordingly, the media indicated that passengers and flight attendants on the 9/11 flights communicated with people on the ground by means of cell phones.

The Best Evidence

Various technological reports between 2001 and 2004 indicated that, given the cell phones available in 2001, cell phone calls from high-altitude airliners—meaning ones above 20,000 feet—were very unlikely.[833]

- The most extensive of these reports were by Canadian mathematician and scientist A. K. Dewdney, who for many years had written a column for *Scientific American*.[834] In 2003, he published reports of experiments he had carried out in single- and twin-engine airplanes, showing that at 20,000 feet, there was a one-in-a-hundred chance of successful calls from a single-engine plane, and in a twin-engine plane (which has greater insulation), the success rate at 7,000 feet was 0 percent. Dewdney also pointed out that cell phone failure would occur at even lower altitudes in large airliners, which are even more insulated.[835]

- When the times of the reported phone calls are compared with the official flight data paths, it is clear that some of the cell phone calls reported in the mainstream press occurred when the planes were above 40,000 feet, and that all of them occurred above 20,000 feet.[836]

- Dewdney's report did not stand alone. Several other articles published between 2001 and 2004 cast doubt on the credibility of the reported cell phone calls.[837]

- In 2004, Qualcomm announced a successful demonstration of a fundamentally new kind of cell phone technology, involving a "picocell," that would allow passengers "to place and receive calls as if they were on the ground." American Airlines announced that this new technology was expected to be commercially available in 2006.[838] This technology, in fact, first became available on commercial flights in March 2008.[839] Given the fact that this picocell technology was not available in 2001, most of the reported cell phone calls could not have occurred.

- The cell phone companies, even before 9/11, kept extensive coded data on each call from the three-sided cell phone towers, and these data provide triangulation location points.[840] Such data are routinely requested for court cases and would have been used in the massive cell phone investigation that ensued.[841]

Therefore the above-reported cell phone calls almost certainly could not have been received from any of the 9/11 planes.

Conclusion

Beginning with the reported cell phone calls by Barbara Olson

aboard AA 77, the first official account of the 9/11 attacks depended heavily on media stories of cell phone calls from the 9/11 planes.

From 2001 until 2006, such stories appeared to be supported
by the FBI and the 9/11 Commission. The commission reported
the stories about Barbara Olson from American 77; Peter Hanson
and Brian Sweeney from United 175; and Mark Bingham, Marion
Britton, Tom Burnett, and Jeremy Glick from United 93. The 9/11
Commission and the FBI, moreover, did nothing to cast doubt on
the belief that these people had, while in 9/11 planes, used cell
phones to talk to people on the ground.[842]

Therefore, the first official account of phone calls from the 9/11
planes, which fleshed out the dramatic public story, is objectively
so improbable as to be unbelievable—a fact that casts doubt on the
credibility of the official account of 9/11 as a whole.

50

The Treatment of the Reported Cell Phone Calls as Authentic: Second Version

Introduction

According to what served as the official account of cell phone usage from the 9/11 planes until July 2004 (when *The 9/11 Commission Report* was released), more than a dozen calls—from a combination of passengers and flight attendants—were made to people on the ground by means of cell phones. The belief that such calls had been made was conveyed to the public by the mass media, with apparent support by the FBI and (later) *The 9/11 Commission Report*. According to the first version of the official story (see the previous chapter), there were reportedly cell phone calls from passengers and/or flight attendants from all four flights, although most of them were from UA 93.

The fact that the first version of the official story about cell phones had been replaced by a second version became obvious in the FBI's testimony for the Moussaoui trial, which occurred in early 2006. This second version was also implicit in *The 9/11 Commission Report*, although this fact did not become obvious until after (a) the FBI presented its report to the Moussaoui trial and (b) a 9/11 staff report of 2004 became available.[843]

The Official Account

According to the second version of the official account, most of the phone calls from the 9/11 planes were made from onboard (seatback) phones; only two of them were made by means of cell phones. This was stated at the trial of Zacarias Moussaoui in 2006, reported journalist Greg Gordon, who was covering the trial for the McClatchy newspapers.[844] Summarizing this part of the FBI testimony, Gordon wrote, "In the back of the plane, 13 of the terrified passengers and crew members made 35 air phone calls and two cell phone calls to family members and airline dispatchers, a member of an FBI Joint Terrorism Task Force testified Tuesday."[845]

Both of the reported cell phone calls were from UA 93, after it had descended (shortly before crashing) to the altitude of 5,000 feet.[846] The two reported cell phone callers were flight attendant CeeCee Lyles and passenger Edward Felt. The FBI's reports about the calls from Lyles and Felt are profiled—like the FBI's reports about all phone calls from the 9/11 planes, whether reportedly made from cell phones or onboard phones—in an interactive computer presentation on the US government website for the Moussaoui trial.[847] Each report consists of a graphic that summarizes the information about the reported call.

The graphic for flight attendant CeeCee Lyles indicates that she made two calls, one of which was a "cell phone call" to a residential number at 9:58:00 AM.[848]

The graphic for the call from Felt, which was also said to have occurred at 9:58:00 AM, says "call placed from bathroom," from which readers can infer that it must have been made from a cell phone. There is an even more explicit—albeit less accessible—graphic, which says, "9:58 AM: Passenger Edward Felt, using his cell phone, (732) 241-XXXX, contacts John Shaw, a 911 Operator from Westmoreland County, PA."[849]

Based on the belief that other phone calls from the 9/11 planes were made from cell phones, some people have argued that the reported calls from the 9/11 planes could not have been received, because in 2001 cell phone calls from high-altitude airliners were impossible. However, given the fact that the only reported cell phone calls were from UA 93 at 9:58:00 AM, after it had descended to 5,000 feet, there is no problem.

The Best Evidence

By stating this second version of the official account—that the only reported cell phone calls from the 9/11 planes were made from UA 93 at 9:58:00 AM, after it had evidently descended to 5,000 feet—the FBI seemingly avoided the problem created by the fact that cell phone calls from high-altitude airliners could in 2001 connect momentarily at best. But five problems remain.

1. The Calls by Lyles and Felt

As stated in Chapter 49 ("The Treatment of the Reported Cell Phone Calls as Authentic: First Version"), A. K. Dewdney reported that he found the success rate of cell phone calls from twin-engine planes fell to zero at 7,000 feet. He also said that the cell phone failure would occur at lower altitudes in airliners, because they are much more insulated.[850] How much lower? According to many anecdotal reports, Dewdney said, "in large passenger jets, one loses contact *during takeoff*, frequently before the plane reaches 1000 feet altitude."[851] The fact that UA 93 was at 5,000 feet does not necessarily show, therefore, that Felt and Lyles could have made successful cell phone calls at 9:58 AM.

Indeed there is evidence to suggest that they did *not* make such calls: The UA 93 phone records for the precisely timed 9:58:00 AM calls by both Lyles and Felt show no cell phone number and no duration—information included on any cell phone bill[852]—in spite of "an exhaustive study. . . of the cell phone records of each of the passengers who owned cell phones."[853]

2. The Falsity of the First Official Account

By virtue of holding that all of the reported cell phone calls, except for those of Felt and Lyles, were made from onboard phones, the FBI's 2006 report implied that one of the chief elements in the story about 9/11 told (or at least allowed) by authorities from the outset—that the presence of hijackers on the 9/11 flights were reported in cell phone calls by *numerous* passengers—was untrue. The question becomes, then, whether the FBI's second account is plausible.

3. A Priori Reason to Doubt the Second Account

The 2006 FBI account entails that all of the reported calls that had been presented in the first official account as cell phone calls had actually been—except for those by Felt and Lyles—calls from onboard phones. That is, the calls by seven passengers—UA 93 passengers Mark Bingham, Marion Britton, Tom Burnett and Jeremy Glick; UA 175 passengers Peter Hanson and Brian Sweeney; and AA 77 passenger Barbara Olson—had been misascribed.

It might be possible that all of these reported calls had involved errors, perhaps due to mishearing, misspeaking, or poor memory (whether by the journalists who reported the calls or the people who received them). The probability of this many errors, all in the same direction, would be extremely low.

Two of the reported calls, moreover, cannot be explained away as errors due to mishearing, misspeaking, or poor memory: the calls to Julie Sweeney and Deena Burnett. (The problem of the reported calls from Barbara Olson is a special case, covered in Chapter 48.)

4. The Call Received by Julie Sweeney

As reported in Chapter 49, *Washington Post* writer David Maraniss said in a discussion of UA 175: "Brian Sweeney called his wife Julie: 'Hi, Jules,' Brian Sweeney was saying into his cell phone. 'It's Brian. We've been hijacked, and it doesn't look too good.'"[854]

However, Chapter 49 did not include information in the FBI's interview with Julie Sweeney on October 2, 2001. Having been out when her husband had called, she "returned home to find that her husband had left a message, made from his cell phone aboard the plane, on their answering machine. The answering machine recorded that the message was left at approximately 8:58 AM." At that time, UA 175 was reportedly at about 25,000 feet.[855]

Given the fact that the phone call (which lasted twenty-seven seconds) was on Julie Sweeney's answering machine, one could not argue that her report—that her husband had called from his cell phone—was based on faulty hearing or memory. How, then, could the FBI have later stated that Brian Sweeney left a voice mail message "using a GTE Airfone"?[856]

5. The Calls Received by Deena Burnett

Deena Burnett, a former Delta Airlines flight attendant, told FBI interviewers that, shortly after the calls had come, she had received three to five calls from her husband, Tom Burnett, on UA 93.[857]

- In the first years after 9/11 (from 2001 through 2006), these calls were described in books[858] and newspaper articles[859] as cell phone calls.

- These UA 93 calls were allegedly made from high altitudes (35,000 and 40,700 feet[860]), so Tom Burnett could not have called his wife on a cell phone at that time. Even Deena Burnett herself, who had been a flight attendant, later wrote, "I didn't understand how he [Tom] could be calling me on his cell phone from the air."[861]

- When the FBI report on phone calls from the 9/11 airliners was issued in connection with the 2006 Moussaoui trial, it indicated that Tom Burnett had made three calls, *none of which were from a cell phone*: All were said to have been made from onboard phones.[862] The FBI report also specified the rows from which the calls were made.[863]

- This FBI 2006 report, according to which Tom Burnett had called his wife from seat back phones, removed the problem of how he could have been using a cell phone at flight UA 93's high elevation. But it introduced a new problem:

- According to Deena Burnett's FBI interview on September 11, she knew that her husband had used his cell phone: "Burnett was able to determine that her husband was using his own cellular telephone because the caller identification showed his number, 925-980-3360. Only one of the calls did not show on the caller identification as she was on the line with another call."[864]

- This creates a seemingly insuperable problem: If Tom Burnett had used onboard phones, his cell phone number could not have shown up even once.

The FBI's categorizing of the Burnett calls as onboard phone calls, in spite of the FBI's early interview with Deena Burnet to the contrary, is contradicted by the FBI's opposite treatment of the case involving UA 93 flight attendant CeeCee Lyles:

- The FBI's summary of her husband's testimony says: "At 9:58 AM, Lorne Lyles received a call at home from her celular [sic] telephone. . . . Lyles commented that CeCe [sic] Lyles' telephone number 941-823-2355 was the number on the caller ID."[865] This account was faithfully reflected in the FBI's telephone report for the Moussaoui trial.

- But even though Deena Burnett provided the same evidence—that her spouse's cell phone number had appeared on her phone's caller ID—the FBI's report for the Moussaoui trial did *not* reflect her testimony.

- This difference in treatment may be explained by the fact that, whereas the reported Burnett call was from an elevation that was clearly too high to make cell phone calls, a cell phone call from 5,000 feet might seem plausible.

- The FBI claim that the Burnett calls were from onboard phones implied that (1) either Deena's memory was faulty or (2) she was lying. However, (1a) Deena gave her FBI interviews within hours of receiving the calls,[866] and (2a) there would seem to be no plausible motive as to why she would have lied.

The FBI has not explained the contradiction between Deena's 2001 FBI interview and the FBI's report that surfaced in 2006; it simply ignored this contradiction. Moreover, the call to Julie Sweeney, cited above, provides additional support for the truth of Deena Burnett's account.

Conclusion

Whereas the first official account of the allegedly hijacked planes rested heavily on reported cell phone accounts by passengers and flight attendants, the second official account—which was implicit in *The 9/11 Commission Report* and became explicit in the FBI's report during the 2006 Moussaoui trial—claimed that all of the phone calls that had been reported in the press as cell phone calls, except the 9:58 AM calls by Edward Felt and CeeCee Lyles, were actually made from onboard phones.

This second official account, if we ignore the problems in the Felt and Lyle accounts, removed the main problem of the first official account, which claimed that cell phone calls were made at high altitudes. But this solution created new problems.

By denying the truth of much of the first account, which had been provided, or at least allowed, by the authorities, the second account raises a question about its own credibility: Why should the new account by these same authorities be trusted?

The idea that all seven of the reported cell phone calls, aside from those by Felt and Lyles, were due to errors is implausible.

Moreover, two of the reported cell phone calls cannot be explained away, because the call to Julie Sweeney at 25,000 feet was recorded on her answering machine and the calls to Deena Burnett were shown by her caller ID to have been received from her husband's cell phone when his plane was above 35,000 feet.

Therefore, the second official account is contradicted by inconvenient evidence: that two of the reported *cell* phone calls were received when the plane was far too high to sustain such calls.

IX.

THE QUESTION OF INSIDER TRADING

Introduction

A week after 9/11, the BBC stated:

> The City watchdog, the Financial Services Authority, has launched an inquiry into unusual share price movements in London before last week's atrocities. *The [London] Times* reports that the American authorities are investigating unusually large sales of shares in airlines and insurance companies. There are said to be suspicions that the shares were sold by people who knew about the impending attacks.[867]

Three econometric studies published in reputable financial journals have reported unusual trades substantiating these suspicions, and they have not been challenged by professional or government responses. (Evidence of other kinds of foreknowledge of the events of 9/11 has been provided in Chapters 16, 21, 26, and 38.)

51

The Claim That There Was No Insider Trading Involving Put Options in Advance of 9/11

Introduction

In the first month after 9/11, there was rather widespread commentary in the press that some people had made enormous profits from foreknowledge of the attacks.[868]

The Official Account

In 2004, *The 9/11 Commission Report* wrote: "Highly publicized allegations of insider trading in advance of 9/11" have been made, and there was "[s]ome unusual trading" involving "put options— investments that pay off only when a stock drops in price."[869] However, the commission said: "Exhaustive investigations by the Securities and Exchange Commission, FBI, and other agencies have uncovered no evidence that anyone with advance knowledge of the attacks profited through securities transactions."[870]

For example, "the volume of put options … surged in the parent companies of United Airlines on September 6 and American airlines on September 10," and this was "highly suspicious trading on its face." However, "further investigation has revealed that the trading had no connections with 9/11. A single U.S.-based institutional investor with no conceivable ties to al-Qaeda purchased 95 percent of the UAL puts on September 6 as part of a trading strategy that also included buying 115,000 shares of American on September 10."[871]

The Best Evidence

There are three reasons to reject the 9/11 Commission's claim that it refuted the belief that huge profits were gained through foreknowledge of the 9/11 attacks.

First, the 9/11 Commission did not show that there was no

insider trading based on foreknowledge about the 9/11 events, but simply asserted this.

Second, the commission used a circular argument with regard to United Airlines: In stating that most of the United Airlines put options were purchased by an investor "with no conceivable ties to al Qaeda," the commission simply presupposed that 9/11 was planned and executed solely by al-Qaeda and that no one else had any advance knowledge of the attacks.

Third, econometricians—who use statistical analyses to produce objective results in economics—have published studies showing the occurrence of very unusual trades shortly before 9/11 that ensured high profits, thereby revealing high probabilities of insider trading.

- For example, an analysis of the purchases of put options on United and American Airlines between the fifth and tenth of September, 2001, carried out by a University of Illinois professor of finance and published in a well-established journal, concluded that the evidence was "consistent with the terrorists or their associates having traded ahead of the September 11 attacks."[872]

- Another econometric study published in a well-respected journal concluded that "abnormal trading volumes . . . provide credible circumstantial evidence in support of the insider trading claim."[873]

- A more comprehensive study, by professors at the Swiss Finance Institute and the Swiss Banking Institute,[874] shows that insiders using put options for Boeing, Merrill Lynch, J.P. Morgan, Citigroup, and Bank of America stocks likely obtained $15 million.[875]

These econometric investigations, which appeared in 2006, 2010, and 2011, have not been challenged in any professional or governmental responses.

Conclusion

The very unusual trades shortly before 9/11 involving millions of dollars in profits imply that there was considerable insider foreknowledge of the 9/11 attacks.

Conclusion

The claim that al-Qaeda operatives, under the inspiration of Osama bin Laden, attacked America on 9/11 was used by the Bush-Cheney administration as a pretext to attack Muslim-majority nations. The wars against Afghanistan and Iraq killed hundreds of thousands (at least) of Muslims and forced many more to become refugees. The assumption that the 9/11 attacks gave America the right to attack Muslims continued during eight years of the Obama administration. Many more Muslims were killed or forced to move.

The belief that Muslims were responsible for the 9/11 attacks also led to a great increase in Islamophobia in the world, especially in the United States. The Trump administration even entered office with a vow to prevent Muslims in other countries from entering America.

One way to challenge the use of 9/11 to attack and ban Muslims would be to point out that it is irrational to blame Muslims in general for the acts of Osama bin Laden and a hand-full of his followers—just as it would be illogical to blame Americans in general for the beliefs and acts of the Ku Klux Klan. However, it has seldom been possible to get people to engage in this kind of rational discussion when they believe that they, their family, their religion, or their country has been attacked.

Another approach to stopping attacks on Muslims because of the 9/11 attacks would be to show how many fundamental aspects of the official account of 9/11 are not true. This approach has been exemplified in the present book. It differs from previous attempts to expose the truth by having a panel of experts from various countries and expertise evaluate claims made by the official account of the 9/11 attacks.

The panel looked at claims made in the official account about nine features of the 9/11 attacks: (1) The destruction of the Twin Towers; (2) the destruction of WTC 7; (3) the attack on the Pentagon; (4) the 9/11 flights; (5) US military exercises that occurred on or before 9/11; (6) the behavior on 9/11 of military and political leaders with roles that put them in positions to affect what happened on 9/11; (7) Osama bin Laden and the men designated as hijackers; (8) the reported phone calls from the 9/11 flights; and (9) the question of whether stock market activity suggested foreknowledge in America of the attacks.

If the official account of 9/11 were true, we would be surprised to find its claims about any of these nine topics to be false. Some of these claims—those involving the Twin Towers, WTC 7, the Pentagon, Osama bin Laden, the alleged hijackers, and the phone calls from the planes—are so crucial to the official account that showing any one of them to be false would show the entire account to be false.

The official account of 9/11 would be even more decisively refuted if its claims in all nine categories were shown to be false. And that is exactly what the international 9/11 review panel concluded. To summarize:

- The Twin Towers could not have been brought down by the airplane impacts and the resulting fires; there had to be materials producing very powerful explosions. Therefore, the Twin Towers could not have been brought down by airplanes flown by al-Qaeda pilots.

- WTC 7 could not have been brought down by office fires caused by inflammatory material from one of the Twin Towers. Therefore, again, al-Qaeda could not have been responsible; the destruction had to have been caused by explosives placed within the building.

- Hani Hanjour lacked the skill to use an airliner to strike the Pentagon.

- In spite of the official account's claims to the contrary, the government and the military were prepared to prevent and respond efficiently to attacks of the type that occurred on 9/11.

- The official account, as summarized in *The 9/11 Commission Report*, gave false accounts of the behavior of political and military leaders on 9/11, including the vice president, the secretary of defense, the acting chairman of the Joint Chiefs of Staff, and the commander-in-chief of NORAD.

- There is no good evidence that Osama bin Laden ordered

the attacks, no good evidence that there were al-Qaeda hijackers on the flights and no good evidence that the alleged hijackers were devout Muslims. Indeed, all of those claims appear to be false.

- There is no good evidence that people on the ground were telephoned by friends and loved ones from the 9/11 flights; indeed, the execution of those calls appears to have been impossible.

- Contrary to the official account's claim that there was no good evidence of insider trading based on foreknowledge of the 9/11 attacks, there was such evidence, meaning that people other than al-Qaeda operatives knew the attacks were coming.

There has been much discussion about "fake news." Some of the claims about false news are themselves false; others are true. The most fateful example of fake news in the twenty-first century thus far has been the official account of 9/11. It is long past the time to set the story straight.

Notes

1   Vincent Warren, "The 9/11 Decade and the Decline of U.S. Democracy," Center for Constitutional Rights, 9 September 2011.

2   Ahad Nil, "9/11 Used to Demonize Muslim World, Justify NSA Spying of US Citizens: Analyst," CNN, 28 February 2015.

3   John W. Whitehead, "The Tyranny of 9/11: The Building Blocks of the American Police State from A–Z," Counterpunch, 8 September 2016.

4   Kevin Drum, "Since 9/11, We've Had 4 Wars in the Middle East. They've All Been Disasters," *Mother Jones*, 17 February 2015.

5   David Ray Griffin, *9/11 Contradictions: An Open Letter to Congress and the Press* (Interlink, 2008).

6   Joe Taglieri, "Bush Advisers Planned Iraq War Since 1990s," From the Wilderness, 1 October 2002; Max Fisher, "America's Unlearned Lesson: The Forgotten Truth about Why We Invaded Iraq," Vox, 16 February 2016.

7   O'Neill is quoted to this effect in Ron Susskind, *The Price of Loyalty: George W. Bush, the White House, and the Education of Paul O'Neill* (Simon & Schuster, 2004). Susskind, whose book also draws on interviews with other officials, said that in its first weeks the Bush administration was discussing the occupation of Iraq and the question of how to divide up its oil; Richard Clarke, *Against All Enemies: Inside America's War on Terror* (Free Press, 2004), 264.

8   Jeffrey Kluger, "Why So Many People Believe Conspiracy Theories," *Time*, 15 October 2017; Emma Young, "Believers in Conspiracy Theories and the Paranormal Are More Likely to see 'Illusory Patterns,'" Research Digest, The British Psychological Society, 16 October 2017; Cliff Kincaid, "Lies of the 9/11 'Truth' Movement," Accuracy in Media, 21 May 2014.

9   Jeremy Jones and Duncan Hunter, "Consensus Methods for Medical and Health Services Research," *British Medical Journal*, 5 August 1995.

10   See Benjamin DeMott, "Whitewash as Public Service: How the 9/11 Commission Report Defrauds the Nation," *Harper's Magazine*, October 2004; Editorial Board, "What the 9/11 Commission Report Ignores: The CIA-Al Qaeda Connection," World Socialist Web Site, 24 July 2004; David Ray Griffin, *The 9/11 Commission Report: Omissions and Distortions* (Interlink, 2005); Peter Tatchell, "9/11—The Big Cover-Up?" *Guardian*, 12 September 2007; Philip Shenon, *The Commission: The Uncensored History of the 9/11 Investigation* (Twelve, 2008); "9/11 Commission Report Questioned by Over 100 Professors," Want to Know.info.

11   Bill Manning, "Selling Out the Investigation," *Fire Engineering*, January 2002.

12   James Glanz and Eric Lipton, *City in the Sky: The Rise and Fall of the World Trade Center* (Times Books/Henry Holt, 2004), 330.

13   Manning, "Selling Out the Investigation."

14   *The 9/11 Commission Report: Final Report of the National Commission on Terrorist Attacks upon the United States*, Authorized Edition (W. W. Norton, 2004), 541 n. 1.

15   NIST, *Final Report on the Collapse of the World Trade Center Towers*, September 2005.

16   "Fact Sheet: NIST's World Trade Center Investigation" (http://www.nist. gov/public_affairs/factsheet/nist_investigation_911.htm).

17   These points have been emphasized in Kevin Ryan, "What is 9/11 Truth? The First Steps," *Journal of 9/11 Studies*, Vol. 2, August 2006: 1–6.

18   This former employee's written statement, dated 1 October 2007, is contained in "NIST Whistleblower" (http://georgewashington.blogspot. com/2007/10/former-nist-employee-blows-whistle.html). Although this person wanted to remain anonymous to prevent possible retaliation, the authenticity of the self-representation has been confirmed by physicist Steven Jones (email from Jones, 3 December 2007).

19   Steven Jones, Robert Korol, Anthony Szamboti, and Ted Walter, "15 Years Later: On the Physics of High-rise Building Collapses," *Europhysics News*, July-August 2016: 22–26, at 26.

20   Peter Michael Ketcham, Letter to the Editor, *Europhysics News*, November 2016.

21   NIST, "Answers to Frequently Asked Questions," 30 August 2006, Question 2.

22   Graeme MacQueen, "118 Witnesses: The Firefighters' Testimony to Explosions in the Twin Towers," *Journal of 9/11 Studies*, Vol. 2, August 2006: 47–106.

23   Reports by journalists, police officers, WTC employees are summarized here: David Ray Griffin, "Explosive Testimony: Revelations about the Twin Towers in the 9/11 Oral Histories," 911Truth.org, 18 January 2006.

24   "NIST found no corroborating evidence for alternative hypotheses suggesting that the WTC towers were brought down by controlled demolition using explosives planted prior to September 11, 2001" (NIST NCSTAR 1, Final Report on the Collapse of the World Trade Center Towers," September 2005: xxxviii).

25   Federal Emergency Management Agency (2002), "World Trade Center Building Performance Study: Data Collection, Preliminary Observations, and Recommendations"; Medserv Medical News, "Towers Collapse

Shocks Engineers," 11 September, 2001; "Twin Towers Engineered to Withstand Jet Collision," *Seattle Times*, 2 February 1993.

26   "Twin Tower Fires Not Hot Enough to Melt or Weaken Steel!" YouTube: 9/11 Truth Videos.

27   Architect Mario Salvadori explains: "The load on the columns increases with the number of floors of the building, and their weight must vary in the same proportion." (Dr. Mario Salvadori, *Why Buildings Stand Up* [W.W. Norton, 1980], 117.) The lower the floors, the stronger the steel structures. So even if the impacts and fires had caused the top sections of these buildings to collapse, the collapses would have been arrested by the lower floors.

28   NIST NCSTAR 1, *Final Report on the Collapse of the World Trade Center Towers*, September 2005:15. Regarding airplane impacts, see 150–51; Jet fuel, 24, 42; Fires, 91, 127, 183.

29   RJ Lee Group, "WTC Dust Signature Report: Composition and Morphology," December 2003: 21; RJ Lee Group, "Expert Report: WTC Dust Signature," May 2004: 12; Heather A. Lowers and Gregory P. Meeker, US Geological Survey, US Department of the Interior, "Particle Atlas of World Trade Center Dust," 2005; Steven E. Jones et al., "Extremely High Temperatures during the World Trade Center Destruction," *Journal of 9/11 Studies* 19 (January 2008). For discussion and summary, see David Ray Griffin, *The Mysterious Collapse of World Trade Center 7: Why the Final Official Report about 9/11 Is Unscientific and False* (Interlink, 2009), 39–44.

30   NIST NCSTAR 1, *Final Report on the Collapse of the World Trade Center Towers*, September 2005:144–45.

31   The Scientists for 9/11 Truth website shows a photo of "Impaled Steel Columns at the 20th Floor of the World Financial Center Building 3 (WFC3)." See also Video 1 (https://www.youtube.com/watch?v=Qa7PN-8T2VY) and Video 2 (https://www.youtube.com/watch?v=DChR1XcYhlw) showing horizontal ejections).

32   In addition to showing that these columns struck WTC 3 (the American Express Building), the FEMA report (*World Trade Center Building Performance Report*) showed in Chapter 7 ("Peripheral Buildings") that similar debris hit the Winter Gardens, 500–600 feet distant. The FEMA report includes a map showing the location of these buildings.

33   "Remains Bring Hope, Frustration for 9/11 Families," *USA Today*, 20 April 2006.

34   Floors 78–84 of the South Tower were impacted by Flight 175 ("2 World Trade Center," 911research.wtc7.net).

35   *The 9/11 Commission Report*, 300.

36   "Answers to Frequently Asked Questions," NIST, "*Question No. 8*: We know that the sprinkler systems were activated because survivors reported

water in the stairwells. If the sprinklers were working, how could there be a 'raging inferno' in the WTC towers?"

37 Jim Dwyer and Ford Fessenden, "Lost Voices of Firefighters, Some on the 78th Floor," 4 August 2002.

38 Jim Dwyer and Kevin Flynn, "9/11 Tape Raises Added Questions on Radio Failures," *New York Times*, 9 November 2002. The transcript has been removed from the article but is cited at http://911research.wtc7.net/cache/wtc/evidence/memoryhole_tapeexcerpts.htm.

39 FDNY; a "10-45 Code One" means "Black tag (deceased)."

40 "Excerpts From Firefighters' WTC Tape on 9/11," typed transcript, posted 22 November 2002 (http://911research.wtc7.net/cache/wtc/evidence/memoryhole_tapeexcerpts.htm). The radio recording can be heard online: "Let me know when you see fire" (https://www.youtube.com/watch?v=hT-po-tmJRc).

41 Jim Dwyer and Kevin Flynn, "9/11 Tape Raises Added Questions," *New York Times*, 2 November 2002.

42 *The 9/11 Commission Report*, 305.

43 Kevin Flynn and Jim Dwyer, "Fire Department Tape Reveals No Awareness of Imminent Doom," *New York Times*, 9 November 2002.

44 Ibid.

45 Jaime Holguin, "Report: FDNY Reached WTC 78th Floor," *CBS News*, 4 August 2002, 12:09 PM.

46 NIST, *Final Report on the Collapse of the World Trade Center Towers*, September 2005: 15. Regarding airplane impacts, see pp. 150-51; Jet fuel, pp. 24, 42; Fires, pp. 91, 127, 183 (http://ws680.nist.gov/publication/get_pdf.cfm?pub_id=909017).

47 NIST NCSTAR 1A, *Final Report on the Collapse of World Trade Center Building 7* (brief report), November 2008, xxxv (http://ws680.nist.gov/publication/get_pdf.cfm?pub_id=861610). In NIST's words, the collapse of WTC 7 was "the first known instance of the total collapse of a tall building primarily due to fires."

48 In a post-report publication (September 2011), NIST wrote: "In no instance did NIST report that steel in the WTC towers melted due to the fires. The melting point of steel is about 1,500 degrees Celsius (2,800 degrees Fahrenheit). Normal building fires and hydrocarbon (e.g., jet fuel) fires generate temperatures up to about 1,100 degrees Celsius (2,000 degrees Fahrenheit). NIST reported maximum upper layer air temperatures of about 1,000 degrees Celsius (1,800 degrees Fahrenheit) in the WTC towers (for example, see NCSTAR 1, Figure 6-36)." NIST Engineering Laboratory, "Questions and Answers about the NIST WTC Towers Investigation (Question 15)," 19 September 2011 (https://www.nist.gov/el/faqs-nist-wtc-towers-investigation).

49   *The 9/11 Commission Report.*

50   NIST NCSTAR 1–9 Vol. 1, *Structural Fire Response and Probable Collapse Sequence of World Trade Center Building 7, Volume 1 and 2* Chapter 8 (http://ws680.nist.gov/publication/get_pdf.cfm?pub_id=861611).

51   NIST NCSTAR 1A, *Final Report on the Collapse of World Trade Center Building 7, Federal Building and Fire Safety Investigation of the World Trade Center Disaster*, NIST NCSTAR 1A, 20 November 2008 (http://www.nist.gov/manuscript-publication-search.cfm?pub_id=861610).

52   Dr. Gross was the co-project leader on *Structural Fire Response and Collapse Analysis.* See "Dr. John L. Gross" (https://web.archive.org/web/20120521082449/http://www.nist.gov/el/building_materials/jgross.cfm).

53   A lecture, 18 October 2006, University of Texas at Austin, on the collapse of the Twin Towers, "Dr. John Gross, N.I.S.T." (http://www.youtube.com/watch?v=7KzAp962t2Q). Date confirmed at http://ut-pnac.blogspot.ca/2007/02/upcoming-meeting-john-gross-of-nist-up.html).

54   NIST Engineering Laboratory, "Questions and Answers about the NIST WTC Towers Investigation (Question 23)," 19 September 2011.

55   "Iron," WebElements: The Periodic Table on the Web.

56   Steven E. Jones, "Why Indeed Did the World Trade Center Buildings Completely Collapse?" *Journal of 9/11 Studies*, Vol. 3, September 2006: 18 (http://www.journalof911studies.com/volume/200609/WhyIndeed-DidtheWorldTradeCenterBuildingsCompletelyCollapse.pdf).

57   James Glanz, "Engineers Suspect Diesel Fuel in Collapse of 7 World Trade Center," *New York Times*, 29 November 2001.

58   Jonathan Barnett, Ronald R. Biederman, and Richard D. Sisson, Jr., "Limited Metallurgical Examination," FEMA, *World Trade Center Building Performance Study*, May 2002, Appendix C (https://www.fema.gov/pdf/library/fema403_apc.pdf).

59   Joan Killough-Miller, "The 'Deep Mystery' of Melted Steel," *WPI Transformations*, Spring 2002 (http://web.archive.org/web/20160119053139/http://www.wpi.edu/News/Transformations/2002Spring/steel.html).

60   James Glanz and Eric Lipton, "A Search for Clues in Towers' Collapse," *New York Times*, 2 February 2002.

61   Thomas Eagar and Christopher Musso, "Why Did the World Trade Center Collapse? Science, Engineering, and Speculation," *JOM: Journal of the Minerals, Metals & Materials Society* 53/12 (2001), 8-11 (http://www.tms.org/pubs/journals/JOM/0112/Eagar/Eagar-0112.html).

62   Thomas Eagar, "The Collapse: An Engineer's Perspective," which is part of "Why the Towers Fell," NOVA, 30 April 2002 (www.pbs.org/wgbh/nova/wtc/collapse.html).

63 RJ Lee Group, "WTC Dust Signature," Expert Report, May 2004 (http://www.ae911truth.org/documents/WTCDustSignature_ExpertReport.051304.1646.mp_.pdf), 5.

64 Ibid., 11.

65 RJ Lee Group, "WTC Dust Signature Study" (December 2003), 5 (http://911research.wtc7.net/essays/thermite/cache/nyenvirolaw_WTC-DustSignatureCompositionAndMorphology.pdf).

66 Ibid., 24.

67 Ibid., 17.

68 Ibid., 21.

69 WebElements: The Periodic Table on the Web.

70 Heather A. Lowers and Gregory P. Meeker, U.S. Geological Survey, U.S. Department of the Interior, "Particle Atlas of World Trade Center Dust," 2005.

71 To see enlarged photos of the iron-rich particles, go to http://pubs.usgs.gov/of/2005/1165/table_1.html, then click on "Yes" at the far right of the lines for "Iron-03" and "Iron-04."

72 Steven E. Jones et al., "Extremely High Temperatures during the World Trade Center Destruction," *Journal of 9/11 Studies*, January 2008 (http://journalof911studies.com/articles/WTCHighTemp2.pdf), 8.

73 Ibid., 1-2.

74 Ibid., 4. On its characteristics, see "Molybdenum" in WebElements: The Periodic Table on the Web.

75 "Firefighter Describes 'Molten Metal' at Ground Zero, Like a 'Foundry'" (http://www.youtube.com/watch?v=uQyIN6OTMyY).

76 Jennifer Lin, "Recovery Worker Reflects on Months Spent at Ground Zero" (https://web.archive.org/web/20170801090443/http://fallenbrothers.com/community/showthread.php?2062-Recovery-worker-reflects-on-months-spent-at-Ground-Zero).

77 "Unflinching Look Among the Ruins," *New York Post*, 3 March 2004.

78 "Les Robertson Confirms Molten Metal in WTC Basement," in a presentation at Stanford University, at 0:40 (http://www.youtube.com/watch?v=r-jmHqES_lto). See also National Conference of Structural Engineers, 5 October 2001; James M. Williams, "WTC: A Structural Success," *SEAU NEWS, The Newsletter of the Structural Engineers Association of Utah*, October 2001: 3 (http://web.archive.org/web/20060909104247/http://www.seau.org/SEAUNews-2001-10.pdf).

79 Quoted in Francesca Lyman, "Messages in the Dust: What Are the Lessons of the Environmental Health Response to the Terrorist Attacks of September 11?" National Environmental Health Association, September

2003 (http://web.archive.org/web/20040330042927/http:/www.neha.org/9-11%20report/index-The.html).

80   "Mobilizing Public Health," *Johns Hopkins Public Health*, Late Fall, 2001.

81   FEMA Director Allbaugh with Bryant Gumbel, CBS Early Show, 4 October 2001 (http://web.archive.org/web/20130730103131/http:/911en-cyclopedia.com/wiki/index.php/Publication:20121014014812).

82   Greg Gittrich, "Fire May Smolder for Months," *New York Daily News*, 1 November 2001.

83   Trudy Walsh, "Handheld APP Eased Recovery Tasks," *Government Computer News* 21, no. 27a, 9 September 2002 (https://gcn.com/articles/2002/09/09/handheld-app-eased-recovery-tasks.aspx).

84   "K-9/11: Tracking the Rescuers' Trauma," PENN Arts & Sciences, Summer 2002 (http://www.sas.upenn.edu/sasalum/newsltr/summer2002/k911.html).

85   Tom Arterburn, "D-Day: NY Sanitation Workers' Challenge of a Lifetime," *Waste Age*, 1 April 2002.

86   NIST, Answers to Frequently Asked Questions (30 August 2006), Question 12.

87   NIST conducted only a hypothetical experiment and "found no evidence of any blast events." NIST NCSTAR 1-9, Structural Fire Response and Probable Collapse Sequence of World Trade Center Building 7, Draft for Public Comment, August 2008: 357.

88   Ibid. The hypothetical "experiment" referred to by NIST is the computation of the sound level of a blast of conventional explosives that could have severed column 79 in a single blast. Since it claims no such sound levels were recorded, NIST concluded that there was no need to investigate the possible use of explosives. This rationale is disingenuous because there is a clear description of the finding of nano-energetic material in the dust. NIST has access to WTC dust but refuses to investigate to confirm or contradict the explicit finding.

89   Dr. Steven Jones discussed the "chain of custody" of the dust samples in "9/11: Explosive Testimony Exclusive, Part 1," at 3:30 and 7:58 minutes, and at zero minutes at Part 2 of 2.

90   Niels H. Harrit, Jeffrey Farrer, Steven E. Jones, et al., "Active Thermitic Material Observed in Dust from the 9/11 World Trade Center Catastrophe," *The Open Chemical Physics Journal*, 2009, 2: 7–31 (http://electricpolitics.com/media/docs/7TOCPJ.pdf).

91   The quoted phrase is from Dr. Niels Harrit, associate professor of chemistry emeritus at the Nano-Science Center, University of Copenhagen. E-mail letter to Elizabeth Woodworth, copied to David Ray Griffin, 19 June 2011.

92   The *Amptiac Quarterly Newsletter* from the spring of 2002 said: "The 221st National Meeting of the American Chemical Society held during April 2001 in San Diego featured a symposium on Defense Applications of Nanomaterials. One of the 4 sessions was titled Nanoenergetics. This session featured speakers from government labs (DOD and DOE) and academia. . . . A number of topics were covered, including . . . Metastable Intermolecular Composites (MICs), sol-gels, and structural nanomaterials. . . . At this point in time, all of the military services and some DOE and academic laboratories have active R&D programs aimed at exploiting the unique properties of nanomaterials that have potential to be used in energetic formulations for advanced explosives and propellant applications. . . . Nanomaterials, especially nanoenergetics, could be used for improving components of munitions. . . . Nanoenergetics hold promise as useful ingredients for the thermobaric (TBX) and TBX-like weapons, particularly due to their high degree of tailorability with regards to energy release and impulse management" (43–44).

93   *World Trade Center Building Performance Study: Data Collection, Preliminary Observations, and Recommendations* (FEMA, 2002: 1–10); William Pitts et al., *Federal Building and Fire Safety Investigation on the World Trade Center Disaster: Visual Evidence, Damage Estimates, and Timeline Analysis* (NIST NCSTAR 1-5A, 22-23).

94   *The 9/11 Commission Report*, 461, n. 168.

95   "[We] recorded numerous seismic signals from two plane impacts and building collapses from the two World Trade Center (WTC) towers. . . . Collapses of the two WTC towers generated large seismic waves, observed in five states and up to 428 km away. . . . The collapse of 7 WTC at 17:20:33 EDT was recorded [as well]. . . . The two largest signals were generated by collapses of Towers 1 and 2." Won-Young Kim et al., "Seismic Waves Generated by Aircraft Impacts and Building Collapses at World Trade Center, New York City," *EOS, Transactions American Geophysical Union*, 20 November 2001 (82/47): 565, 570–71.

96   "For collapses 1 and 2, values of ML [local magnitude] determined from E-W components are 2.1 and 2.3. . . . The seismic energy of a ML 0.7 to 0.9 [was] computed for the impacts" (ibid).

97   "Scientists at Lamont-Doherty Earth Observatory . . . were able to determine accurate times of the plane impacts and building collapses using the seismic signals recorded at numerous seismographic stations in the Northeastern United States," Won-Young Kim and Gerald R. Baum, "Seismic Observations during September 11, 2001 Terrorist Attack," Maryland Geological Survey Earth Science Information Center Publications.

98   Craig T. Furlong and Gordon Ross, "Seismic Proof—9/11 Was An Inside Job (Updated Version II)," *Journal of 9/11 Studies*, September, 2006.

99   André Rousseau, "Were Explosives the Source of the Seismic Signals Emitted from New York on September 11, 2001?" *Journal of 9/11 Studies*, vol.

34, November 2012. This peer-reviewed article has not been challenged in the scientific literature.

100 Kim et al., "Seismic Waves Generated by Aircraft Impacts and Building Collapses at World Trade Center, New York City." The report also treated the collapse of WTC7, but it is not relevant here.

101 "The problem of the 'displacements' between the times of origin of the seismic waves and the times at which the planes crashed into the Towers, particularly that for WTC1, is certainly a key question and one that is emblematic of all the contradictions of the official version of September 11, 2001," as already pointed out by Furlong and Ross in 2006. Rousseau also wrote: "*There is a hiatus of 15 seconds between the plausible time of the origin of the Rayleigh wave based on the Palisades data and the time—afterwards—of the crash of the plane into WTC1 based on the ground radar data.* . . . A similar discrepancy exists in the data for the seismic wave and impact times for WTC2"; Rousseau, "Were Explosives the Source of the Seismic Signals Emitted from New York on September 11, 2001?" p. 6.

102 Rousseau, "Were Explosives the Source of the Seismic Signals Emitted from New York on September 11, 2001?" Abstract, p. 1.

103 As indicated by wave amplitudes.

104 A 2.1 magnitude shock releases 89 MJ (mega Joules), while a 2.3 event releases 178 MJ. These values are equivalent to 21 and 42 kilograms of TNT. One can check this on a calculator of energy released by magnitudes.

105 Rousseau, "Were Explosives the Source of the Seismic Signals Emitted from New York on September 11, 2001?"

106 "Three minutes of continuous data shown starting at 09:36:30 EDT (13:36:30 UTC). Data were sampled at 40 times/s and passband filtered from 0.6 to 5 Hz"; Kim and Baum, "Seismic Observations during September 11, 2001, Terrorist Attack"; Rousseau, "Were Explosives the Source of the Seismic Signals Emitted from New York on September 11, 2001?" p. 4.

107 FEMA, *World Trade Center Building Performance Study: Executive Summary*, May 2002 (https://s3-us-gov-west-1.amazonaws.com/dam-production/uploads/20130726-1512-20490-7075/403_execsum.pdf).

108 *The 9/11 Commission Report.*

109 NIST, *Final Report on the Collapse of the World Trade Center Towers*, September 2005 (http://fire.nist.gov/bfrlpubs/fire05/art119.html).

110 "Answers to Frequently Asked Questions," Question 2, NIST, 30 August 2006 (http://wtc.nist.gov/pubs/factsheets/faqs_8_2006.htm).

111 Quoted in Christopher Bollyn, "New Seismic Data Refutes Official Explanation," 14 December 2004.

112   9/11 oral history of Edward Cachia, 6 December 2001: 5 (http://graphics8.
      nytimes.com/packages/pdf/nyregion/20050812_WTC_GRAPH-
      IC/9110251.PDF).

113   9/11 oral history of Kenneth Rogers, 10 December 2001: 3–4 (http://
      graphics8.nytimes.com/packages/pdf/nyregion/20050812_WTC_
      GRAPHIC/9110290.PDF).

114   "9/11 BBC Correspondent Steven Evans—A Series of Explosions," BBC, 11
      September 2001.

115   Greg Szymanski, "NY Fireman Lou Cacchioli Upset that 9/11 Commission
      'Tried to Twist My Words,'" Arctic Beacon.com, 19 July 2005.

116   Greg Szymanski, "WTC Basement Blast and Injured Burn Victim Blows
      'Official 9/11 Story' Sky High," Arctic Beacon.com, 24 June 2005.

117   Greg Szymanski, "Second WTC Janitor Comes Forward with Eye-Witness
      Testimony of 'Bomb-Like' Explosion in North Tower Basement," Arctic-
      Beacon.com, 12 July 2005.

118   "We Will Not Forget: A Day of Terror," *The Chief Engineer*, July, 2002.
      "Some of the burning fuel shot up and down the elevator shafts, blowing
      out doors and walls on other floors all the way down to the basement."
      But besides providing an implausible answer to reports such as the one
      by Louie Cacchioli above, it provides an even more implausible response
      to Pecoraro's report about the door and the hydraulic press, which weighs
      about 650 lbs.

119   9/11 oral history of Lonnie Penn, 9 November 2001: 5 (http://graphics8.
      nytimes.com/packages/pdf/nyregion/20050812_WTC_GRAPH-
      IC/9110203.PDF).

120   9/11 oral history of Paul Curran, 18 December 2001: 11 (http://graphics8.
      nytimes.com/packages/pdf/nyregion/20050812_WTC_GRAPH-
      IC/9110369.PDF).

121   9/11 oral history of Bradley Mann, 7 November 2001: 5–7 (http://graph-
      ics8.nytimes.com/packages/pdf/nyregion/20050812_WTC_GRAPH-
      IC/9110194.PDF). See also Graeme MacQueen, "Did the Earth Shake
      Before the South Tower Hit the Ground?" *Journal of 9/11 Studies*, 9 July
      2009: 26–28.

122   Richard Gage, the founder of Architects and Engineers for 9/11 Truth,
      emphasizes the rapid onset of the buildings in his various presentations.
      See video with discussion on "911 Truth on the Fifth Estate Part 1 of 4
      Richard Gage—Architects & Engineers For 911 Truth—CBC Canada." For
      Gage's full-length presentation, see "Blueprint for Truth." See also "WTC
      North Tower Exploding, David Chandler, AE911Truth"), or Chandler,
      "Downward Acceleration of the North Tower."

123   Liz Else, "Baltimore Blasters," *New Scientist*, 24 July 2004: 48.

124 See David Chandler, "Acceleration + Serendipity" (http://www.youtube.com/watch?v=AJf7pWVyvIw&list=PL3705E482383CCA91).

125 See David Chandler, "Downward Acceleration of the North Tower" (http://www.youtube.com/watch?v=ZjSd9wB55zk) and "Destruction of the World Trade Center North Tower and Fundamental Physics," *Journal of 9/11 Studies*, February 2010.

126 See Graeme MacQueen and Anthony Szamboti, "The Missing Jolt: A Simple Refutation of the NIST-Bazant Collapse Hypothesis" *Journal of 9/11 Studies*, January 2009.

127 See David Chandler, "What a Gravity-Driven Demolition Looks Like" (http://www.youtube.com/watch?v=NiHeCjZlkr8).

128 See Gregory Szuladzinski, Anthony Szamboti, and Richard Johns, "Some Misunderstandings Related to WTC Collapse Analysis," *International Journal of Protected Structures*, 4/2, June 2013 (http://911speakout.org/wp-content/uploads/Some-Misunderstandings-Related-to-WTC-Collapse-Analysis.pdf).

129 See "9/11: Blueprint for Truth—The Architecture of Destruction," and "WTC North Tower Exploding, David Chandler."

130 "The World Trade Center: Rise and Fall of an American Icon," *History Channel*, 8 September 2002 (https://newflixhd.com/subscriptions/flowplayer?&theme=owl&a_aid=507c686605b4a&a_bid=72491354&chan=&pubid=77231&sid=&clickid=&subid=&g=47e2c20850a2d-37694681de58a4054d7&).

131 See "9/11: Blueprint for Truth—The Architecture of Destruction."

132 NIST, "Answers to Frequently Asked Questions," Question 2, NIST, 30 August 2006.

133 Jones, "Why Indeed Did the WTC Buildings Collapse?" *Journal of 9/11 Studies*, September 2006/Vol. 3: 26.

134 See "A Word about Our Poll of American Thinking Toward the 9/11 Terrorist Attacks," Zogby International, 24 May 2006 (http://www.zogby.com/features/features.dbm?ID=231).

135 "WTC 7 Collapse," NIST, 5 April 2005 (http://wtc.nist.gov/pubs/WTC%20Part%20IIC%20-%20WTC%207%20Collapse%20Final.pdf).

136 NIST, "Answers to Frequently Asked Questions," 30 August 2006 (http://wtc.nist.gov/pubs/factsheets/faqs_8_2006.htm), Question 14.

137 "NIST Releases Final WTC 7 Investigation Report," NIST, 25 November 2008.

138 "A Nation Challenged: The Site; Engineers Have a Culprit in the Strange Collapse of 7 World Trade Center: Diesel Fuel," *New York Times*, 29 November 2001.

139 Peter Michael Ketcham, "Thoughts from a Former NIST Employee," Letter to the Editor of *Europhysics News*, November, 2016.

140 FEMA, *World Trade Center Building Performance Study*, Ch. 5, Sect. 6.2, "Probable Collapse Sequence"; *Debunking 9/11 Myths: Why Conspiracy Theories Can't Stand Up to the Facts: An In-Depth Investigation by "Popular Mechanics,"* ed. David Dunbar and Brad Reagan (Hearst Books, 2006), 53–58. (This semi-official book contained quotations from NIST showing what it was thinking at the time.)

141 NIST NCSTAR 1A, *Final Report on the Collapse of World Trade Center Building 7*, November 2008: 49. In NIST's words, the collapse of WTC 7 was "the first known instance of the total collapse of a tall building primarily due to fires."

142 "Building 7 Implosion: The Smoking Gun of 9/11," Architects and Engineers for 9/11 Truth," 24 August 2010; David Llewelyn, "Let's Start with Science, Not Conspiracies, When It Comes to 9/11," Architects and Engineers for 9/11 Truth, 14 November 2017.

143 NIST NCSTAR 1-9, *Structural Fire Response and Probable Collapse Sequence of World Trade Center Building 7. Draft for Public Comment*, August 2008.

144 "[Y]ou had a sequence of structural failures that had to take place. Everything was not instantaneous" ("WTC 7 Technical Briefing," NIST, 26 August 2008). Although NIST originally had a video and a transcript of this briefing at its Internet website, it removed both of them. However, the video is now available elsewhere. Also available is its transcript, under the title "NIST Technical Briefing on Its Final Draft Report on WTC 7 for Public Comment."

145 David Chandler, "WTC7: NIST Finally Admits Freefall (Part I)," 7 December 2008, at 9:07. Chandler's report of free fall was eventually supported by NIST itself: NIST NCSTAR 1A, *Final Report on the Collapse of World Trade Center Building 7*, November 2008: 45–46.

146 NIST NCSTAR 1A, *Final Report on the Collapse of World Trade Center Building 7*, November 2008: 45–46.

147 Ibid., 45.

148 Chandler, "WTC7: NIST Finally Admits Freefall (Part III)," 2 January 2009, at 1:19 minutes. This analysis has been confirmed by NIST itself, in "Questions and Answers about the NIST WTC 7 Investigation," NIST, August 2008. This version of the document, which was posted at NIST's website at the time its draft version of its WTC 7 report was published, has been replaced by a version that was updated 17 September 2010 (https://www.nist.gov/pba/questions-and-answers-about-nist-wtc-7-investigation), in which NIST continues to acknowledge a 2.25-second stage of "gravitational acceleration (free fall)."

149 Sunder said: "A free fall time would be (the fall time of) an object that has no structural components below it. . . . . The . . . time that it took . . . for those 17 floors to disappear (was roughly 40 percent longer than free fall).

And that is not at all unusual, because there was structural resistance that was provided in this particular case. And you had a sequence of structural failures that had to take place. Everything was not instantaneous" ("WTC 7 Technical Briefing," NIST, 26 August 2008). Although NIST originally had a video and a transcript of this briefing at its Internet website, it removed both of them. However, the video is now available at Vimeo (https://vimeo.com/11941571). Also available is its transcript, under the title "NIST Technical Briefing on Its Final Draft Report on WTC 7 for Public Comment."

150 David Chandler, "WTC 7: Sound Evidence for Explosions," 5 July 2010 (http://www.youtube.com/watch?v=ERhoNYj9_fg&rel=0).

151 "9/11: WTC 7 East Penthouse Collapse," You Tube (http://www.youtube.com/watch?v=OUkvnfV606w).

152 David Chandler, "WTC 7 in Freefall No Longer Controversial" (http://www.youtube.com/watch?v=kX8Qd0Mmk20). NIST measured 2.25 seconds of absolute free fall with a gradual transition into free fall (NIST NCSTAR 1A, November 2008: 46 (http://www.nist.gov/customcf/get_pdf.cfm?-pub_id=86161), but NIST's measurements were taken near the midpoint of the roofline using video from a street-level camera. The horizontal folding of the roofline at that point was erroneously interpreted as downward motion, giving the appearance of a gradual transition into free fall.

153 Statement by Shyam Sunder on 20 March 2006, in answer to reporters' questions. Reported in Mark Jacobson, "The Ground Zero Grassy Knoll," *New York Magazine*, 20 March 2006); also in "Profile: Shyam Sunder" at *History Commons*.

154 NIST NCSTAR 1-9, Vol. 1, Structural Fire Response and Probable Collapse Sequence of World Trade Center Building 7, Volume 1 and 2, Chapter 8 (http://www.nist.gov/el/disasterstudies/wtc/wtc_finalreports.cfm); NIST NCSTAR 1A, Executive Summary, November 2008: xxxvi.

155 NIST NCSTAR 1-9 Vol. 2, Chapter 12: 588–97. A picture of the distorted collapsing model is emphasized on the cover of NIST's report (http://www.nist.gov/el/disasterstudies/wtc/wtc_finalreports.cfm). NIST has not released the actual simulation data.

156 The videos showing the models have been removed from the NIST website but they have been widely downloaded and reposted. They are available, for example, here: "NIST WTC7 Models" (http://www.youtube.com/watch?v=TNEKtvB80us).

157 David Chandler, "WTC7 in Freefall: No Longer Controversial," 12 February 2010 (http://www.youtube.com/watch?v=rVCDpL4Ax7I).

158 The deformations may also be seen at this official source: NIST NCSTAR 1A, "Final Report on the Collapse of World Trade Center Building 7," November 2008: 42.

159 The collapse of the west penthouse is plainly visible. It begins to collapse, but gets only about half way to the main roofline when the whole building collapses. After that, the penthouse and main building move together with the penthouse continuing to be visible during the free fall part of the collapse.

160 NIST NCSTAR 1-9, *Structural Fire Response and Probable Collapse Sequence of World Trade Center Building 7*, Vol. 1: 526-27 (http://www.nist.gov/customcf/get_pdf.cfm?pub_id=861611).

161 Ron Brookman obtained the drawings in late 2011. David Cole of the Nine Eleven Accountability Team discovered, in February 2012, that Frankel Fabrication Shop Drawing #9114 showed stiffeners providing support to a girder that had allegedly buckled. The full significance of the discovery of stiffeners that had been missing from the NIST report was first understood by mechanical engineer Tony Szamboti.

162 The 2008 NIST report did not identify this girder as A2001, a designation that did not become available until two FOIA requests from Ron Brookman—FOIA #11-209 and 12-009—led to the release of Frankel drawing #E12/13 in November 2011. This drawing is available in attorney William F. Pepper's letter of 12 December 2013 to the US Department of Commerce Inspector General: "The NIST Report on the Collapse of WTC Building 7 Challenged by 2,100 Architects and Engineers," *Journal of 9/11 Studies*, January 2014 (http://www.journalof911studies.com/resources/2014JanLetterPepper.pdf). It may also be downloaded in one of two zip files located in an article titled "WTC 7 Blueprints Exposed Via FOIA Request: Building Plans Allow for Deeper Analysis of Skyscraper's Destruction" (http://www.ae911truth.org/en/news-section/41-articles/611-wtc-7-blueprints-exposed-via-foia-request.html).

163 William F. Pepper, "The NIST Report on the Collapse of WTC Building 7 Challenged by 2,100 Architects and Engineers," *Journal of 9/11 Studies*, January 2014.

164 Ibid., Figure 11: 11.

165 Ibid., Figures 12–16: 12–14.

166 William F. Pepper, whose primary work is international commercial law, is a barrister in the United Kingdom and admitted to the bar in numerous jurisdictions in the United States. He has represented governments in the Middle East, Africa, South America, and Asia. Pepper, who had been a friend of Martin Luther King, Jr., represented the King family in a wrongful death civil trial, which the family won. He is heavily involved in human rights law, for a time convening the International Human Rights Seminar at Oxford University.

167 William F. Pepper, "The NIST Report on the Collapse of WTC Building 7 Challenged by 2,100 Architects and Engineers," *Journal of 9/11 Studies*, January 2014.

168   The following statements were made in "Mechanical and Metallurgical
       Analysis of Structural Steel," NCSTAR 1-3, September 2005 (http://www.
       nist.gov/customcf/get_pdf.cfm?pub_id=101016):

1.   "Although no steel was recovered from WTC 7, a 47-story building
       that also collapsed on September 11, properties for steel used in its
       construction were estimated based on literature and contemporane-
       ous documents" (iii).

2.   "The steel used in the construction of WTC 7 is described based solely
       on data from the literature, because no steel from the building was
       recovered" (xxxvii).

3.   "No steel was recovered from WTC 7; however, construction-related
       documents describe the structural steel as conventional 36 ksi, 42 ksi,
       and 50 ksi steels" (xliv).

4.   "Since no steel from WTC 7 was recovered from the site, the steel
       used in the construction of this building is described based on data
       from the literature of the period" (1).

5.   "Because NIST recovered no steel from WTC 7, it is not possible to
       make any statements about its quality" (114).

6.   "No metallography could be carried out because no steel was
       recovered from WTC 7" (115).

       The following statement was made in "Mechanical Properties of Structural
       Steels," NCSTAR 1-3D, September 2005 (http://www.nist.gov/customcf/
       get_pdf.cfm?pub_id=101021):

7.   "Because NIST recovered no steel from WTC 7, it is not possible to
       make any statements about its quality" (273).

       The following statement was taken from "Physical Properties of Structural
       Steels," NCSTAR 1-3E, September 2005 (http://www.nist.gov/customcf/
       get_pdf.cfm?pub_id=101022):

8.   "These analyses were made only for steel from WTC 1 and WTC 2 as
       no steel was recovered from WTC 7" (1).

       The following statement was taken from a NIST Progress Re-
       port of June 2004 (http://911encyclopedia.com/wiki/index.php/
       NIST_Claims_To_Have_No_Steel_Samples_From_WTC7):

9.   "No steel from WTC 7 has been identified from the pieces of recov-
       ered WTC steel in NIST's possession.... Properties were estimated
       from available test data in the literature" (vol. 1: 17).

169   "Final Report on the Collapse of World Trade Center Building 7, Federal
       Building and Fire Safety Investigation of the World Trade Center Disaster,"
       NIST NCSTAR 1A, 20 November 2008 (http://www.nist.gov/manu-
       script-publication-search.cfm?pub_id=861610).

170   *The 9/11 Commission Report.*

171 "Mechanical and Metallurgical Analysis of Structural Steel," NIST, NC-STAR 1-3, September 2005: 115 (http://www.nist.gov/customcf/get_pdf.cfm?pub_id=101016).

172 "Because NIST recovered no steel from WTC 7, it is not possible to make any statements about its quality," "Mechanical and Metallurgical Analysis of Structural Steel," NIST, NCSTAR 1-3, September 2005: 114 (http://www.nist.gov/customcf/get_pdf.cfm?pub_id=101016).

173 "Mechanical and Metallurgical Analysis of Structural Steel," NC-STAR 1-3, September 2005 (http://www.nist.gov/customcf/get_pdf.cfm?pub_id=101016):

 1. "Although no steel was recovered from WTC 7, a 47-story building that also collapsed on September 11, properties for steel used in its construction were estimated based on literature and contemporaneous documents" (iii).

 2. "The steel used in the construction of WTC 7 is described based solely on data from the literature, because no steel from the building was recovered" (xxxvii).

 3. "Since no steel from WTC 7 was recovered from the site, the steel used in the construction of this building is described based on data from the literature of the period" (1).

174 *JOM* is the journal of the Minerals, Metals, and Materials Society.

175 J.R. Barnett, R.R. Biederman, and R.D. Sisson, Jr., "An Initial Microstructural Analysis of A36 Steel WTC Building 7," *JOM*, 53(12), 2001: 18.

176 Jonathan Barnett, Ronald R. Biederman, and Richard D. Sisson, Jr., "Limited Metallurgical Examination," FEMA, World Trade Center Building Performance Study, May 2002, Appendix C.

177 Michael E. Newman, Senior Communications Officer, NIST, letter of 24 June 2010 (http://ae911good-job-nist.org/wp-content/uploads/2012/10/FiniteElementAnalysis_Data_Witheld.pdf). The FEMA Report is by Jonathan Barnett, Ronald R. Biederman, and Richard D. Sisson, Jr., "Limited Metallurgical Examination," FEMA, World Trade Center Building Performance Study, May 2002, Appendix C, and includes the photograph. See FIG 3.

178 Professor Jonathan Barnett reported, "It came from a much larger beam. . . . This was the size of steel that they used in the construction of Tower 7. They didn't use this particular kind of steel in Tower 1 or Tower 2. So that's why we know its pedigree. It was a surprise to me because it was so eroded and deformed and so we took it for analysis in the lab." BBC, "The Third Tower," 2008 (48-minute mark) (https://www.youtube.com/watch?v=oTZ3XXO7wNA).

179 Ramon Gilsanz and Audrey Massa, "WTC Steel Data Collection," FEMA, World Trade Center Building Performance Study, May 2002, Appendix D (http://www.fema.gov/media-library-data/20130726-1512-20490-6875/403_apd.pdf).

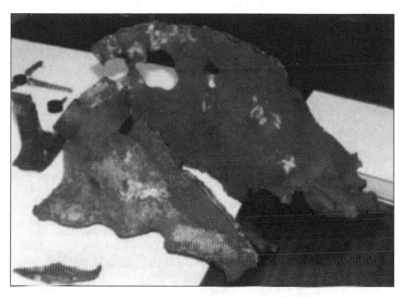

FIG 3: *Curled up Swiss cheese appearance of steel from WTC 7*

180 "Damage and Failure Modes of Structural Steel Components," NIST
NCSTAR 1-3C, September 2005: 233 (http://www.nist.gov/customcf/
get_pdf.cfm?pub_id=101019). This reference was cited in Andrea Dreger,
"How NIST Avoided a Real Analysis of the Physical Evidence of WTC
Steel," n.d. (http://www.ae911truth.org/documents/How_NIST_Avoid-
ed_a_Real_Analysis_of_the_Physical_Evidence_of_WTC_Steel.pdf).

181 World Trade Center Investigation Team Members; "Dr. John L. Gross"
(http://web.archive.org/web/20140407053156/http://www.nist.gov/el/
building_materials/jgross.cfm).

182 This photo is taken from NIST FOIA Request #12-057, 7 February 2012.
Its file number is DSCN0397_Iwankiw, from file WTC7_Beam_Pho-
tos_Scrap_Yard_OCT 2001. It may be found online, buried in the dataset
at http://www.911datasets.com/index.php/SFolder:WQEO747PTQ-
6JALMVDD5HYIWULETIKJ2H.183   "Final Report on the Collapse
of World Trade Center Building 7," NIST NCSTAR 1A, November 2008:
xxviii (http://www.nist.gov/customcf/get_pdf.cfm?pub_id=861610). These
photos were obtained by NIST FOIA #12-057, 7 February 2012, and are
available in an online dataset: NIST FOIA 12-057 Feb 07 2012 (http://
www.911datasets.com/index.php/NIST_FOIA_12-057_Feb_07_2012).
The name of the WTC 7 photographs file is FEMA Photographs of
WTC7_Beam_Photos_Scrap_Yard_OCT_2001.rar—RAR archive,
unpacked size 11,280,860 bytes. David Cole wrote in an email to Elizabeth
Woodworth (4 April 2014) "that while these [photos] were obtained from
NIST, they are actually FEMA created records."

184 James Glanz, "Engineers Suspect Diesel Fuel in Collapse of 7 World Trade Center," *New York Times*, 29 November 2001.

185 James Glanz and Eric Lipton, "A Search for Clues in Towers' Collapse; Engineers Volunteer to Examine Steel Debris Taken to Scrapyards," *New York Times*, 2 February 2002.

186 Joan Killough-Miller, "The 'Deep Mystery' of Melted Steel," *WPI Transformations*, Spring 2002.

187 "Damage and Failure Modes of Structural Steel Components," NIST NCSTAR 1-3C, September 2005: 233 (http://www.nist.gov/customcf/get_pdf.cfm?pub_id=101019).

188 In failing to seek peer review from the scientific community, NIST had ignored the recommendation of Dr. James G. Quintiere, a professor of Fire Protection Engineering at the University of Maryland and a member of the advisory committee for NIST's WTC project. In a lecture on the WTC investigations at the 2007 World Fire Safety Conference, Quintiere said: "I wish that there would be a peer review of this. . . . I think all the records that NIST has assembled should be archived. I would really like to see someone else take a look at what they've done; both structurally and from a fire point of view." Speaking directly to a NIST representative, Quintiere said: "I found that throughout your whole investigation it was very difficult to get a clear answer. And when anyone went to your advisory panel meetings or hearings, where they were given five minutes to make a statement; they could never ask any questions. And with all the commentary that I put in, and I spent many hours writing things . . . , I never received one formal reply." Alan Miller, "Former Chief of NIST's Fire Science Division Calls for Independent Review of World Trade Center Investigation," *OpEdNews*, 21 August 2007.

189 See Chapter 14, "The Assumption That NIST's Analysis of the Collapse Initiation of WTC 7 Is Valid."

190 Many such sources are given below under "The Best Evidence."

191 Sivaraj Shyam Sunder and C. Sawyer, "June 2004 Progress Report of the Federal Building and Fire Safety Investigation of the World Trade Center Disaster NIST SP 1000-5," National Institute of Standards and Technology, 30 June 2004: xxxviii (http:/www.nist.gov/manuscript-publication-search.cfm?pub_id=860567). A 2005 article in *Popular Mechanics*, "Debunking the 9/11 Myths: Special Report—The World Trade Center," illustrates the way NIST's early investigations were used to counter the claims of critics of the official narrative of 9/11.

192 Richard Gann, *Final Report on the Collapse of World Trade Center Building 7 NIST NCSTAR 1A*, National Institute of Standards and Technology, 20 November 2008.

193 Shyam Sunder and C. Sawyer, "June 2004 Progress Report"; "Debunking the 9/11 Myths: Special Report."

194 NIST has tended to avoid the issue of foreknowledge, but various "debunkers" have built on NIST statements in their arguments. Ryan Mackey's attempt was addressed in Graeme MacQueen, "Waiting for Seven: WTC 7 Collapse Warnings in the FDNY Oral Histories," *Journal of 9/11 Studies*, January 2008.

195 "Other than initiating the fires in WTC 7, the damage from the debris from WTC 1 had little effect on initiating the collapse of WTC 7." Richard Gann, *Final Report on the Collapse of World Trade Center Building 7 NIST NCSTAR 1A*: xxxvii.

196 "[F]uel oil fires did not play a role in the collapse of WTC 7" (ibid, xxxvi).

197 "This was the first known instance of the total collapse of a tall building primarily due to fires" (ibid., xxxv).

198 The mechanism behind the collapse is supported by graphical output, which is included in the NIST Final Report, NIST NCSTAR 1-9 Vol. 2, Chapter 12: 588-97. A picture of the distorted collapsing model is emphasized on the cover (http://www.nist.gov/el/disasterstudies/wtc/wtc_finalreports.cfm).

199 Richard Gann, *Final Report on the Collapse of World Trade Center Building 7 NIST NCSTAR 1A*, National Institute of Standards and Technology, 20 November 2008.

200 Some firefighters on the scene made collapse predictions based on their own observations, but they were outnumbered 7 to 1 by firefighters who derived their confidence in the imminence of collapse from others, typically superior officers. MacQueen, "Waiting for Seven: WTC 7 Collapse Warnings in the FDNY Oral Histories."

201 Reporter at WTC 7: "That is the building that is going to go down next!" (https://www.youtube.com/watch?v=O-WZpXiEKAo, 0:17).

202 The oral histories recording the personal 9/11 accounts of approximately 503 members of the Fire Department of New York (World Trade Center Task Force Interviews) can be found on the website of the *New York Times* (http://graphics8.nytimes.com/packages/html/nyregion/20050812_WTC_GRAPHIC/met_WTC_histories_full_01.html).

Additional reports to those listed below include:

- "The rest of the day we were unloading trucks. We were just doing whatever little things we could do, but they were waiting for 7 World Trade Center to fall." Firefighter Timothy Burke, p. 17.

- "[T]hey pulled everyone back, and everybody stood there and we actually just waited and just waited and waited until it went down." EMT Joseph Fortis, p. 15.

- "I remember later on in the day as we were waiting for seven to come down, they kept backing us up Vesey, almost like a full block."

- "The whole time while we were waiting—there were hours that went by." Vincent Massa, pp. 17, 19.

- "They had figured they knew that building was going to come down. It was just a question of time, and everybody was awaiting that." Lieutenant Russell Stroebel, p. 5.

- "Once they got us back together and organized somewhat, they sent us back down to Vesey, where we stood and waited for Seven World Trade Center to come down. Firefighter Frank Sweeney, p. 14.

203 Fire Department of New York, World Trade Center Task Force Interview—Firefighter Thomas Donato (Interview Date: 17 January 2002), *New York Times*, 5 (http://graphics8.nytimes.com/packages/pdf/nyregion/20050812_WTC_GRAPHIC/9110471.PDF).

204 World Trade Center Task Force Interview—Firefighter James Wallace (Interview Date: 17 January 2002), *New York Times*, 4 (http://graphics8.nytimes.com/packages/pdf/nyregion/20050812_WTC_GRAPHIC/9110409.PDF).

205 World Trade Center Task Force Interview—Assistant Commissioner James Drury (Interview Date: 16 October 2001), 10 (http://graphics8.nytimes.com/packages/pdf/nyregion/20050812_WTC_GRAPHIC/9110098.PDF).

206 World Trade Center Task Force Interview—Chief Thomas McCarthy (Interview Date: 11 October 2001), p. 11 (http://graphics8.nytimes.com/packages/pdf/nyregion/20050812_WTC_GRAPHIC/9110409.PDF).

207 World Trade Center Task Force Interview—Paramedic Steven Pilla (Interview Date: 17 October 2001), p. 13 (http://graphics8.nytimes.com/packages/pdf/nyregion/20050812_WTC_GRAPHIC/9110409.PDF).

208 MacQueen, "Waiting for Seven: WTC 7 Collapse Warnings in the FDNY Oral Histories."

209 World Trade Center Task Force Interview—Vincent Nassa (Interview Date: 4 December 2001), p. 19 (http://graphics8.nytimes.com/packages/pdf/nyregion/20050812_WTC_GRAPHIC/9110222.PDF).

210 MacQueen, "Waiting for Seven: WTC 7 Collapse Warnings in the FDNY Oral Histories."

211 David Ray Griffin, *The Mysterious Collapse of World Trade Center 7: Why the Final Official Report About 9/11 is Unscientific and False* (Interlink, 2010), 113.

212 Ibid., 114.

213 CNN's premature announcement is available at Dailymotion as "CNN Announces WTC7 Collapse Too Early."

214 For CNN's full day 9/11 coverage, see the September 11 Television Archive (https://archive.org/details/sept_11_tv_archive).

215 The BBC's premature announcement is available at Dailymotion as "BBC REPORT ON EARLY WTC7 COLLAPSE."

216 Barry Jennings interviews have been posted at "Barry Jennings Interviews (WABC-TV, 2001/LTW, 2007)" (https://www.youtube.com/watch?v=OmeY2vJ6ZoA). Transcripts of these interviews are available at http://s1.zetaboards.com/LooseChangeForums/topic/451652/1/.

217 History Commons—Profile: Barry Jennings (shortly before 9:03 a.m.) http://www.historycommons.org/entity.jsp?entity=barry_jennings_1).

218 Soon after his escape, Hess told Frank Ucciardo of UPN 9 News: "I was trapped in World Trade Center 7 for an hour and a half," 1:37 min. at "Michael Hess, WTC7 explosion witness" (https://www.youtube.com/watch?v=6e3K9jcPdXc).

219 Jennings and Hess testified to NIST in 2004, but this testimony was never released and FOIA requests have been declined. For example, NIST declined a request on the basis of a provision allowing for exemption from FOIA disclosure if the information is "not directly related to the building failure," letter of 12 August 2009, from Catherine S. Fletcher, Freedom of Information Act Officer, NIST, to a FOIA request of 8 August 2009, from Ms. Susan Peabody, for "[t]he complete texts of NIST's 2004 interviews of Michael Hess and Barry Jennings, which are cited in NIST NCSTAR 1-8. . . , 109, n. 380, as 'WTC 7 Interviews 2041604 and 1041704.'" Quoted in David Ray Griffin, "9/11 Truth: The Mysterious Collapse of WTC Seven," *Global Research*, 14 September 2009.

220 J. Randall Lawson and Robert L. Vettori, "NIST NCSTAR 1-8. Federal Building and Fire Safety Investigation of the World Trade Center Disaster. The Emergency Response Operations," NIST, September 2005: 109–10 (https://archive.org/details/emergencyrespons181laws).

221 Ibid., NIST Ref. 368. FDNY Interview 54, Winter 2004: 109.

222 Ibid., NIST Ref. 369. FDNY Interview 54, Winter 2004: 109.

223 Ibid., NIST Ref. 370. WTC 7 Interview 1110402, Fall 2002: 109.

224 NIST here did not provide a reference.

225 Ibid., NIST Ref. 376. FDNY Interview 45, Winter 2004: 109.

226 Ibid., Ref. 377. PAPD Interview 1, Fall 2003: 109.

227 Ibid., NIST Ref. 378. FDNY Interview 3, Winter 2004: 109.

228 Ibid., NIST Ref. 379. FDNY Interview 19, Winter 2004: 109.

229 Ibid., NIST Ref. 380. Interviews 2041604 and 1041704, Spring 2004: 109.

230 NIST here did not provide a reference.

231 Ibid., NIST Ref. 381. WTC 7 Interviews 2041604 and 1041704, Spring 2004: 110.

232 NIST, "Appendix L: Interim Report on WTC 7" (http://web.archive.org/
web/20041016105411/http://wtc.nist.gov/progress_report_june04/appen-
dixl.pdf), L-18. No source for this claim is cited.

233 Bob Weaver, the Assistant Special Agent in charge of the US Secret Service
New York Field Office, said: "When the first plane hit we looked up out of
our building and saw the fire and explosion. It was easy to see that it was
time to evacuate," in Richard Thieme, "More Than Human: The Network
Is More Than the Sum of Its Parts when Disaster Hits," 2001 (http://web.
archive.org/web/20030725001156/http://www.thiemeworks.com/write/
archives/MoreThanHuman.htm). After WTC 7 shook, Chief Engineer
Michael Catalano said: "The plane had already hit and there was a big
gouge." He returned to his crew and ordered an evacuation. The second
plane hit and they were thrown to the ground. While the building was
emptying, Catalano and his crew worked to maintain the building's vital
systems." In "First On the Scene: 2 of 3. The Unsung Heroes of September
11," 8 July 2002 (http://www.buildings.com/article-details/articleid/925/
title/first-on-the-scene-2-of-3.aspx). Other supervisors "knew not to take
the elevators" and instructed staff to head downstairs, *Arizona Republic*, 8
September 2011: 4 (https://www.newspapers.com/newspage/122873627/).

234 NIST, "Questions and Answers about the NIST WTC 7 Investigation
(09/17/2010, ARCHIVE, incorporated into 9/19/2011 update)" (http://
www.nist.gov/public_affairs/factsheet/wtc_qa_082108.cfm).

235 See the grey and green diagram showing staircases based on Cantor
structural drawings, half way down (http://www.abovetopsecret.com/
forum/thread1112758/pg1.

236 Hess is visible calling for help through a broken north window of the 8th
floor, amidst sounds of explosions outside (1:52 minutes). At 2:34, Hess
yells down to the firefighters, "An explosion," in "WTC 7, Michael Hess
Calls For Help" (https://www.youtube.com/watch?v=VFuWlLP0jz8).

237 Michael Hess 2008 BBC interview, "In an instant five different things happened," 0:55 min. at https://www.youtube.com/watch?v=hy5lpp6yADw.

238 Barry Jennings transcript from 2007 "Uncut" interview (http://s1.ze-
taboards.com/LooseChangeForums/topic/451652/1/).

239 "Barry Jennings Interviews (WABC-TV, 2001/LTW, 2007)," 0:24 min.
(https://www.youtube.com/watch?v=OmeY2vJ6ZoA).

240 Ibid., 1:00 min.

241 "Michael Hess, WTC7 Explosion Witness," 0:30 minutes (https://www.
youtube.com/watch?v=6e3K9jcPdXc).

242 Michael Hess 2008 BBC interview: "In an instant five different things happened," 1:30 min. at https://www.youtube.com/watch?v=hy5lpp6yADw.

243 Paul Vallely "Inside the Towers, They Scrambled for Their Lives. The
Survivors," *The Independent*, 13 September 2001.

244 "NIST FOIA: WTC 7 Lobby Shots and South Face Around 10:15 a.m." (https://www.youtube.com/watch?v=4YdNclhdzSo). The note below the video reads: "All of the footage was recorded between the tower collapses, roughly around 10:15 a.m. (estimate by NIST in sub-report "NIST NCSTAR 1-9, Vols. 1-2", Nov. 2008). Videographer: Mark LaGanga, CBS Source of video excerpt: 911datasets.org, NIST FOIA #09-42 Release 25 Subfolder: 42A0120—G25D31 File: DVD Video Container Total File Size: 3.82 GB Subfolder Link: http://911datasets.org/index.php/ SFolder:3IAGVZVIFRCYCZVEEMC4QG2NSIE3UGAF

245 David Ray Griffin, "Michael Hess, Barry Jennings. The 9/11 Interview with Evidence that NIST Lied about When Michael Hess and Barry Jennings Were Rescued," 18 September 2008, WantToKnow.info.

246 *The 9/11 Commission Report*, 225, 334.

247 Marc Fisher and Don Phillips, "On Flight 77: 'Our Plane Is Being Hijacked,'" *Washington Post*, 12 September 2001.

248 John Hanchette, "Clues to Attackers Lie in Wreckage, Computer Systems," *Detroit News*, 13 September 2001.

249 "Primary Target: The Pentagon," *CBS News*, 21 September 2001.

250 "'Get These Planes on the Ground': Air Traffic Controllers Recall Sept. 11," *20/20*, ABC News, 24 October 2001.

251 Justin Paprocki, "Airport Owners Panic over Plummeting Profits," *Maryland Newsline*, 19 September 2001.

252 Amy Goldstein et al., "Hanjour: A Study in Paradox," *Washington Post*, 15 October 2001.

253 Jim Yardley, "A Trainee Noted for Incompetence," *New York Times*, 4 May 2002.

254 Baxter Dmitry, "Pilot Who Flew 9/11 Planes Says Official Narrative Is Impossible," YourNewsWire.com, 6 September 2016.

255 Email from Ralph Omholt to David Ray Griffin, 17 October 2006.

256 "By 8:57 a.m., it was evident that Flight 77 was lost." Matthew L. Wald and Kevin Sack, "'We Have Some Planes,' Hijacker Told Controller," *New York Times*, 16 October 2001.

257 "NORAD's Response Times," North American Aerospace Defense Command, 18 September 2001 (www.standdown.net/noradseptember182001pressrelease.htm); "Officials: Government Failed to React to FAA Warning," CNN, 17 September 2001 (http://web.archive.org/web/20080311023952/http://archives.cnn.com/2001/US/09/16/inv.hijack.warning/).

258 Pentagon sources said that Andrews "had no fighters assigned to it" (*USA Today*, 17 September 2001). Major General Larry Arnold—the

commanding general of NORAD's Continental Region—said: "We [didn't] have any aircraft on alert at Andrews" (ibid.).

259 Michael Bronner, "9/11 Live: The NORAD Tapes," *Vanity Fair*, August 2006: 262–285, at 268. (Bronner, who had been an associate producer of the film *United 93* [which had faithfully portrayed the 9/11 Commission's new account of this flight], was able to write this article because he was the first journalist to be given access to tapes provided by NORAD, which were used by the 9/11 Commission for its new account of American 77 [as well as the other accounts]). After 9/11, Colonel Robert Marr, the head of NEADS, said: "I have determined . . . that with only four aircraft, we cannot defend the whole northeastern United States" (James Bamford, *A Pretext for War* [Doubleday, 2004], 60–61). The 9/11 Commission said that calling on other air bases would not have helped, because these "[o]ther facilities, not on 'alert,' would need time to arm the fighters and organize crews," *9/11 Commission Report*, 17.

260 "NORAD's Response Times."

261 "NORAD's Response Times," 18 September 2001; "Air Attack on Pentagon Indicates Weaknesses," *Newsday*, 23 September 2001.

262 "FAA Communications with NORAD on September 11, 2001: FAA Clarification Memo to 9/11 Independent Commission," 21 May 2003.

263 "FAA Communications with NORAD on September 11th, 2001," read into the record by Commissioner Richard Ben-Veniste, *9/11 Commission Hearing*, 23 May 2003.

264 *The 9/11 Commission Report*, 24.

265 Scoggins was cited three times in *The 9/11 Commission Report*, 458, and in a *Vanity Fair* article by Michael Bronner, "9/11 Live: The NORAD Tapes," August 2006.

266 E-mail from Scoggins to David Ray Griffin, 20 December 2006.

267 Email from Scoggins, 20 December 2006.

268 William B. Scott, "Exercise Jump-Starts Response to Attacks," *Aviation Week and Space Technology*, 3 June 2002 (http://web.archive.org/web/20020917072642/http://www.aviationnow.com/content/publication/awst/20020603/avi_stor.htm). The more complete statement was: "At Syracuse, N.Y., an ANG commander told [Col. Robert] Marr [the battle commander of NEADS (the Northeast Air Defense Sector of NORAD)]: "Give me 10 min. and I can give you hot guns. Give me 30 min. and I'll have heat-seeker [missiles]. Give me an hour and I can give you slammers [Amraams]." Marr replied, "I want it all." The point is that, if Marr had not insisted on having "it all," he could have had fighters with hot guns within 10 minutes.

269 *The 9/11 Commission Report*, 34.

270 Both General Arnold and General Ralph E. "Ed" Eberhart testified that FAA notified NORAD at 9:24 (National Commission on Terrorist Attacks Upon the United States, Public Hearing, 23 May 2003). The NORAD News Release of 18 September 2001 had reported the time of the FAA Notification to NEADS as 9:24.

271 *The 9/11 Commission Report*, 34.

272 Some members of the 9/11 Commission argued that General Arnold and other military leaders had lied; see Michael Bronner, "9/11 Live: The NORAD Tapes," *Vanity Fair*, August 2006: 262–285, at 285; *Vanity Fair*, 17 October 2006. Co-chairs Thomas Kean and Lee Hamilton, in their 2006 book *Without Precedent*, said that NORAD's behavior "bordered on willful concealment," adding: "Fog of war could . . . not explain why all of the after-action reports . . . and public testimony by FAA and NORAD officials advanced an account of 9/11 that was untrue" (261).

273 Matthew Wald, "Pentagon Tracked Deadly Jet but Found No Way to Stop It," *New York Times*, 15 September 2001.

274 9/11 Commission Hearing, 17 June 2004: 91.

275 White House News Release, "President Meets with Muslim Leaders," 26 September 2001.

276 "Text: Rumsfeld on NBC's 'Meet the Press,'" *Washington Post*, 30 September 2001.

277 American Free Press Service, US Department of Defense, 23 October 2001.

278 Ari Fleischer Press Briefing, 16 May 2002 (http://web.archive.org/web/20020814201635/http:/www.whitchouse.gov/news/releases/2002/05/20020516-4.html).

279 "National Security Advisor Holds Press Briefing," 16 May 2002 (http://web.archive.org/web/20020806160231/http:/www.whitehouse.gov/news/releases/2002/05/20020516-13.html).

280 "Air Attack on Pentagon Indicates Weaknesses," by Sylvia Adcock, Brian Donovan and Craig Gordon, *Newsday*, 23 September 2001.

281 When a statement is made about the Pentagon being "attacked," it is often assumed that this means that the Pentagon was struck by an airliner. But evidence has not been adequate to establish the nature of the attack. What is known for certain is that there was an attack of some type, resulting in dozens of deaths.

282 Steven Komarow and Tom Squitieri, "NORAD Had Drills of Jets as Weapons," *USA Today*, 18 April 2004; see also Barbara Starr, "NORAD Exercise Had Jet Crashing into Building," CNN Washington Bureau, 19 April 2004 (http://www.cnn.com/2004/US/04/19/norad.exercise/).

283   US Army, Military District of Washington, "Contingency Planning Pentagon MASCAL Exercise Simulates Scenarios in Preparing for Emergencies," 3 November 2000 (http://web.archive.org/web/20041214161246/http://www.mdw.army.mil/content/anmviewer.asp?a=290).

284   Matt Mienka, "Pentagon Medics Trained for Strike," *US Medicine*, 1 October 2001 (https://web.archive.org/web/20090417183205/http:/www.usmedicine.com/article.cfm?articleID=272&issueID=31).

285   Mark Hosenball, "Bush: 'We're at War,'" *Newsweek*, 23 September 2001. *The 9/11 Commission Report* omitted this report.

286   Phillip Matier and Andrew Ross, "Willie Brown Got Low-key Early Warning about Air Travel," *San Francisco Chronicle*, 12 September 2001.

287   James Doran, "Rushdie's Air Ban," *London Times* (Times Online), 27 September 2001 (http://911research.wtc7.net/cache/sept11/london-times_rushdieairban.htm).

288   "Secretary Rumsfeld Interview with Larry King," Larry King Live, CNN, 5 December 2001. Transcript available (http://archive.defense.gov/Transcripts/Transcript.aspx?TranscriptID=2603).

289   "Chairman Cox's Statement on the Terrorist Attack on America," Tuesday, 11 September 2001. The quote from his press release was picked up by Associated Press the same day: Robert Burns, "Pentagon Attack Came Minutes after Rumsfeld Predicted: 'There Will Be Another Event,'" *The Topeka-Capitol Journal* (Associated Press), 11 September 2001.

290   William Langley, "Revealed: What Really Went on During Bush's 'Missing Hours,'" *The Telegraph*, 16 December 2001.

291   For sound only, see "9/11 News Oddities—Reporter Pre-Warned of Pentagon Attacks," NBC News, 11 September 2001 (https://www.youtube.com/watch?v=TmzM3g-mxSs). For face-to-face footage of Miklaszewski, see video documentary by Massimo Mazzucco, *9/11—The New Pearl Harbor* (https://www.youtube.com/watch?v=O1GCeuSr3Mk, 1:15:22 to 1:16:18 min.).

292   "Pentagon Eyewitnesses' Traffic Descriptions: Witnesses Described Heavy Traffic Conditions Around the Pentagon," n.d. [© 2003-2004].

293   "Arlington County After-Action Report on the Response to the September 11 Terrorist Attack on the Pentagon," Titan Systems Corporation under contract to Dept. of Justice, n.d. [2002], Annex A, p. A-22. "The Crime Scene Team [was] onsite 30 minutes after the attack. Special Agent John Adams began organizing the FBI Evidence Recovery Team on a grassy site" (p. C-45).

294   Patrick Creed and Rick Newman, "Firefight: Inside the Battle to Save the Pentagon on 9/11," Presidio Press, 2008: 80.

295   Bill McKelway, "Three Months On, Tension Lingers Near the Pentagon," *Richmond Times-Dispatch*, 11 December 2001.

296 Bill Gertz and Rowan Scarborough, "Inside the Ring," *Washington Times*, 11 September 2001 (http://web.archive.org/web/20010921200613/www. washtimes.com/national/20010921-90259475.htm).

297 *The 9/11 Commission Report*, Chapter 1.

298 "To facilitate NORAD tracking, every attempt shall be made to ensure that the hijacked aircraft is squawking Mode 3/A, code 7500." Source: Federal Aviation Administration, "Order 7610.4J: Special Military Operations, Chapter 7. ESCORT OF HIJACKED AIRCRAFT," 12 July 2001; "Hijack Code a Secret Signal of Distress," ABC News, 3 June 2005.

299 The *Christian Science Monitor* reported the failure to squawk as an "anomaly" (Peter Grier, "The Nation Reels," *Christian Science Monitor*, 12 September 2001).

300 "Flight 11 was hijacked apparently by knife-wielding men. Airline pilots are trained to handle such situations by keeping calm, complying with requests, and if possible, dialing in an emergency four digit code on a device called a transponder. ... The action takes seconds, but it appears no such code was entered" ("America Under Attack: How could It Happen?" CNN Live Event, 12 September 2001).

301 According to the purported tapes from the cockpit recorder of United 93, it took over 30 seconds for the intruders to break into the pilot's cabin (Richard A. Serrano, "Heroism, Fatalism Aboard Flight 93," *Los Angeles Times*, 12 April 2006). Flight 11's failure to squawk is discussed in "America Under Attack: How Could It Happen?" CNN Live Event/Transcript, 12 September 2001 (http://transcripts.cnn.com/TRANSCRIPTS/0109/12/ se.60.html). It clearly would have been *possible* for the pilots to have squawked the hijack code. According to a famous Sherlock Holmes story, the theory about an intruder in a racing stable was disproved by "the dog that didn't bark." The intruder theory about the 9/11 airliners, one could say by analogy, is disproved by the pilots that didn't squawk.

302 For discussion, see David Ray Griffin, *The New Pearl Harbor Revisited* (Interlink, 2008), 175–79.

303 *The 9/11 Commission Report*, 14.

304 "9/11 Flight 93 Shanksville: Mayor Says No Plane Crashed!"(https:// www.youtube.com/watch?v=pPkpvc-9wFM&NR=1); "9/11 Flight 93 Shanksville: No Plane! No Crash!" A 1994 US Geological Survey showed the same crater and scar that was allegedly left by the crash of Flight 93 (https://www.youtube.com/watch?v=OumTBrSayqw); "Flight 93 Crash Exposed: Rare Footage Never Again Seen on TV," *Dailymotion*, 4 May 2013; "Nothing There Except a Hole in the Ground," VIDEO: Rare Footage—Flight 93 Crashes in Pennsylvania—September 11 2001, *Global Research*, 17 December 2007.

305 Bill Heltzel and Tom Gibb, "2 Planes Had No Part in Crash of Flight 93," *Pittsburgh Post-Gazette*, 16 September 2001: "Debris from the Crash

Has Been Found up to 8 Miles from the Crash Site."; "America Under Attack: FBI and State Police Cordon Off Debris Area Six to Eight Miles from Crater Where Plane Went Down," CNN, 13 September 2001; Debra Erdley, "Crash Debris Found 8 Miles Away," *Pittsburgh Tribune-Review*, 14 September 2001.

306 Richard Wallace, "What Did Happen to Flight 93?" *Daily Mirror*, 12 September 2002. For further discussion, see David Ray Griffin, *The New Pearl Harbor Revisited* (Interlink, 2008), 120–21.

307 *The 9/11 Commission Report*, Chapter 1.

308 Ibid., 16.

309 Ibid., 18.

310 Ibid., 20.

311 Ibid., 21.

312 Ibid., 9.

313 Ibid., 25.

314 Ibid., 454.

315 Rising Up Aviation, "Federal Aviation Regulations. Sec. 135.152—Flight Data Recorders," (showing amendments from 1988 to 2009).

316 Mark Clayton, "Controllers' Tale of Flight 11," *Christian Science Monitor*, 13 September 2001.

317 Tom Watkins and Steve Almasy, "Transponder's Fate May Prove Key to Solving Malaysia Airlines Puzzle," CNN World, 13 March 2014.

318 See for example, Chapter 18, "The Claim That Hani Hanjour Piloted AA 77 into the Pentagon"; Chapter 22, "The Claim that the 9/11 Flights Were Hijacked"; Chapter 42, "The Claim that a Video Showed 5 Hijackers at Dulles Airport on September 11"; Chapter 45, "The Assumption That the Todd Beamer 'Let's Roll' Call from United 93 Was Authentic: Part I"; Chapter 47, "The Assumption That the Reported Phone Calls from Barbara Olson Were Authentic."

319 Rising Up Aviation, "Federal Aviation Regulations. Sec. 135.152—Flight Data Recorders" (showing amendments from 1988 to 2009).

320 "Flight Recorder," (http://en.wikipedia.org/wiki/Flight_recorder) (accessed 3 February 2017).

321 "The CVRs and FDRs from American 11 and United 175 were not found," *The 9/11 Commission Report*, 456, n. 76 (no ref. given by Commission); Brian Dakss, "Speed Likely Factor in WTC Collapse," *CBS News*, 25 February 2002.

322 The 9/11 Commission, "Memorandum for the Record: John S. Adams, Special Agent, FBI, November 3, 2003"; "Flight 77's black box was found

on the first floor near the A&E Drive by the night shift team" (http://
media.nara.gov/9-11/MFR/t-0148-911MFR-00472.pdf); "3:29 PM UAL 93
black box located at Sommerset [sic], PA.," 9/11 Commission, Chronology
of Events, undated; "Flight Data and Voice Recorders Found at Pentagon,"
PBS Online Newshour, 14 September 2001; "Feds Would Have Shot Down
Pa. Jet," *CBS News*, 12 September 2001.

323   "The CVRs and FDRs from American 11 and United 175 were not found,"
The 9/11 Commission Report, 456, n. 76 (no ref. given by Commission).

324   Transcript of Flight 93's Cockpit Voice Recorder (http://911research.wtc7.
net/planes/evidence/flight93cvr.html).

325   ASCE, *Pentagon Building Performance Report*, 40.

326   Gail Swanson, *Behind-the-Scenes: Ground Zero: A Collection of Personal
Accounts* (Unknown Binding, 2003); Will Bunch, "New Coverup Revealed? Black Boxes Found," *Philadelphia News*, 28 October 2004.

327   Edward F. Jacoby, Jr., "Sept. 18, 2001, memo to Gov. George Pataki," OEM
FOIL Sec. 4: 16. Jacobi was the director of the New York State Emergency
Management Office, responsible for marshalling 22 state agencies and
nearly 17,000 personnel, including 5,200 National Guardsmen and 500
state police officers.

328   General Paul J. Kern, "AMC: Accelerating the Pace of Transformation,"
AUSA: Army Magazine, 1 February 2002. Kern headed the US Army
Materiel Command from October 2001 to November 2004 (http://en.wiki-
pedia.org/wiki/Paul_J._Kern, accessed 3 February 2014).

329   National Commission on Terrorist Attacks Upon the United States, Public
Hearing, 26 January 2004.

330   Ronald Hamburger et al., "WTC1 and WTC2," FEMA World Trade Center
Building Performance Study, FEMA, n.d., 2-16.

331   "List of Unrecovered Flight Recorders," Wikipedia (accessed February 3, 2017) (http://en.wikipedia.org/wiki/
List_of_unrecovered_flight_recorders).

332   ASCE, *Pentagon Building Performance Report*, Section 6.2: 40; passage
quoted in David Dunbar and Brad Reagan, eds., *Debunking 9/11 Myths:
Why Conspiracy Theories Can't Stand Up to the Facts* (Hearst Books, 2006),
70.

333   "Washington's Heroes: On the Ground at the Pentagon on Sept. 11,"
Newsweek and MSNBC News, 28 September 2001.

334   "Black Boxes from Hijacked Plane Found at Pentagon," Associated Press,
14 September 2001 (http://web.archive.org/web/20070615063705/http://
www.chron.com/disp/story.mpl/front/1047680.html).

335 Aidan Monaghan, "Pentagon 9/11 Flight 'Black Box Data File' Created Before Actual 'Black Box' Was Recovered?" 911blogger.com, 18 May 2008; "Searchers Find Pentagon Black Boxes," *USA Today*, 14 September 2001.

336 National Transportation Safety Board, Vehicle Recorder Division, "Flight Data Recorder Handbook for Aviation Accident Investigations: A Reference for Safety Board Staff," December, 2002.

337 Aidan Monaghan, "9/11 Aircraft 'Black Box' Serial Numbers Mysteriously Absent," 911blogger.com, 26 February 2008.

338 Colonel George Nelson, USAF (ret.), "Impossible to Prove a Falsehood True: Aircraft Parts as a Clue to Their Identity," Physics 911, 23 April 2005.

339 President George Bush said, "al Qaeda struck in a way that was unimaginable." White House News Release, "President Meets with Muslim Leaders," 26 September 2001. And there were many more similar statements:

  • Secretary of Defense Donald Rumsfeld said, "Never would have crossed anyone's mind." "Text: Rumsfeld on NBC's 'Meet the Press,'" 30 September 2001.

  • General Richard Myer, Deputy commander of the Joint Chiefs of Staff, said, "You hate to admit it, but we hadn't thought about this." American Free Press Service, 23 October 2001 (http://www.defenselink.mil/news/newsarticle.aspx?id=44621).

  • White House Press Secretary Ari Fleischer said, "Never did we imagine what would take place on September 11th, where people used those airplanes as missiles and weapons" (http://web.archive.org/web/20020814201635/http://www.whitehouse.gov/news/releases/2002/05/20020516-4.html).

  • National Security Advisor Condoleezza Rice said, "I don't think anybody could have predicted that these people would take an airplane and slam it into the World Trade Center, take another one and slam it into the Pentagon; that they would try to use an airplane as a missile, a hijacked airplane as a missile" (http://web.archive.org/web/20020806160231/http://www.whitehouse.gov/news/releases/2002/05/20020516-13.html).

340 "In sum, the protocols in place on 9/11 for the FAA and NORAD to respond to a hijacking presumed that. . . the hijacking would take the traditional form: that is, it would not be a suicide hijacking designed to convert the aircraft into a guided missile." *The 9/11 Commission Report*, 18.

341 "America's homeland defenders faced outward. NORAD itself was barely able to retain any alert bases. Its planning scenarios occasionally considered the danger of hijacked aircraft being guided to American targets, but only aircraft that were coming from overseas." *The 9/11 Commission Report*, 352.

342   Kevin Howe, "Expert Stresses Need for Intelligence," *Monterey County Herald*, 18 July 2002. Ken Merchant, NORAD's joint exercise design manager, told the 9/11 Commission in 2003 that he could not "remember a time in the last 33 years when NORAD has not run a hijack exercise." Interview, 14 November 2003 (http://media.nara.gov/9-11/MFR/t-0148-911MFR-00790.pdf).

343   Dennis Ryan, "Contingency Planning Pentagon MASCAL Exercise Simulates Scenarios in Preparing for Emergencies," 3 November 2000.

344   Matt Mientka, "Pentagon Medics Trained for Strike," U.S. Medicine, October 2001. (Although this story has been removed from the Internet, a portion of it has been retained by Aldeilis.net.)

345   National Transportation Security Summit, Washington, DC, 30 October 2001, "MTI Report S-01-02," Mineta Transportation Institute, San José State University, 2001.

346   Steven Komarow and Tom Squitieri, "NORAD Had Drills of Jets as Weapons," *USA Today*, 18 April 2004.

347   "Airborne Anti-Terrorist Operation Getting Underway," CNN.com, 4 June 2002 (http://transcripts.cnn.com/TRANSCRIPTS/0206/04/lt.08.html); Gerry J. Gilmore, "NORAD-Sponsored Exercise Prepares For Worst-Case Scenarios," American Forces Press Service (http://www.defense.gov/news/newsarticle.aspx?id=43789).

348   Steven Komarow and Tom Squitieri, "NORAD Had Drills of Jets as Weapons," *USA Today*, 19 April 2004.

349   "Global Guardian," GlobalSecurity.org. (http://www.globalsecurity.org/military/ops/global-guardian.htm).

350   *The 9/11 Commission Report*, 20.

351   *The 9/11 Commission Report*, 458, n. 116.

352   Ibid.

353   Ibid.

354   Myers said: "The important thing to realize is that North American Aerospace Defense Command was responsible [for managing the wargames]. These are command post exercises; what that means is that all the battle positions that are normally not filled are indeed filled; so it was an easy transition from an exercise into a real world situation. It actually enhanced the response; otherwise, it would take somewhere between 30 minutes and a couple of hours to fill those positions, those battle stations, with the right staff officers." Transcript of Representative Cynthia McKinney's Exchange with Defense Secretary Donald Rumsfeld, Chairman of the Joint Chiefs of Staff Richard Myers, and Under Secretary of Defense (Comptroller) Tina Jonas, 11 March 2005 (http://web.archive.org/web/20050319093812/http://www.copvcia.com/free/ww3/031505_mckinney_transcript.shtml).

355 NORAD Exercises Hijack Summary, 1998–2001, a "Commission Sensitive" document (http://www.scribd.com/doc/16411947/NORAD-Exercises-Hijack-Summary). Vigilant Guardian hijack exercises took place October 25-27, 1998, and October 16-23, 2000. See Senate Hearing 108-875, "Implications for the Department of Defense and Military Operations of Proposals to Reorganize the United States Intelligence Community," 16 and 17 August 2004 (http://www.gpo.gov/fdsys/pkg/CHRG-108shrg24495/html/CHRG-108shrg24495.htm).

356 "Vigilant Guardian," Global Security (http://www.globalsecurity.org/military/ops/vigilant-guardian.htm).

357 A command-post exercise (CPX) is one "in which the forces are simulated, involving the commander, the staff, and communications within and between headquarters." See "Dictionary of Military and Associated Terms" (US Department of Defense), 2005 (http://www.dtic.mil/doctrine/dod_dictionary/?zoom_query=command+post+exercise&zoom_sort=0&zoom_per_page=10&zoom_and=1).

358 See the August 20, 2001, Memorandum from Col. Robert Marr at the NEADS Command Center, outlining the 24/7 Operations that would be conducted September 10-13, 2001 (http://www.scribd.com/doc/26080483/GSA-B116-RDOD-03013141-Fdr-Entire-Contents-Vigilant-Guardian-Docs-760). The exercise included injects, or simulated track inputs, onto NORAD radar screens.

359 "Exercise Global Guardian 2001-2 Joint After Action Report, US Strategic Command, Offutt AFB, Nebraska (http://www.scribd.com/doc/54399941/FOIA-11-023-Response-Pgs-1-30).

360 Examples of U.S. Strategic Command Nuclear Exercise Activities (http://www.dod.gov/pubs/dswa/document.html).

361 Hans N. Kristensen, "Taking the Pulse of the US Nuclear Arsenal," Washington, DC, Basic (British American Security Information Council), 1998 (http://web.archive.org/web/20020919232754/http://www.basicint.org/pubs/Research/taking_pulse-3.htm#Planning). *Global Guardian* began on October 22, 2003. See Hans M. Kristensen, "Global Strike: A Chronology of the Pentagon's New Offensive Strike Plan," Federation of American Scientists, 2006 (http://www.fas.org/ssp/docs/GlobalStrikeReport.pdf).

362 *Global Guardian* had been originally scheduled for October 22–31, 2001, according to NBC military analyst William M. Arkin in his book *Code Names: Deciphering U.S. Military Plans, Programs and Operations in the 9/11 World* (Steerforth, 2005), 379. See also the dates October 17 to 25, 2002, at (http://www.globalsecurity.org/military/ops/global-guardian.htm), which provides online evidence that these exercises were moved.

363 "Global Guardian," GlobalSecurity.org (http://www.globalsecurity.org/military/ops/global-guardian.htm).

364 *Amalgam Warrior* took place October 15-20, 1996 (http://www.globalse-curity.org/military/ops/amalgam-warrior.htm). It included the 101st Fighter Squadron from Otis Air Force Base (http://irvingshapiro.tripod.com/cgi-bin/Flight_93/AB_Otis.htm). It took place on 27 October 2000 (http://web.archive.org/web/20040229152154/http://www.eielson.af.mil/library/news/00nsvs/oct00/001027a.html).

365 9/11 Commission interview with Merchant and Goddard, "Memorandum for the Record: NORAD Field Site Visit: Interview with Major Paul Goddard (Canadian Forces)and Ken Merchant, 4 March 2004 (http://www.scribd.com/doc/18990372/DH-B5-DODNORAD-Notes-Fdr-3404-MFR-Maj-Paul-Goddard-Canada-and-Ken-Merchant-Military-Exercises).

366 Lieutenant-General Ken Pennie, Deputy Commander-in-Chief of NORAD, said that "NORAD-allocated forces will remain in place until the end of the Russian exercise. NORAD conducted operation Northern Denial from December 1 to 14, 2000 in response to a similar, but smaller scale, Russian deployment"; see also "NORAD Maintains Northern Vigilance," NORAD News, 9 September 2001 (http://www.norad.mil/News/2001/090901.html), and *Toronto Star*, 9 December 2001, "Northern Guardian" and "Northern Vigilance" (NORAD exercises on 911/2001) (https://web.archive.org/web/20050826012232/http://ringnebula.com/northern-vigilance.htm).

367 9/11 Commission, "Memorandum for the Record," interview with NORAD Deputy Commander, Lieutenant General Rick Findley, Canadian Forces (CF)," 1 March 2004 (http://media.nara.gov/9-11/MFR/t-0148-911MFR-00789.pdf).

368 9/11 Commission interview with Merchant and Goddard.

369 See TSgt. Bruce Vittner, "Historian's Report for Sept. 11, 2001," 2 (http://www.scribd.com/doc/13653185/T8-B16-Miles-Kara-Work-Files-Otis-Langley-1-of-2-Fdr-Historians-Report-for-Sept-11-2001-by-TSgt-Bruce-Vittner); 9/11 Commission, "Memorandum for the Record: Initial overview of Otis AFB operations by Colonel Paul Worcester," 14 October 2003 (http://www.scribd.com/doc/20954930/Mfr-Nara-t8-Dod-usaf-Worcester-Paul-10-14-03-00914).

370 Lynn Spencer, *Touching History: The Untold Story of the Drama That Unfolded in the Skies Over America on 9/11* (Free Press, 2008), 156.

371 9/11 Commission, "Memorandum for the Record: Visit to Reagan National Airport Control Tower in Alexandria, VA and Andrews Air Force Base Control Tower," 28 July 2003 (http://media.nara.gov/9-11/MFR/t-0148-911MFR-00245.pdf).

372 Mary Lou Vocale, "Guard Tempo of Operation Noble Eagle," *Code One Magazine*, Fourth Quarter 2002 (http://web.archive.org/web/20021226062700/http://www.codeonemagazine.com/archives/2002/articles/oct_02/guard/index.html).

373 Center of Military History, United States Army, "Interview of CW2 (Chief Warrant Officer)(name deleted)" (tape transcription), n.d. (http://web.archive.org/web/20090301023718/http://aal77.com/cmh_foia/neit322.pdf).

374 Jody T. Fahrig, "Davison Army Airfield Hosts Open House," 7 May 1999 (http://web.archive.org/web/20030902231146/http://www.dcmilitary.com/army/pentagram/archives/may7/pt_i5799.html).

375 9/11 Commission, "Early Morning Flight Activity, September 11, 2001: Exercise Concept" (Commission Sensitive Document), Faxed 3 July 2003, 07:39 AM (http://www.scribd.com/doc/18663225/T8-B16-Misc-Work-Papers-Fdr-NRO-Exercise-Plane-Crash-Into-Building). John J. Lumpkin, "Agency Planned Exercise on Sept. 11 Built around a Plane Crashing into a Building," *Associated Press*, 21 August 2002 (http://web.archive.org/web/20020925073028/http://www.sfgate.com/cgi-bin/article.cgi?f=/news/archive/2002/08/21/national1518EDT0686.DTL).

376 "NORAD Exercises Hijack Summary" (Commission Sensitive), 9/11 Commission, n.d. (http://www.scribd.com/doc/16411947/NORAD-Exercises-Hijack-Summary).

377 "Memorandum for the Record," interview with NORAD Deputy Commander, Lieutenant General Rick Findley, Canadian Forces (CF)," 9/11 Commission, 1 March 2004 (http://media.nara.gov/9-11/MFR/t-0148-911MFR-00789.pdf).

378 "Memorandum for the Record: Visit to Reagan National Airport Control Tower in Alexandria, VA and Andrews Air Force Base Control Tower," 9/11 Commission, 28 July 2003 http://media.nara.gov/9-11/MFR/t-0148-911MFR-00245.pdf).

379 "Conversation With Major General Larry Arnold, Commander, 1st Air Force, Tyndall AFB, Florida," *Code One*, January 2002 (http://web.archive.org/web/20031121154045/http:/www.codeonemagazine.com/archives/2002/articles/jan_02/defense/).

380 "Chilling Audio from 9/11 Hijack Played at Hearing," aired 17 June 2004 (https://web.archive.org/web/20050423220113/http://transcripts.cnn.com/TRANSCRIPTS/0406/17/pzn.00.html).

381 "Memorandum for the Record," 9/11 Commission, 24 November 2003 (http://www.scribd.com/doc/15937127/DH-B1-FAA-MFRs-Fdr-Monte-Belger-MFR-w-Underlining-and-Bracketing-809).

382 Shoestring 9/11, "The Many False Hijackings of 9/11," 10 April 2011 (http://shoestring911.blogspot.com/2011/04/many-false-hijackings-of-911.html).

383 *The 9/11 Commission Report*, 39.

384 Mitch Stacy, "Florida School Where Bush Learned of the Attacks Reflects on Its Role in History," Associated Press, 19 August 2002.

385 *The 9/11 Commission Report*, 38.

386 Ibid., 38.

387 Ibid., 38.

388 Ibid., 39.

389 "One of the many unanswered questions about that day is why the Secret Service did not immediately hustle Bush to a secure location, as it apparently did with Vice President Dick Cheney," Susan Taylor Martin, "Of Fact, Fiction: Bush on 9/11," *St. Petersburg Times*, 4 July 2004. This issue had been raised the day after 9/11 in one of Canada's leading newspapers, which wrote: "For some reason, Secret Service agents did not bustle [Bush] away," John Ibbitson, "Action, Not Overreaction, Prudent Course," *Globe and Mail*, 12 September, 2001.

390 Thomas H. Kean and Lee H. Hamilton, *Without Precedent: The Inside Story of the 9/11 Commission* (Knopf, 2006), 54.

391 *The 9/11 Commission Report*, 39.

392 Philip H. Mclanson, *Secret Service: The Hidden History of an Enigmatic Agency* (Carroll & Graf, 2002), as quoted in Susan Taylor Martin, "Of Fact, Fiction: Bush on 9/11."

393 Mike Riopell, "Educator's History Lesson," *Arlington Heights Daily Herald*, 11 September 2006. The event had been known by county school officials since early August. Much preparation had been done. "George W. Bush at Booker Elementary School(9/11/01)" (YouTube: Matty). Concern was expressed by Sarasota County Sheriff Colonel Steve Burns, who was in charge of security at Booker Elementary school that day and was working with the Secret Service; see "Sarasota County Sheriff's Office—Behind the Scenes on 9/11" (YouTube: SarasotaSheriff, at 2:30).

394 Richard A. Clarke, *Against All Enemies: Inside America's War on Terror* (Free Press, 2004), 4.

395 Tom Bayles, "The Day Before Everything Changed, President Bush Touched Locals' Lives," *Sarasota Herald-Tribune*, 10 September 2002; Blakewill's statement was later quoted in Susan Taylor Martin, "Of Fact, Fiction: Bush on 9/11," *St. Petersburg Times*, 4 July 2004.

396 Bush's speech was reported live on CNN (YouTube: slipstick99).

397 *The 9/11 Commission Report*, 38.

398 Andrew Card, "What If You Had to Tell the President," *San Francisco Chronicle*, 11 September 2002. Likewise, Card had told NBC's Brian Williams: "I pulled away from the president, and not that many seconds later, the president excused himself from the classroom, and we gathered in the holding room and talked about the situation," NBC News, 9 September 2002; reported in Scott Paltrow, "Government Accounts of 9/11 Reveal Gaps, Inconsistencies," *Wall Street Journal*, 22 March 2004.

Card similarly told ABC News: "The president waited for a moment for the students to finish, then said, 'Thank you all so very much for showing me your reading skills,' and headed for the empty classroom next door," in "Sept. 11's Moments of Crisis: Part 1: Terror Hits the Towers," ABC News, 14 September 2002.

399   "9/11 Interview with Campbell Brown," NBC News, 11 September 2002.

400   Sandra Kay Daniels, "9/11: A Year After/Who We Are Now," *Los Angeles Times*, 11 September 2002.

401   Jennifer Barrs, "From a Whisper to a Tear," *Tampa Tribune*, 1 September 2002. On the importance of this story, plus the fact that it has become virtually unavailable on the Internet, see Elizabeth Woodworth, "President Bush at the Florida School: New Conflicting Testimonies," 7 July 2007, 911Blogger.com.

402   Barrs, "From a Whisper to a Tear."

403   Ibid.; Bill Adair and Stephen Hegarty, "The Drama in Sarasota," *St. Petersburg Times*, 8 September 2002.

404   Bill Sammon, *Fighting Back: The War on Terrorism: From Inside the Bush White House* (Regnery, 2002), 89-90.

405   "5-Minute Video of George W. Bush on the Morning of 9/11," YouTube.

406   Scot J. Paltrow, "Government Accounts of 9/11 Reveal Gaps, Inconsistencies," *Wall Street Journal*, 22 March 2004.

407   Ibid.

408   *9/11 Commission Report*, 464, n. 213.

409   "911 Commission: Trans. Sec. Norman Mineta Testimony."

410   Richard Clarke, *Against All Enemies* (Free Press, 2004), 2–5.

411   See "9/11: Interviews by Peter Jennings," ABC News, 11 September 2002.

412   "The Vice President Appears on Meet the Press with Tim Russert," MSNBC, 16 September 2001.

413   *The 9/11 Commission Report*, 29. The three Secret Service reports about Cheney: (1) A September 12, 2012, memorandum, "Actions of TSD [Technical Services Division] Related to Terrorist Incident," stated that when Danny Spriggs, the Secret Service assistant division chief, entered the PEOC at 9:30, Cheney and Condoleezza Rice, along with ten other "Presidential and Vice Presidential staff," were already there. (2) According to minutes of 9/11 Commission interviews with members of the Secret Service, Carl Truscott, the Special Agent In Charge who escorted Condoleezza Rice down to the PEOC shortly before 9:30 AM, wrote this brief report: "Upon arrival at the shelter the VP and Mrs were present; VP on the phone." (3) A memorandum by Special Agent In Charge Anthony Zotto, who was in charge of Cheney's safety, reported that Cheney was in

the PEOC at least eight minutes prior to the attack on the Pentagon. (All three documents contained in Aidan Monaghan, *Declassifying 9/11: A Between the Lines and Behind the Scenes Look at the September 11 Attacks* [iUniverse, 2012]).

414   *The 9/11 Commission Report*, 29.

415   Ibid., 40.

416   Ibid., 41.

417   Ibid., 34.

418   Ibid., 41. (The movie *United 93*, which follows the timeline of *The 9/11 Commission Report*, says that the shoot-down authorization was given at 10:18.)

419   Ibid., 37.

420   "By 10:03, when United 93 crashed in Pennsylvania, there had been no mention of its hijacking [to the military]" (ibid., 38).

421   Richard A. Clarke, *Against All Enemies: Inside America's War on Terror* (Free Press, 2004).

422   Ibid., 7.

423   Clarke reported that the call came while the president's plane was still "getting ready to take off" (ibid., 8).

424   Ibid., 8.

425   Chitra Ragavan and Mark Mazzetti, "Pieces of the Puzzle: A Top-Secret Conference Call on September 11 Could Shed New Light on the Terrorist Attacks," *U.S. News & World Report*, 31 August 2003.

426   "'The Pentagon Goes to War': National Military Command Center," *American Morning with Paula Zahn*, CNN, 4 September 2002.

427   Quoted in Leslie Filson, *Air War over America: Sept. 11 Alters Face of Air Defense Mission*, Foreword by Larry K. Arnold (Public Affairs: Tyndall Air Force Base, 2003,) 68. Marr also said that, after he received the shoot-down authorization, he "passed that on to the pilots" ("9/11: Interviews by Peter Jennings," ABC News, 11 September 2002).

428   Filson, *Air War Over America*, 71.

429   "9/11: Interviews by Peter Jennings," ABC News, 11 September 2002.

430   *The 9/11 Commission Report*, 34.

431   Ibid.

432   9/11 Commission Hearing, 23 May 2003 (http://www.9-11commission.gov/archive/hearing2/9-11Commission_Hearing_2003-05-23.htm).

433   The 9/11 Commission acknowledged that FAA headquarters had realized by 9:34 that United 93 had been hijacked (*The 9/11 Commission Report*,

28). Also, when General Arnold was asked by the 9/11 Commission what NORAD was doing on 9/11 at 9:24 AM, he said: "Our focus was on United 93, which was being pointed out to us very aggressively, I might say, by the FAA" (9/11 Commission Hearing, 23 May 2003).

434 9/11 Commission Hearing, 23 May 2003.

435 In *The 9/11 Commission Report* (40–41), the commission's skepticism is muted, limited to stating that there was no documentary evidence for the call to President Bush that, according to Cheney, he made shortly after entering the PEOC, during which Bush gave him the authorization. According to *Newsweek* magazine, however, this statement was a "watered down" version of an earlier draft, which had reflected the fact that "some on the commission staff were . . . highly skeptical of the vice president's account." That earlier draft, which evidently expressed more clearly the belief that the vice president and the president were lying, was reportedly modified after vigorous lobbying from the White House (Daniel Klaidman and Michael Hirsh, "Who Was Really in Charge?" *Newsweek*, 20 June 2004).

436 See Chapter 31, "The Claim That Vice President Cheney Did Not Enter the PEOC Until Shortly Before 10 AM."

437 Donna Miles, "Vice Chairman: 9/11 Underscored Importance of DoD Transformation," American Forces Press Service, 8 September 2006.

438 "Rumsfeld's War," *Frontline*, PBS, 26 October 2004.

439 *The 9/11 Commission Report*, 35.

440 Ibid., 37.

441 *The 9/11 Commission Report*, 43–44. The commission's account corresponds to one given by Rumsfeld himself, in which he said: "I was in my office with a CIA briefer and I was told that a second plane had hit the other tower. Shortly thereafter, at 9:38, the Pentagon shook with an explosion of then unknown origin. I went outside to determine what had happened. I was not there long because I was back in the Pentagon with a crisis action team shortly before or after 10:00 A.M. On my return from the crash site and before going to the Executive Support Center, I had one or more calls in my office, one of which was with the president. I went to the National Military Command Center where General Myers . . . had just returned from Capitol Hill. . . . I joined the air threat telephone conference call that was already in progress" (9/11 Commission Hearing, 23 March 2004).

442 *The 9/11 Commission Report*, 34.

443 Ibid., 36. The commission added: "And none of the information conveyed in the White House video teleconference, at least in the first hour, was being passed to the NMCC [National Military Command Center]."

444 Ibid., 34.

445 Richard A. Clarke, *Against All Enemies: Inside America's War on Terror* (Free Press, 2004). MSNBC said: "The publishing phenomenon of the year. . . . Sales soar for book by former terrorism adviser."

446 Clarke reported that, having arrived at the White House shortly after 9:03 (when the second World Trade Center building was hit), he started his videoconference shortly after having a brief meeting with Dick Cheney and Condoleezza Rice (Clarke, *Against All Enemies*, 1–3). Clarke indicated that, several minutes after the conference had begun, Secretary of Transportation Norman Mineta arrived, and Clarke "suggested he join the Vice President [who had gone down to the PEOC]" (ibid., 5). Mineta told the 9/11 Commission that he "arrived at the PEOC at about 9:20 AM" (9/11 Commission Hearing, 23 May 2003). Clarke's account agrees with that of Mineta; see "Statement of Secretary of Transportation Norman Y. Mineta before the National Commission on Terrorist Attacks upon the United States, May 23, 2003." It takes a few minutes to get down to the PEOC from the Situation Room, so if Mineta is right about getting to the PEOC by 9:20, he must have started down at roughly 9:15. And if this is correct, the videoconference must have begun at about 9:10.

447 Clarke, *Against All Enemies*, 3.

448 Ibid., 7.

449 Ibid., 8–9.

450 The fact that *The 9/11 Commission Report* did not mention Richard Clarke's treatment of Rumsfeld does not mean that this treatment did not influence its account of Rumsfeld. According to early (2001 and 2002) discussions of Rumsfeld's movements by him and his assistant Torie Clarke (no relation to Richard Clarke), Rumsfeld went, after going to the reported crash site, directly from his office to the NMCC; the ESC was not mentioned ("Assistant Secretary Clarke Interview with WBZ Boston"; "Secretary Rumsfeld Interview with John McWethy, ABC," U.S. Department of Defense, 12 August 2002). But Clarke's book appeared on 10 March 2004, two weeks before Rumsfeld's March 23 testimony to the 9/11 Commission. During this testimony, Rumsfeld modified his story, saying: "On my return from the crash site and before going to the Executive Support Center, I had one or more calls in my office. . . . I went to the National Military Command Center" (9/11 Commission Hearing, 23 March 2004). This modification allowed the 9/11 Commission to soften the contradiction between its story and Clarke's: The commission wrote that Rumsfeld "went from the parking lot to his office . . . , then to the Executive Support Center, where he participated in the White House video teleconference. He moved to the NMCC shortly before 10:30" (*The 9/11 Commission Report*, 43).

451 As shown by his biographical statement, "Robert Andrews, Consultant," Andrews has received the Department of Defense Award for Outstanding

Public Service (2007) and the medal for Distinguished Civilian Service to the United States Army (2009).

452 "The moment I saw the second plane strike 'live,'" said Andrews, "I knew Secretary Rumsfeld would need the most up-to-date information, and ran down to our counterterrorism center [CTC] to get maps of New York and other data to take to him in the Executive Support Center [ESC]." Quoted in Barbara Honegger, "Special Operations Policy Expert and Veteran Robert Andrews Gives Distinguished Visiting Guest Lectures at NPS," 4 September 2004. Honegger could not publish this interview (it belongs to the Naval Postgraduate School, her former employer), but she will supply it on request.

453 Honegger, "Special Operations Policy Expert." Andrews hence said that Rumsfeld was in the ESC when he talked to President Bush, not—as *The 9/11 Commission Report* said—in his office.

454 "Pentagon Attack: Interview with Paul Wolfowitz," by Alfred Goldberg and Rebecca Cameron, 19 April 2002.

455 Alfred Goldberg et al., *Pentagon 9/11*, Defense Studies Series (Historical Office of the Secretary of Defense: Washington, DC, 2007).

456 "Pentagon Attack: Interview with Paul Wolfowitz."

457 *The 9/11 Commission Report*, 36.

458 General Hugh Shelton, Ronald Levinson, and Malcolm McConnell, *Without Hesitation: The Odyssey of an American Warrior* (St. Martin's Press, 2010), 430, 433.

459 Richard B. Myers, *Eyes on the Horizon: Serving on the Front Lines of National Security* (Threshold Editions, 2009), 7. See also "Interview: General Richard B. Myers," Armed Forces Radio and Television Services, 17 October 2001 (http://web.archive.org/web/20011118060728/http://www.dtic.mil/jcs/chairman/AFRTS_Interview.htm), and *The 9/11 Commission Report*, 463n199, citing an interview of 17 February 2004.

460 Sen. Max Cleland said: "General, it's a good thing that . . . you and I were meeting . . . here [on Capitol Hill] and not us meeting in the Pentagon"; quoted in "General Myers Confirmation Hearing," 13 September 2001.

461 "Interview: General Richard B. Myers" (2001).

462 Myers, *Eyes on the Horizon*, 8.

463 Ibid., 9.

464 Ibid., 9.

465 Jim Garamone, "Former Chairman Remembers 9/11 Attacks," American Forces Press Service, 8 September 2006.

466 *The 9/11 Commission Report*, 38.

467 Ibid., 37. At 9:29 AM, a "significant event" conference had begun, but it was canceled at 9:34, which "resumed at 9:37 as an air threat conference call." (*The 9/11 Commission Report* added: "All times given for this conference call are estimates, which we and the Department of Defense believe to be accurate within a ± minute margin of error" [ibid.].)

468 Ibid., 34.

469 Richard A. Clarke, *Against All Enemies: Inside America's War on Terror* (Free Press, 2004), which appeared and became a best-seller while the 9/11 Commission was holding public hearings.

470 Clarke reported that he had a brief meeting with Dick Cheney and Condoleezza Rice, which began after his arrival at the White House shortly after 9:03. The starting time of approximately 9:10 is further supported by Clarke's statement that this conference had been going on for several minutes before Norman Mineta arrived, combined with Mineta's statement that, after he arrived, he spent "four or five minutes" (see http://www.achievement.org/autodoc/page/min0int-8) talking with Clarke before going down to the Presidential Emergency Operations Emergency Center, which he reached "at about 9:20 AM" (9/11 Commission Hearing, 23 May 2003).

471 Clarke, *Against All Enemies*, 3.

472 "CAP" is the Combat Air Patrol, used here as a verb.

473 Clarke, *Against All Enemies*, 5.

474 Alfred Goldberg et al., *Pentagon 9/11*, Defense Studies Series (Historical Office of the Secretary of Defense: Washington, D.C., 2007).

475 "Pentagon Attack: Interview with Paul Wolfowitz," by Alfred Goldberg and Rebecca Cameron, 19 April 2002 (http://www.scribd.com/doc/51086776/GSA-B115-RDOD03012843-Fdr-Entire-Contents-Intvw-2002-04-19-Wolfowitz-Paul-054).

476 "Deputy Secretary Wolfowitz Interview with PBS NewsHour," PBS, 14 September 2001.

477 "General Myers Confirmation Hearing."

478 "Orientation and Tour of the National Military Command Center (NMCC): Secret Memorandum for the Record," 21 July 2003 (http://media.nara.gov/9-11/MFR/t-0148-911MFR-00756.pdf).

479 "Statement of Capt. Charles J. Leidig, Jr., Before the National Commission on Terrorist Attacks Upon the United States," 17 June 2004.

480 An FAA transcript shows that Delta 1989 was reported hijacked at 9:23 but then shortly reported as OK at 9:26 (http://www.scribd.com/doc/13484888/Transcript-of-FAA-Open-Line-on-911).

481 Ibid.

482   Gen. Hugh Shelton et al., *Without Hesitation*, 432–33. Just before that statement by Shelton, he had written: "Until I crossed back into United States airspace, all the decisions would be Dick's to make" (ibid., 432). There is no hint in these pages that Myers was not in the Pentagon.

483   Ibid., 433.

484   This meeting is mentioned in Robert Burns, "Pentagon Attack Came Minutes After Rumsfeld Predicted: 'There Will Be Another Event,'" Associated Press, 12 September 2001.

485   "Rumsfeld's War," *Frontline*, PBS, 26 October 2004.

486   See Chapter 35, "The Claim That General Shelton Returned to the Pentagon from an Aborted Flight in the Early Afternoon."

487   In June 2004, Myers said he learned that the Pentagon was hit while he was on his "way back to the Pentagon," 9/11 Commission Hearing, 17 June 2004. In his 2009 book, Myers likewise said that he was told "the Pentagon's just been hit" as he "raced away from Capitol Hill" (*Eyes on the Horizon*, 9).

488   At his confirmation hearing, Myers said: "I was with Senator Cleland when this [attack on the Pentagon] happened" ("General Myers Confirmation Hearing"). In an interview of 17 October 2002, Myers said that when he and Cleland came out of his office, the fact that the second tower had been hit "was obvious. Then right at that time someone said the Pentagon has been hit" ("Interview: General Richard B. Myers," Armed Forces Radio and Television Services, 17 October 2001).

489   "I was called out by Gen. Eberhart . . . and my executive assistant," Myers wrote. He then immediately got into his car and rushed back to the Pentagon. "Before we even got to the 14th Street Bridge, the Pentagon was hit," he said. "The scene coming across the bridge was the Pentagon with black smoke rolling out of it." Jim Garamone, "Former Chairman Remembers 9/11 Attacks," American Forces Press Service, 8 September 2006. In his 2009 book, Myers also said that the call from Eberhart came before he learned that the Pentagon had been hit (*Eyes on the Horizon*, 9).

490   In 2001, Myers said: "Sometime during that office call the second tower was hit. Nobody informed us of that. But when we came out, that was obvious. Then right at that time somebody said the Pentagon has been hit. . . . [S]omebody handed me a cell phone, and it was General Eberhart out at NORAD in Colorado Springs," Armed Forces Radio and Television Service Interview, General Richard B. Myers, 17 October 2001.

491   "I was called out by Gen. (Ralph) Eberhart . . . and my executive assistant," he said. Myers immediately got into his car and rushed back to the Pentagon. "Before we even got to the 14th Street Bridge, the Pentagon was hit," he said. "The scene coming across the bridge was the Pentagon with black smoke rolling out of it." Jim Garamone, "Former Chairman Remembers 9/11 Attacks," American Forces Press Service, 8 September 2006. In his

2009 book, Myers also said that the call from Eberhart came before he learned that the Pentagon had been hit (*Eyes on the Horizon*, 9).

492 "Sometime during that office call the second tower was hit. Nobody informed us of that. But when we came out, that was obvious. Then right at that time somebody said the Pentagon has been hit. I immediately, somebody handed me a cell phone, and it was General Eberhart" ("Interview: General Richard B. Myers").

493 "General Myers Confirmation Hearing."

494 Tom Baxter and Jim Galloway, "Max Returns, With Fire in His Eyes," *Atlanta Journal-Constitution*, 16 June 2003. This talk is also available as "Max Cleland Speech," St. Mark's Episcopal Church, Raleigh N.C. Although this document spelled Myers's name "Meyers," it otherwise appears to be an accurate transcription of a speech given by Cleland.

495 "Interview: General Richard B. Myers," Armed Forces Radio and Television Services, 17 October 2001 (http://web.archive.org/web/20011118060728/http://www.dtic.mil/jcs/chairman/AFRTS_Interview.htm).

496 Ibid.

497 In his 2009 book, Myers said: "He [Cleland] had started preparing a pot of tea, but we hadn't taken a sip when a staff person came in from the outer office and informed us that the second tower had been hit. We both knew the interview was over" (Myers, *Eyes on the Horizon*, 8).

498 Baxter and Galloway, "Max Returns."

499 Suzanne Giesemann, *Living a Dream: A Journey from Aide to the Chairman of the Joint Chiefs of Staff on 9/11 to Full-Time Cruiser* (Paradise Cay Publications, 2008).

500 Shelton, *Without Hesitation*, 432; Myers, *Eyes on the Horizon*, 10.

501 "At around 7:30 we were wheels up" (Shelton, *Without Hesitation*, 431). The flight-tracking strip (see note 19, below) indicated that the plane took off at 7:09 AM. (The difference between the two times might simply reflect two different ways of reporting the departure time: 7:09 may have been when the plane was given the signal to begin moving, whereas 7:30 might have been when the plane was "wheels up.")

502 Shelton usually flew in a VIP Boeing 757 often used by the vice president, but it was reportedly unavailable (Shelton, *Without Hesitation*, 431; Giesemann, *Living a Dream*, 21).

503 Shelton, *Without Hesitation*, 431; Giesemann, *Living a Dream*, 22–23. (Shelton said he was told of the first WTC attack "about an hour and a half into the flight" and then learned of the second strike "[t]en minutes later" [*Without Hesitation*, 431].)

504 Myers, *Eyes on the Horizon*, 10.

505 Shelton's executive director, Col. Doug Lute, told him: "[W]e've been denied permission to return. All US airspace has been shut down."

506 Shelton said: "Doug, tell the pilot we'll ask for forgiveness instead of permission, so have him turn us around. We're going home." Shelton added: "I knew there was no way they were going to shoot down a 707 with UNITED STATES AIR FORCE emblazoned along the side" (Shelton, *Without Hesitation*, 432). Giesemann wrote: "Every other passenger plane across the nation now sat on the ground, but with the uniformed leader of the United States military aboard, our aircraft flew on unimpeded" (*Living a Dream*, 24).

507 "Ten minutes later they called back with confirmation that we had been officially cleared to fly through the shutdown airspace" (Shelton, *Without Hesitation*, 433). A draft FAA document said: "Gen. Shelton, upon hearing of the events ordered his plane to return to Washington, but was initially denied this request by air traffic controllers who had already begun diverting inbound oceanic traffic for non-U.S. destinations. Minutes later, however, clearance was granted and Gen. Shelton's plane reversed course and headed for Washington" ("The Air Traffic Organization's Response to the September 11th Terrorist Attack: ATC System Assessment, Shutdown, and Restoration," 21 March 2002, Appendix G, "Key Personnel Movement," G-1).

508 Immediately after the previous quotation, Shelton wrote: "One of our pilots stuck his head out of the cockpit and announced, 'Sir, our flight path will take us right over Manhattan, if you'd like to come up here about ten minutes from now'" (Shelton, *Without Hesitation*, 433).

509 Ibid.; Giesemann wrote: "I stared at the place where the twin towers should have been" (*Living a Dream*, 26).

510 Shelton, *Without Hesitation*, 432.

511 "Within an hour of passing New York City, we landed at Andrews Air Force Base" (Giesemann, *Living a Dream*, 27).

512 Shelton, *Without Hesitation*, 434. See also Giesemann, *Living a Dream*, 27–28.

513 Shelton, *Without Hesitation*, 434.

514 Myers, *Eyes on the Horizon*, 159.

515 Giesemann, *Living a Dream*, 27.

516 Shelton wrote: "Until I crossed back into the United States airspace, all the decisions would be Dick's [Myers's] to make in conjunction with Secretary Rumsfeld and the president" (Shelton, *Without Hesitation*, 432).

517 Ibid., 434.

518 "At 5:40 PM, the Chairman, Gen. Hugh Shelton, having just returned from an aborted flight to Europe, arrived in the NMCC" (Myers, *Eyes on the Horizon*, 159).

519 See previous note.

520 The Andrews AFB flight-tracking strips for September 11, 2001, were obtained by the 911 Working Group of Bloomington, Indiana (http://data.911workinggroup.org/), by means of a FOIA request made by Kevin Ryan and two other members. A tool for reading flight-tracking strips is available online.

521 As shown by a photo at Airliners.Net.

522 Flight-tracking strips are in Zulu time, which is four hours ahead of US Eastern time. The flight track strip for Andrews AFB on September 11, 2001, shows that Trout 99 landed at 2040, i.e., 4:40 PM Eastern time (just as it shows that this flight took off at 1109, i.e., 7:09 AM Eastern time). We are grateful to Kevin Ryan and Matthew Everett for providing this information.

523 Shelton, *Without Hesitation*, 434; Giesemann, *Living a Dream*, 27.

524 Giesemann, *Living a Dream*, 27.

525 An interview-based section on Lt. Col. Rob Pedersen constitutes one of 10 sections of "Airmen on 9/11," *Air Force Magazine*, September 2011: 61 (Pedersen is now executive officer for the Air Force Strategic Deterrence and Nuclear Integration Division at the Pentagon, ibid.).

526 Ibid., 60.

527 Ibid., 60, 61.

528 Ibid., 61.

529 Although Pedersen states that this flight made it to Andrews "by early afternoon," the flight-tracking strip says that it landed at 4:40 PM (which cannot be considered "early afternoon"). Also, Pedersen states that the Speckled Trout crew "was wheels up around 5 AM," whereas the flight-tracking strip shows that this did not occur until after 7:00 (see note 522, above). These errors do not, however, ruin the credibility of Pedersen's account: Ten years later, he might have forgotten the exact departure and return times, about which he would have had no decisions to make. But as the navigator, he would have had the task of planning the return route, so his memories about this feature of the trip should have been firmly fixed in his memory.

530 *The 9/11 Commission Report: Final Report of the National Commission on Terrorist Attacks Upon the United States* (W. W. Norton, 2004), 37.

531 For example, Air Force Col. Susan Kuehl, "the self-described 'mayor of NMCC,'" is "a trained DDO and supervises the operation of the NMCC." See "Orientation and Tour of the National Military Command Center

(NMCC): Secret Memorandum for the Record," 21 July 2003 (https://web.
archive.org/web/20150911202959/http://media.nara.gov/9-11/MFR/t-
0148-911MFR-00756.pdf).

532   "Orientation and Tour of the National Military Command Center
      (NMCC)." One of those nine members was the 9/11 Commission's
      executive director, Philip Zelikow.

533   "'The Pentagon Goes to War': National Military Command Center," CNN
      American Morning with Paula Zahn, 4 September 2002.

534   "9/11: Interviews by Peter Jennings," ABC News, 11 September 2002.

535   Richard B. Myers, *Eyes on the Horizon: Serving on the Front Lines of
      National Security* (Threshold Editions, 2009), 152.

536   Brigadier General W. Montague "Que" Winfield, Commander, JPAC
      (Joint POW/MIA Accounting Command) (http://web.archive.org/
      web/20041011040723/www.jpac.pacom.mil/CommandStaff.htm).

537   "Orientation and Tour of the National Military Command Center
      (NMCC)."

538   "Taped Interview of Captain Charles Joseph Leidig: Commission Sensitive
      Memorandum for the Record," 29 April 2004 (https://web.archive.
      org/web/20110309231347/http://media.nara.gov/9-11/MFR/t-0148-
      911MFR-00684.pdf). The members of the staff were Miles Kara, Dana
      Hyde, Kevin Shaeffer, John Azzarello, and John Farmer. The interview was
      held in Joint Chiefs of Staff offices, with Col. Kuehl and a JCS legal officer
      present.

539   DH B2 Cmdr Gardner DOD Fdr, Entire Contents, Handwritten Interview
      Notes, 5 May 2004, NOIWON (http://www.scribd.com/doc/14274408/
      DH-B2-Cmdr-Gardner-DOD-Fdr-Entire-Contents-Handwritten-Inter-
      view-Notes-May-5-2004-064); DH B2 Cmdr Gardner DOD Fdr, Entire
      Contents, Handwritten Interview Notes, 12 May 2004, NOIWON (http://
      www.scribd.com/doc/14274414/DH-B2-Cmdr-Gardner-DOD-Fdr-En-
      tire-Contents-Handwritten-Interview-Notes-May-12-2004-NOIWON).

540   "Orientation and Tour of the National Military Command Center
      (NMCC)."

541   "Taped Interview of Captain Charles Joseph Leidig."

542   Ibid.

543   Ibid.

544   Ibid.

545   Ibid.]

546   For the (hand-written) notes for the two Gardner interviews, see note 538,
      above.

547 Kean described Leidig as having "served as deputy director of operations in the National Military Command Center on 9/11," 9/11 Commission Hearing, 17 June 2004.

548 "Statement of Capt. Charles J. Leidig, Jr., before the National Commission on Terrorist Attacks upon the United States," 17 June 2004.

549 "Taped Interview of Captain Charles Joseph Leidig."

550 "'The Pentagon Goes to War': National Military Command Center" (CNN); "9/11: Interviews by Peter Jennings" (ABC).

551 Winfield continued: "We started receiving reports from the fighters that were heading to, to intercept. The FAA kept us informed with their time estimates as the aircraft got closer and closer. . . . And at some point, the closure time came and went, and nothing had happened. So you can imagine everything was very tense in the NMCC."

552 *The 9/11 Commission Report*, 30, 38.

553 "Taped Interview of Captain Charles Joseph Leidig." Four more examples: (1) "He could not say whether it was he or Gardner who had made notification calls to the offices of the Secretary of Defense and the Chairman of the Joint Chiefs." (2) "He did not recall if there has been a call to the White House." (3) "He . . . did not recall who was notified that the ATCC [air threat conference call] was convened." (4) "He did not recall phone calls to NORAD prior to the advent of the SIEC. At this point Staff turned to the transcript of the Air Threat Conference Call (ATCC) and recalled for him his update."

554 "Orientation and Tour."

555 "Taped Interview of Captain Charles Joseph Leidig."

556 "Interview with General Winfield" (http://www.scribd.com/doc/14274468/DH-B3-Gen-Winfield-Interview-Fdr-Questions-and-Withdrawal-Notice-Handwritten-Interview-Notes-Classified-088). The handwritten notes for this interview were withdrawn from the publicly available file, with a handwritten note: "national security withdrawn."

557 *The 9/11 Commission Report*, 463 n. 190.

558 Gerry J. Gilmore, "Eberhart Tabbed to Head U.S. Northern Command," American Forces Press Service, 8 May 2002; the Northern Command (NORTHCOM) is considered "the nation's premier military homeland defense organization"; NORAD and USNORTHCOM Public Affairs, "NORAD and USNORTHCOM Honour 9/11 Heroes," 15 October 2012 (http://web.archive.org/web/20130118114658/http://www.rcaf-arc.forces.gc.ca/v2/nr-sp/index-eng.asp?id=13272).

559 *The 9/11 Commission Report*, 465 n. 228.

560 "Memorandum for the Record: Interview with CINCNORAD (Commanded in Chief NORAD), General Edward 'Ed' Eberhart," 9/11 Commission,

1 March 2004: 4 (https://web.archive.org/web/20111202093712/http://media.nara.gov/9-11/MFR/t-0148-911MFR-00788.pdf).

561 9/11 Commission "Memorandum for the Record," Interview with NORAD Deputy Commander, Lieutenant General Rick Findley, Canadian Forces (CF)," 1 March 2004 (https://web.archive.org/web/20110224024217/http://media.nara.gov/9-11/MFR/t-0148-911MFR-00789.pdf).

562 Ibid., 2.

563 "Memorandum for the Record: Interview with CINCNORAD (Commanded in Chief NORAD), General Edward 'Ed' Eberhart," 9/11 Commission, 1 March 2004: 4.

564 General Myers said that shortly after Eberhart's call, the Pentagon was hit on his [Myers's] way back to it. Source: Panel I, Day II of the Twelfth Public Hearing of the National Commission on Terrorist Attacks Upon the United States. Chaired by Thomas Kean, Chairman, 17 June 2004: 43–44 (http://govinfo.library.unt.edu/911/archive/hearing12/9-11Commission_Hearing_2004-06-17.pdf).

565 Richard Myers (with Malcolm McConnell), *Eyes on the Horizon: Serving on the Front Lines of National Security* (Threshold Editions, 2009), 9.

566 "Memorandum for the Record: Interview with Richard Myers, Affiliated with NORAD, 9/11 Commission," 17 February 2004 (http://media.nara.gov/9-11/MFR/t-0148-911MFR-00751.pdf).

567 "Richard Myers, Interview by Jim Miklaszewski," NBC News, 11 September 2002; Myers, *Eyes on the Horizon*, 9.

568 "Memorandum for the Record: Interview with CINCNORAD," 1 March 2004.

569 *The 9/11 Commission Report*, 465; T.R. Reid, "Military to Idle NORAD Compound," *Washington Post*, 29 July 2006.

570 Bruce Finley, "Military to Put Cheyenne Mountain on Standby," Denver Post, 27 July 2006.

571 *The 9/11 Commission Report*, 42; Pam Zubeck, "Cheyenne Mountain's Fate May Lie in Study Contents," *The Gazette*, 16 June 2006; Lynn Spencer, *Touching History: The Untold Story of the Drama That Unfolded in the Skies Over America on 9/11* (Free Press, 2008), 240.

572 *The 9/11 Commission Report*, 38, 463, citing "DOD transcript, Air Threat Conference Call, Sept. 11, 2001."

573 William B. Scott, "Exercise Jump-Starts Response to Attacks," *Aviation Week & Space Technology*, 3 June 2002; 9/11 Commission, Twelfth Public Hearing, 17 June 2003; Spencer, *Touching History*, 269.

574 Chapter 34, "The Claim That General Myers Was Not at the Pentagon During the Attacks."

575 Chapter 22, "The Claim That the 9/11 Flights Were Hijacked."

576 Researcher Kevin Ryan concluded: "No reason was ever given (or requested) for why Eberhart did not fly directly to CMOC from Peterson, making use of the Cheyenne Mountain helicopter port" ("The Case Against Ralph Eberhart, NORAD's 9/11 Commander," 12 January 2013).

577 *The 9/11 Commission Report*, 38, citing "DOD transcript, Air Threat Conference Call, Sept. 11, 2001."

578 Leslie Filson, *Air War Over America: Sept. 11 Alters Face of Air Defense Mission* (Tyndall Air Force Base: 1st Air Force, 2003), 55; Lynn Spencer, *Touching History*, 27.

579 Bob Arnot, "What Was Needed to Halt the Attacks? Cockpit Security, Quick Response Not in Evidence Tuesday," MSNBC, 12 September 2001.

580 NORAD, "NORAD'S Response Times, Sept. 11, 2001," 18 September 2001 (http://web.archive.org/web/20030809155434/http:/www.norad.mil/index.cfm?fuseaction=home.news_rel_09_18_01).

581 *The 9/11 Commission Report*, 18–30.

582 Ibid., 34.

583 Transcript of Hearing Before the Committee on Armed Services, United States Senate, 25 October 2001 (http://web.archive.org/web/20020321022318/http://www.public-action.com/911/eberhart-testimony.html).

584 "FAA Communications with NORAD on September 11, 2001: FAA clarification Memo to 9/11 Independent Commission, May 22, 2003," published by 911Truth.org, 12 August 2004.

585 9/11 Commission, Twelfth Public Hearing, 17 June 2004.

586 "Memorandum for the Record: Interview with CINCNORAD (Commanded in Chief NORAD), General Edward 'Ed' Eberhart," 9/11 Commission, 1 March 2004.

587 *The 9/11 Commission Report*, 26-27, 34; "Memorandum for the Record: Interview with CINCNORAD," 1 March 2004.

588 1st Fighter Wing History Excerpt, July through December 2001: 61 (https://web.archive.org/web/20100805024701/http://www.scribd.com/doc/33866487/T8-B8-Kara-Docs-3-Timelines-Fdr-1st-Fighter-Wing-History-Excerpt-Jul-Dec-01-w-Logs).

589 9/11 Commission, "Memorandum for the Record," Interview with NORAD Deputy Commander, Lieutenant General Rick Findley, Canadian Forces (CF)," 1 March 2004.

590 Vigilant Guardian 01-02 Planning Document (https://web.archive.org/web/20110509072119/http://www.scribd.com:80/doc/26080483/GSA-B116-RDOD-03013141-Fdr-Entire-Contents-Vigilant-Guardian-

Docs-760); "'Real-World or Exercise': Did the U.S. Military Mistake the 9/11 Attacks for a Training Scenario?" Shoestring 9/11, 22 March 2012; "'Let's Get Rid of This Goddamn Sim': How NORAD Radar Screens Displayed False Tracks All Through the 9/11 Attacks," Shoestring 9/11, 12 August 2010; 9/11 Commission, Twelfth Public Hearing, 17 June 2004. Chapter 27, above, "The Claim that the Military Exercises Did Not Delay the Response to the Attacks."

591 Kane spoke to Eberhart following the Commission's Twelfth Public Hearing, 17 June 2004. Source: Don Jacobs, "The Military Drills on 9-11: 'Bizarre Coincidence or Something Else?'" In Paul Zarembka, ed., *The Hidden History of 9-11-2001* (Elsevier, 2006), 129.

592 9/11 Commission interview with Lt. Col. Dawne Deskins, North Eastern Air Defense Sector (NEADS) field site visit, 30 October 2003: 3 (https://web.archive.org/web/20110224025153/http://media.nara.gov/9-11/MFR/t-0148-911MFR-00778.pdf).

593 Dereliction of duty is a specific offense under United States Code Title 10,892, Article 92, and applies to all branches of the US military. A service member who is derelict has willfully refused to perform his duties or has incapacitated himself in such a way that he cannot perform his duties [as when Eberhart took his long drive without a functioning cell phone]. Article 92 applies to service members whose acts or omissions rise to the level of criminally negligent behavior ("Dereliction of Duty," Wikipedia, accessed August 2015).

594 9/11 Commission Hearing, 19 May 2004 (http://www.9-11commission.gov/archive/hearing11/9-11Commission_Hearing_2004-05-19.htm).

595 This statement, made on 9/11 to Peter Jennings of ABC News, can be read and heard at "Who Told Giuliani the WTC Was Going to Collapse on 9/11?" What Really Happened (Updated), 27 August 2010.

596 A televised video of this encounter, titled "Activists Confront Giuliani over 9/11," can be viewed on YouTube as "WeAreChange Confronts Giuliani on 9/11 Collapse Lies."

597 Ibid.

598 James Glanz, "Engineers Have a Culprit in the Strange Collapse of 7 World Trade Center: Diesel Fuel" (originally titled "Engineers Are Baffled Over the Collapse of 7 WTC"), *New York Times*, 29 November 2001.

599 "Interstate Bank Building Fire, Los Angeles, California," FEMA, May 1988.

600 "High-Rise Office Building Fire, One Meridian Plaza Philadelphia, Pennsylvania," FEMA, 19.

601 *World Trade Center Building Performance Study*, FEMA, May 2002, Appendix A: "Overview of Fire Protection in Buildings," A-9 (http://www.fema.gov/pdf/library/fema403_apa.pdf).

602 Robin Nieto, "Fire Practically Destroys Venezuela's Tallest Building," 18 October 2004.

603 "Learning from 9/11: Understanding the Collapse of the World Trade Center," Hearing before the Committee on Science, House of Representatives, 6 March 2002 (http://commdocs.house.gov/committees/science/hsy77747.000/hsy77747_0f.htm). Of course, WTC 7 was different: Many people became convinced that it would come down, but this was after the Twin Towers had come down and after they had been *told* that it was going to come down. See Chapter 16, above, "The Claim That Foreknowledge of WTC 7's Fall Was Based on Observations."

604 To give a few examples:

- John Skilling, the architect primarily responsible for the structural design of the Twin Towers, when asked in 1993 what would happen if one of the towers were to suffer a strike by an airliner loaded with jet-fuel, replied that "there would be a horrendous fire" and "a lot of people would be killed," but "the building structure would still be there." (Eric Nalder, "Twin Towers Engineered to Withstand Jet Collision," *Seattle Times*, 27 February 1993.)

- An investigator with the Bureau of Investigations and Trials said that "no one ever expected it to collapse like that" (Oral History: Lieutenant Murray Murad, 20 (http://graphics8.nytimes.com/packages/pdf/nyregion/20050812_WTC_GRAPHIC/9110009.PDF).

- A firefighter battalion chief said that after "everything blew out on . . . one floor," he thought that the top of the South Tower was going to come off and fall down, but "there was never a thought that this whole thing is coming down" (Oral History: Lieutenant Murray Murad, 20 (http://graphics8.nytimes.com/packages/pdf/nyregion/20050812_WTC_GRAPHIC/9110009.PDF).

- Another firefighter said: "You just couldn't believe that those buildings could come down. . . . [T]here's no history of these buildings falling down" (Oral History: Lieutenant Warren Smith: 14-15, 30-31, 32 [http://www.nytimes.com/packages/html/nyregion/20050812_WTC_GRAPHIC/Smith_Warren.txt]).

- Even the 9/11 Commission said that, to its knowledge, "none of the [fire] chiefs present believed that a total collapse of either tower was possible" (*The 9/11 Commission Report*, 302). One apparent exception was Chief Ray Downey, who was a collapse expert, but he had become convinced that explosives had been placed in the buildings; see Tom Downey, *The Last Men Out: Life on the Edge of Rescue 2 Firehouse* (Henry Holt, 2004).

- Likewise, NIST (the National Institute of Standards and Technology) wrote: "No one interviewed indicated that they thought that the buildings would completely collapse" (*The 9/11 Commission Report*, 302).

605   Oral History: Chief Albert Turi, 13-14 (http://graphics8.nytimes.com/packages/pdf/nyregion/20050812_WTC_GRAPHIC/9110142.PDF).

606   Oral History: EMT Richard Zarrillo, 5-6 (http://graphics8.nytimes.com/packages/pdf/nyregion/20050812_WTC_GRAPHIC/9110161.PDF).

607   "Rotanz was assigned to the Mayor's Office of Emergency Management in 2000," Urban Hazards Forum, FEMA, 2002 (https://web.archive.org/web/20160313044341/http://christianregenhardcenter.org/urban-hazards/Papers/rotanz.PDF).

608   Oral History: Chief John Peruggia, 4, 17 (http://www.nytimes.com/packages/html/nyregion/20050812_WTC_GRAPHIC/Peruggia_John.txt).

609   Oral History: Chief John Peruggia, 17 (http://www.nytimes.com/packages/html/nyregion/20050812_WTC_GRAPHIC/Peruggia_John.txt).

610   A document titled a "Brief History of New York City's Office of Emergency Management" said: "1996: By executive order, the Mayor's Office of Emergency Management is created. The Director reports directly to the Mayor."

611   *The 9/11 Commission Report*, 302.

612   Roemer's statement was made during a 9/11 Commission hearing (www.9-11commission.gov/archive/hearing11/9-11Commission_Hearing_2004-05-18.htm).

613   9/11 Commission Hearing, 18 May 2004 (www.9-11commission.gov/archive/hearing11/9-11Commission_Hearing_2004-05-18.htm). Von Essen had already told this story in his book, *Strong of Heart: Life and Death in the Fire Department of New York* (William Morrow, 2002), 22.

614   Oral History: Father John Delendick, 5. Delendick added: "As we've since learned, it was the jet fuel that was dropping down that caused all this." But what is important is what he reported that Downey, the expert, had said.

615   *The 9/11 Commission Report*, Chap. 5.

616   Federal Bureau of Investigation, "Most Wanted Terrorists" (http://web.archive.org/web/20101011161759/http:/www.fbi.gov/wanted/topten/usama-bin-laden).

617   Ed Haas, "FBI says, 'No Hard Evidence Connecting Bin Laden to 9/11,'" Muckraker Report, 6 June 2006 (http://web.archive.org/web/20090207113442/http:/teamliberty.net/id267.html).

618   (1) Federal German Judge Dieter Deiseroth, in a December 2009 statement, stated that no independent court has verified the evidence against bin Laden (https://www.heise.de/tp/features/Das-schreit-gerade-zu-nach-Aufklaerung-3383769.html). (2) "Bush Rejects Taliban Offer to

Hand Bin Laden Over," *Guardian*, 14 October 2001. (3) "Taliban Met With U.S. Often: Talks Centered on Ways to Hand over bin Laden," *Washington Post*, 29 October 2001 (the Taliban said they would turn bin Laden over if the US provided evidence of his guilt, but it was not forthcoming). (4) "The Investigation and the Evidence," *BBC News*, 5 October 2001, said: "There is no direct evidence in the public domain linking Osama Bin Laden to the 11 September attacks."

619   "Meet the Press," NBC, 23 September 2001; Tony Blair, Office of the Prime Minister, "Responsibility for the Terrorist Atrocities in the United States," *BBC News*, 4 October 2001.

620   "Remarks by the President, Secretary of the Treasury O'Neill and Secretary of State Powell on Executive Order," White House, 24 September 2001; Seymour M. Hersh, "What Went Wrong: The C.I.A. and the Failure of American Intelligence," *The New Yorker*, 1 October 2001; Office of the Prime Minister, "Responsibility for the Terrorist Atrocities in the United States," *BBC News*, 4 October 2001, which stated that it "does not purport to provide a prosecutable case against Osama Bin Laden in a court of law."

621   *The 9/11 Commission Report*, 145; Chap. 5, notes 1, 10, 11, 16, 32, 40, and 41.

622   Thomas H. Kean and Lee H. Hamilton, *Without Precedent: The Inside Story of the 9/11 Commission* (Vintage, 2006), 119.

623   *The 9/11 Commission Report*, 1.

624   Ibid., 2.

625   Robert Mueller, "Statement for the Record" (https://fas.org/irp/congress/2002_hr/092602mueller.html).

626   Richard Bernstein et al., "The Hijackers' Long Road to Infamy," *New York Times*, 11 September 2002.

627   "No physical, documentary, or analytical evidence provides a convincing explanation of why Atta and Omari drove to Portland, Maine, from Boston on the morning of September 10, only to return to Logan on Flight 5930 on the morning of September 11" (*The 9/11 Commission Report*, 451 n. 1).

628   See "The Night Before Terror—The FBI Describes Hijacking Suspects' Overnight Stay in Greater Portland," *Portland Press Herald*, 5 October 2001, which said: "After checking in at the motel, Atta and Alomari were seen several times between 8 PM and 9:30 PM. Between 8 and 9 PM, they were seen at Pizza Hut; at 8:31 PM, they were videotaped by a KeyBank automatic teller machine, and videotaped again at 8:41 PM at a Fast Green ATM next to Pizzeria Uno. . . . At 9:15 PM, the two stopped at Jetport Gas on Western Avenue, where they asked for directions."

629 "Affidavit and Application for Search Warrant," signed by FBI special agent James K. Lechner and US Magistrate Judge David M. Cohen, dated 12 September 2001, *Four Corners: Investigative TV Journalism.*

630 Mueller, "Statement for the Record."

631 Peter Finn and Charles Lane, "Will Gives a Window Into Suspect's Mind," *Washington Post*, 6 October 2001.

632 9/11 Commission Staff Statement No. 16, 16 June 2004. Stating that Atta's luggage "contained far more than what the commission report cited," a 2006 news story added: "Former federal terrorism investigators say [that this luggage] provided the Rosetta stone enabling FBI agents to swiftly unravel the mystery of who carried out the suicide attacks and what motivated them. . . . [T]he government was able to identify all 19 hijackers almost immediately after the attacks . . . through those papers in the luggage;" see Michael Dorman, "Unraveling 9-11 Was in the Bags," *Newsday*, 16 April 2006.

633 Dorman, "Unraveling 9-11 Was in the Bags."

634 Evidently, the 9/11 Commission had originally planned to explain that Atta's bags were not loaded because he had just barely caught the plane. According to the 9/11 Commission's Staff Statement No. 16 (dated 2004): "The Portland detour almost prevented Atta and Omari from making Flight 11 out of Boston. In fact, the luggage they checked in Portland failed to make it onto the plane." But the 9/11 Commission, having evidently realized later that this claim could not be credibly made, wrote in its final *Report*: "Atta and Omari arrived in Boston at 6:45 [A.M.] . . . . Between 6:45 and 7:40, Atta and Omari . . . checked in and boarded American Airlines Flight 11 . . . scheduled to depart at 7:45 [AM]" (*The 9/11 Commission Report*, 1-2). The 9/11 Commission ended up offering no explanation as to why the luggage was not loaded, simply letting the mystery stand.

635 Paul Sperry, "Airline Denied Atta Paradise Wedding Suit," WorldNetDaily. com, 11 September 2002.

636 See "Two Brothers among Hijackers," CNN, 13 September 2001 (http:// en.people.cn/200109/13/eng20010913_80131.html), which said: "Investigators have leads on four hijackers. . . . Two of the men were brothers, . . . Adnan Bukhari and Ameer Abbas Bukhari. . . . The two rented a car, a silver-blue Nissan Altima, from an Alamo car rental at Boston's Logan Airport and drove to an airport in Portland, Maine, where they got on US Airways Flight 5930 at 6 AM Tuesday headed back to Boston, the sources said. . . . Portland Police Chief Mike Chitwood said, 'I can tell you those two individuals did get on a plane and fly to Boston early yesterday morning.'" (This story later disappeared from the CNN website.)

637 The previously quoted CNN story—"Two Brothers among Hijackers"— said: "A Mitsubishi sedan impounded at Logan Airport was rented by

Atta, sources said. The car contained materials, including flight manuals, written in Arabic that law enforcement sources called 'helpful' to the investigation." Another story, "Hijack Suspect Detained, Cooperating with FBI," said: "Federal law enforcement in the United States was led to the Hamburg connection by way of information linked to a car seized at Logan Airport. It was a Mitsubishi. It was rented by Mohammed (sic) Atta, who lived in an apartment in Hamburg. . . . Inside was a flight manual in Arabic language material that law enforcement investigators say was very helpful," CNN, 13 September 2001.

638 See "Feds Think They've Identified Some Hijackers," which said: "We would like to correct a report that appeared on CNN. Based on information from multiple law enforcement sources, CNN reported that Adnan Bukhari and Ameer Bukhari of Vero Beach Florida, were suspected to be two of the pilots who crashed planes into the World Trade Center. CNN later learned that Adnan Bukhari is still in Florida, where he was questioned by the FBI. We are sorry for the misinformation. . . . Ameer Bukhari died in a small plane crash last year," CNN, 13 September 2001.

639 "According to law enforcement sources, . . . [a] Mitsubishi sedan [Atta] rented was found at Boston's Logan Airport. Arabic language materials were found in the car. . . . [Adnan] Bukhari and Ameer Bukhari . . . had been tied to a car found at an airport in Portland, Maine"; Mike Fish, "Fla. Flight Schools May Have Trained Hijackers," CNN, 14 September 2001 (http://archives.cnn.com/2001/US/09/13/flight.schools).

640 "Portland Police Eye Local Ties," Associated Press, *Portsmouth Herald*, 14 September 2001.

641 Joel Achenbach, "'You Never Imagine' A Hijacker Next Door," *Washington Post*, 16 September 2001.

642 "The Night Before Terror: The FBI Describes Hijacking Suspects' Overnight Stay in Greater Portland," *Portland Press Herald*, 5 October 2001.

643 For example, one of the images circulated by the FBI showed Atta and al-Omari at the Jetport gas station at 8:28:29 PM. But this photo had been cropped to hide the date https://web.archive.org/web/20170717130031/http://www.abc.net.au:80/4corners/atta/resources/photos/gas.htm), and the uncropped version reveals the date to have been 11-10-01, rather than 9-10-01 (https://web.archive.org/web/20081022051431/http://www.rcfp.org/moussaoui/jpg/FO07011-1.jpg). Also, although the video was stamped "8:28 PM," the FBI timeline reported that Atta and al-Omari were at the Jetport station on September 10 at 9:15 PM. Another example: A photo showing Atta and al-Omari passing through the security checkpoint is marked both 05:45 and 05:53 (https://web.archive.org/web/20170325001605/http://www.historycommons.org/context.jsp?item=a553portlandfilmed&scale=0). See Point Video-1, "The Alleged Security Videos of Mohamed Atta."

644 If the affidavit had been signed on September 12, CNN's reports on the 12th (according to which the Bukharis had driven the Nissan to Portland) and the 13th (according to which the materials incriminating al-Qaeda were found in a Mitsubishi that Atta had left in the airport at Boston) would be inexplicable. CNN and other media outlets were getting their information from law enforcement officials (as we saw, CNN said on September 13 that the misinformation it had received about the Bukharis had been "[b]ased on information from multiple law enforcement sources"). If the FBI affidavit in its present form had been signed on the morning of September 12, CNN and other outlets would not have been reporting things to the contrary for several days. It is especially impossible to believe that, if the FBI affidavit had been signed on the morning of September 12, no one in the media would have reported before September 16 that the incriminating materials had been found in Atta's luggage inside the airport. We could hardly imagine stronger evidence that the affidavit was backdated.

645 *The 9/11 Commission Report*, 253.

646 FBI Director Robert S. Mueller III, "Statement for the Record," Joint Intelligence Committee Inquiry, 26 September 2002 (http://www.fas.org/irp/congress/2002_hr/092602mueller.html).

647 *The 9/11 Commission Report*, 1, 253.

648 FBI National Press Office, "Boston Division Seeks Assistance," Washington DC, 4 October 2001 (http://www.fbi.gov/news/pressrel/press-releases/boston-division-seeks-assistance/).

649 Rowland Morgan, *Voices*, unpublished manuscript, 2008: 91-92 (available from author).

650 United States v. Zacarias Moussaoui, Prosecution Trial Exhibits, Exhibit Number FO07011: Security camera photo from Jet Tech gas station, Portland, Maine (http://www.vaed.uscourts.gov/notablecases/moussaoui/exhibits/prosecution/FO07011.html).

651 FBI National Press Office, "Boston Division Seeks Assistance," Washington DC, 5 October 2001 (http://www.fbi.gov/news/pressrel/press-releases/boston-division-seeks-assistance/).

652 Ibid., "9:22 p.m.: Atta was at Wal-Mart, 451 Payne Road, Scarborough, Maine, for approximately 20 minutes."

653 Ibid.

654 Ibid.

655 Ibid.

656 Adding the earlier 5:45 AM time in its strange position in the middle of the frame, thereby obscuring the image, would have given the men more than six minutes to board the plane before it took off on time at 6:00 AM.

657 "Tape Shows Terror Suspects at Airport," *Sun Journal*, Lewiston, Maine, 20 September 2001 (http://news.google.com/newspapers?id=qDxHAAAAI-BAJ&sjid=ivMMAAAAIBAJ&pg=1118,3014556).

658 United States v. Zacarias Moussaoui, *Prosecution Trial Exhibits, Exhibit Number FO07021*, "Still from a security camera at the Portland airport security checkpoint on 11 September 2001 at 05:53:37 showing Mohamed Atta" (http://www.vaed.uscourts.gov/notablecases/moussaoui/exhibits/prosecution/FO07021.html). The other three image exhibits—FO07022, FO07023, and FO07024—are also available (http://www.vaed.uscourts.gov/notablecases/moussaoui/exhibits/prosecution.html).

659 FBI National Press Office, "Boston Division Seeks Assistance," Washington DC, 5 October 2001.

660 Mel Allen, "5 Years after 9/11: Former Portland Ticket Agent Mike Tuohey Is Still Haunted by His Meeting with Mohamed Atta," *Yankee*, 26 September 2006 (http://web.archive.org/web/20061126072733/http://www.yankeemagazine.com/thisissue/features/fiveyears911.php).

661 Ibid.

662 "Tuohey asked about the security camera behind his counter position, noting it would have caught the men's picture as they dealt with him. But he was told that camera was broken and had been out of service for some time." David Hench, "TICKET AGENT HAUNTED BY BRUSH WITH 9/11 HIJACKERS," *Portland Press Herald*, 6 March 2005 (http://web.archive.org/web/20050308004944/http://pressherald.mainetoday.com/news/local/050306terror.shtml)

663 *The 9/11 Commission Report*, 8-9.

664 *The 9/11 Commission Report*, 3.

665 See *The 9/11 Commission Report*, 2-4; also 452, notes 11, 14, 15, and the *Associated Press*, 22 July 2004 (http://web.archive.org/web/20040803061628/http://foi.missouri.edu/terrorintelligence/survvideo.html). The security checkpoint video was never made public by the government, but was reportedly released by a law firm representing victims' families in 2004, and is now available on You Tube (http://www.youtube.com/watch?v=uLEqjpHVPhM).

666 According to the above-cited Associated Press story about the release of the Dulles video, the video showed only four, not five, of the alleged hijackers. (Nick Grimm, "Commission Report Finalized as 9/11 Airport Video Released," ABC Radio [Australia], 22 July 2004 [http://www.abc.net.au/pm/content/2004/s1159804.htm].)

667 David Brent, a technical information engineer for IT systems, stated: "In 2001, I worked for a manufacturer that at the time had its CCTV system in the Washington Dulles International Airport and the Pentagon. After the 9/11 attacks, I was part of a team that had the laborious task

of reviewing all the video from the airport with several federal agents looking over our shoulders. Did you notice I said all the video? That's every frame from over 300 cameras with 30 days of retention time. The task took three weeks of 15-hour days," David Brent, "The CSI Effect: How TV is Changing Video Surveillance," *Security InfoWatch*, 15 February 2011 (http://www.securityinfowatch.com/article/10489184/the-csi-effect-how-tv-is-changing-video-surveillance?page=3).

668 Ibid.

669 *The 9/11 Commission Report*, 452, n. 11.

670 Rowland Morgan and Ian Henshall, *9/11 Revealed: The Unanswered Questions* (Carroll & Graf, 2006), 118.

671 Jay Kolar, "What We Now Know about the Alleged 9-11 Hijackers," in Paul Zarembka, ed., *The Hidden History of 9-11*, updated and revised second edition (Seven Stories, 2008), 3–44.

672 Nick Grimm, "Commission Report Finalized as 9/11 Airport Video Released," ABC Radio (Australia), 22 July 2004 (http://www.abc.net.au/pm/content/2004/s1159804.htm). The video may now be found on YouTube (http://www.youtube.com/watch?v=uLEqjpHVPhM).

673 *The 9/11 Commission Report*, 451.

674 Ibid., 3.

675 Ibid., 3.

676 FBI, "T7 B17 Screeners 9-11 and Check-In Fdr- FBI 302s- Screener and Check-In Interviews" (http://www.scribd.com/doc/13950309/ 7 T7-B1-Screeners-911-and-CheckIn-Fdr-FBI-302s-Screener-and-CheckIn-Interviews). Allex Vaughn Interview, 26 September 2001.

677 Ibid., Trainee Interview (name redacted), 12 September 2001.

678 Ibid., Allex Vaughn Interview, 26 September 2001.

679 *The 9/11 Commission Report*, 3.

680 FBI, "T7 B17 Screeners 9-11 and Check-In Fdr- FBI 302s- Screener and Check-In Interviews," Brenda Brown Interview, 17 September 2001.

681 *The 9/11 Commission Report: Final Report of the National Commission on Terrorist Attacks upon the United States*, authorized edition (W. W. Norton, 2004), 160. The text says: "When Atta arrived in Germany, he appeared religious, but not fanatically so. This would change."

682 Ibid., 154.

683 Eric Bailey, "It Was a Little Strange. Most People Want to Do Take-Offs and Landings. All They Did Was Turns," *Daily Mail*, 16 September 2001.

684 David Wedge, "Terrorists Partied with Hooker at Hub-Area Hotel," *Boston Herald*, 10 October 2001.

685 Kevin Fagan, "Agents of Terror Leave Their Mark on Sin City," *San Francisco Chronicle*, 4 October 2001.

686 "Terrorist Stag Parties," *Wall Street Journal*, 10 October 2001.

687 Jody A. Benjamin, "Suspects' Actions Don't Add Up," *South Florida Sun-Sentinel*, 16 September 2001.

688 *The 9/11 Commission Report*, 248.

689 *The 9/11 Commission Report: Final Report of the National Commission on Terrorist Attacks upon the United States*, authorized edition (W. W. Norton, 2004), 160.

690 Ibid., 154.

691 Ibid., 160. The text says: "When Atta arrived in Germany, he appeared religious, but not fanatically so. This would change."

692 Daniel Hopsicker, "The Secret World of Mohamed Atta: An Interview With Atta's American Girlfriend," *InformationLiberation*, 20 August 2006.

693 Jody A. Benjamin, "Suspects' Actions Don't Add Up," *South Florida Sun-Sentinel*, 16 September 2001.

694 Ken Thomas, "Feds Investigating Possible Terrorist-Attack Links in Florida," Associated Press, 12 September 2001.

695 Barry Klein et al., "FBI Seizes Records of Students at Flight Schools," *St. Petersburg Times*, 13 September 2001.

696 David Wedge, "Terrorists Partied with Hooker at Hub-Area Hotel," *Boston Herald*, 10 October, 2001.

697 Sander Hicks, "No Easy Answer: Heroin, Al Qaeda and the Florida Flight School," *Long Island Press*, 26 February 2004.

698 Elias Davidsson, "The Atta Mystery: Double Agent or Multiple Attas?" Aldeilis.net, 5 October 2011.

699 "Professor Dittmar Machule," Interview by Liz Jackson, A Mission to Die For, Four Corners, 18 October 2001.

700 Carol J. Williams et al., "Mainly, They Just Waited," *Los Angeles Times*, 27 September, 2001.

701 Ibid.

702 Peter Finn, "Suspects Used German Rental As Headquarters," *Washington Post*, 15 September 2001.

703 Ibid.

704 Bundeskriminalamt, Zeugenvernehmung von Bejaoui, Bechir, Hamburg, 5-10-2001.

705 Interview of Quentin McDermott with Rudy Dekkers, ABC Australia, 21 October 2001.

706   *The 9/11 Commission Report*, 224.

707   Stephen J. Hedges and Jeff Zeleny, "Hijacker Eluded Security Net," *Chicago Tribune*, 16 September 2001.

708   Elaine Allen-Emrich and Jann Baty, "Hunt for Terrorists Reaches North Port," *Charlotte Sun*, 14 September 2001.

709   Jackson, "Professor Dittmar Machule."

710   There is considerable evidence that the man who was calling himself "Mohamed Atta" in the United States prior to 9/11, and who after 9/11 was accused of being one of the (alleged) hijackers, was not the real Mohamed Atta. In the first place, the behavior and attitudes of the two men were reportedly very different. See Chapter 44, above.

711   See Sections II and IV under *Best Evidence*.

712   "Lt. Col. Shaffer's Written Testimony: Able Danger and the 9/11 Attacks," Armed Services Committee, US House of Representatives, 15 February 2006 (http://www.abledangerblog.com/2006/02/lt-col-shaffers-written-testimony.html); information is also found in additional articles (http://fas.org/irp/congress/2006_hr/021506shaffer.pdf) and (http://www.historycommons.org/context.jsp?item=a092501attaidentified#a092501attaidentified).

713   "Lt. Col. Shaffer's Written Testimony: Able Danger and the 9/11 Attacks," Armed Services Committee, US House of Representatives, 15 February 2006; see also http://fas.org/irp/congress/2006_hr/021506shaffer.pdf.

714   Representative Curt Weldon (R-Penn.), US House of Representatives, 27 June 2005 (www.fas.org/irp/congress/2005_cr/s062705.html) and "Lt. Col. Shaffer's Written Testimony: Able Danger and the 9/11 Attacks," Armed Services Committee, US House of Representatives, 15 February 2006.

715   Jacob Goodwin, "Inside Able Danger—The Secret Birth, Extraordinary Life and Untimely Death of a U.S. Military Intelligence Program," *Government Security News*, circa 23 August 2005 (http://web.archive.org/web/20050924164439/http://www.gsnmagazine.com/sep_05/shaffer_interview.html).

716   Keith Phucas, "Missed chance on Way to 9/11," *Times Herald*, 19 June 2005.

717   *US Congressional Record*, 25 June 2005: H5249, (www.fas.org/irp/congress/2005_cr/s062705.html).

718   "Kean-Hamilton Statement on Able Danger," 12 August 2005 (http://web.archive.org/web/20050819153451/http://www.9-11pdp.org/press/2005-08-12_pr.pdf).

719   See Senator Joe Biden's comment during the 21 September 2005, Senate Hearing (http://fas.org/irp/congress/2005_hr/shrg109-311.html). See

also Shaun Waterman, "Pentagon Gags 'Able Danger' Team," *UPI Business News*, 20 September 2005.

720 "Able Danger and Intelligence Information Sharing," Hearing before the Committee on the Judiciary, United States Senate, 21 September 2005 (http://fas.org/irp/congress/2005_hr/shrg109-311.html).

721 "Curt Weldon Address to the House: Able Danger Failure," *US Congressional Record*, 19 October 2005: H8983 (www.fas.org/irp/congress/2005_cr/weldon101905.html).

722 US Department of Defense, Office of Inspector General, "Report of Investigation, Alleged Misconduct by Senior DOD Officials Concerning the Able Danger Program and Lieutenant Colonel Anthony A. Shaffer, U.S. Army Reserve," 18 September 2006 (http://fas.org/irp/agency/dod/ig-abledanger-alt.pdf).

723 *The 9/11 Commission Report*, July 2004: 434.

724 Thomas R. Eldridge et al., "9/11 and Terrorist Travel: Staff Report of the National Commission on Terrorist Attacks Upon the United States, 11 (http://www.9-11commission.gov/staff_statements/911_TerrTrav_Monograph.pdf). See also *The 9/11 Commission Report*, 519, and "Kean-Hamilton Statement on Able Danger."

725 Philip Shenon, "Second Officer Says 9/11 Leader Was Named Before Attacks," *New York Times*, 23 August 2005.

726 Philip Shenon and Douglas Jehl, "9/11 Panel Seeks Inquiry on New Atta Report," *New York Times*, 10 August 2005 (http://web.archive.org/web/20150403064739/http://www.nytimes.com/2005/08/10/politics/10intel.html).

727 "Kean-Hamilton Statement on Able Danger," 12 August 2005.

728 Ibid.

729 Devlin Barrett, "Panel Rejects Assertion US Knew of Atta before Sept. 11," *Associated Press*, 15 September 2005.

730 Philip Shenon, "Pentagon Bars Military Officers and Analysts From Testifying," *New York Times*, 21 September 2005.

731 US Department of Defense, Office of Inspector General, "Report of Investigation, Alleged Misconduct by Senior DOD Officials Concerning the Able Danger Program and Lieutenant Colonel Anthony A. Shaffer, U.S. Army Reserve," 18 September 2006.

732 "Able Danger and Intelligence Information Sharing," Hearing before the Committee on the Judiciary, United States Senate, 21 September 2005.

733 Brian Ross, "Face to Face with a Terrorist: Government Worker Recalls Mohamed Atta Seeking Funds Before Sept. 11," 6 June 2002 (http://web.archive.org/web/20020725114958/http://abcnews.go.com/sections/wnt/DailyNews/ross_bryant020606.html).

734   "The Night before Terror," *Portland Press Herald*, 5 October 2001.

735   Pat Milton, "Investigator: Hijack leader Atta Visited New York before Attacks," Associated Press, 10 December 2001.

736   Keith Phucas, "Able Danger Source Goes Public," *The Times Herald*, 17 August 2005. Shaffer's attorney, Mark Zaid, testified: "It is Lt Col Shaffer's specific recollection that he informed those in attendance, which included Defense Department personnel, that Able Danger had identified two of the three successful 9/11 cells to include Atta." See "Prepared Statement of Mark S. Zaid," hearing ("Able Danger and Intelligence Information Sharing") before the Committee on the Judiciary, United States Senate, 21 September 2005.

737   The 9/11 Commission, "Memorandum for the Record: Interview— Commander Scott Phillpott," 13 July 2004 (http://cryptome.org/nara/phill-04-0713.pdf).

738   "Kean-Hamilton Statement on Able Danger," 12 August 2005.

739   Lt. Col. Shaffer's written testimony to the Senate Hearing, 15 February 2006.

740   "An Incomplete Investigation: Why did the 9/11 Commission Ignore 'Able Danger'?" *Wall Street Journal*, 17 November 2005 (http://web.archive.org/web/20061022130507/http://www.opinionjournal.com/extra/?id=110007559).

741   Philip Shenon, "Pentagon Bars Military Officers and Analysts from Testifying," *New York Times*, 21 September 2005.

742   David Morgan, "Pentagon Blocking September 11 Inquiry: Senator," posted 23 September 2005 (http://veteransforcommonsense.org/2005/09/23/pentagon-blocking-september-11-inquiry-senator-2/). Originally published by Reuters, 21 September 2005 (no longer available but picked up by *Pravda* (http://english.pravda.ru/news/world/americas/22-09-2005/66445-0/).

743   Curt Weldon, Address to the House, *Congressional Record*, 27 June 2005: H5250.

744   Keith Phucas, "Able Danger Source Goes Public," *The Times Herald*, 17 August 2005.

745   Philip Shenon, "Naval Officer Says Atta's Identity Known Pre-9/11: Captain is Second Military Man to Say Terrorist Was Named," *New York Times*, 23 August 2005, picked up by *San Francisco Chronicle* (http://www.sfgate.com/news/article/Naval-officer-says-Atta-s-identity-known-pre-9-11-2614972.php).

746   "Third Source Backs 'Able Danger' Claims about Atta," Fox News, 28 August 2005 (http://www.foxnews.com/story/2005/08/28/third-source-backs-able-danger-claims-about-atta.html). Note that Christopher Kojm's name was incorrectly reported as "Cojm" in the news story.

747   James Rosen, "Able Danger Hearing Sets Intelligence Officers at Odds,"
      The News & Observer, 16 February 2006. (http://web.archive.org/
      web/20090506125755/http://www.newsobserver.com/114/story/400682.
      html).

748   US Department of Defense, Office of Inspector General, "Report of
      Investigation, Alleged Misconduct by Senior DOD Officials Concerning
      the Able Danger Program and Lieutenant Colonel Anthony A. Shaffer,
      U.S. Army Reserve," 18 September 2006: 32.

749   Joint Hearing on the Able Danger Program, Subcommittees on Strategic
      Forces and on Terrorism, Unconventional Threats, and Capabilities, House
      Armed Services Committee, 15 February 2006(http://web.archive.org/
      web/20170622073459/http://www.abledangerblog.com/hearing.pdf).

750   Associated Press, "More Remember Atta ID'd as Terrorist Pre-9/11," 1
      September 2005; Thom Shanker, "Terrorist Known Before 9/11, More Say,"
      New York Times, 2 September 2005.

751   Sherman de Brosse, "Able Danger, Mohamed Atta and Ali Mohammed," 5
      November 2010 (https://therearenosunglasses.wordpress.com/2010/11/05/
      able-danger-mohamed-atta-and-ali-mohammed/).

752   David Ray Griffin, *The New Pearl Harbor Revisited: 9/11, the Cover-Up,
      and the Exposé* (Interlink, 2008), 187–95.

753   US Department of Defense, Office of Inspector General, "Report of
      Investigation, Alleged Misconduct by Senior DOD Officials Concerning
      the Able Danger Program and Lieutenant Colonel Anthony A. Shaffer,
      U.S. Army Reserve," 18 September 2006: 32.

754   "Weldon Rejects DOD Report on Able Danger & Harassment of Military
      Officer," 21 September 2006 (www.fas.org/irp/news/2006//09/wel-
      don092106.html).

755   Tim O'Brien, "Wife of Solicitor General Alerted Him of Hijacking from
      Plane," CNN, 12 September 2001.

756   *The 9/11 Commission Report*, 5; Charles Lane and John Mintz, "Bid
      to Thwart Hijackers May Have Led to Pa. Crash," *Washington Post*, 13
      September 2001; David Maraniss, "Another Workday Becomes a Surreal
      Plane of Terror," *Washington Post*, 21 September 2001.

757   *The 9/11 Commission Report*, 8.

758   David Ray Griffin, *9/11 Ten Years Later: When State Crimes Against
      Democracy Succeed* (Interlink, 2011), Chapter 5, "Phone Calls from the
      9/11 Planes: How They Fooled America."

759   Greg Gordon, "Jurors Hear Final Struggle of Flight 93: Moussaoui Trial
      Plays Cockpit Tape of Jet that Crashed Sept. 11," *Sacramento Bee*, 13 April
      2006.

760 Lisa D. Jefferson and Felicia Middlebrooks, *Called: Hello, My Name Is Mrs. Jefferson. I Understand Your Plane Is Being Hijacked. 9:45 AM, Flight 93, September 11, 2001* (Northfield Publishing, 2006), 53; Jim McKinnon, "13-Minute Call Bonds Her Forever with Hero," *Pittsburgh Post-Gazette*, 22 September 2001.

761 *The 9/11 Commission Report*, 13, 456 note 80, 457 note 81.

762 Jefferson and Middlebrooks, *Called*, 47–48.

763 The 9/11 Commission, "Memorandum for the Record," 13 May 2004 (http://www.scribd.com/doc/19987615/Mfr-Nara-t7-Doj-Doj-Briefing-on-Ua93-Calls-51304-00217). The graphics produced by the US prosecution for the trial of Zacarias Moussaoui in 2006 are easily accessed here: "Detailed Account of Telephone Calls From September 11th Flights: Todd Beamer" (http://911research.wtc7.net/planes/evidence/calldetail.html).

764 Beamer talked to Phyllis Johnson, a GTE operator, for a few minutes, after which he was transferred to Lisa Jefferson, with whom he talked, she said, for "approximately fifteen more minutes" (Jefferson and Middlebrooks, *Called*, 53); McKinnon, "13-Minute Call Bonds Her Forever With Hero."

765 FBI Interview with Lisa Jefferson, 11 September 11 2001 (http://intelfiles.egoplex.com/2001-09-11-FBI-FD302-lisa-jefferson.pdf).

766 "Bush: 'My Fellow Americans, Let's Roll,'" Jessica Reaves, *Time* magazine, 9 November 2001.

767 Peter Perl, "Hallowed Ground," *Washington Post*, 12 May 2002 (http://www.washingtonpost.com/wp-srv/liveonline/02/magazine/magazine_perl051302.htm).

768 The thirteen minutes is referenced in Jefferson's interview with staff writer Jim McKinnon, "13-Minute Call Bonds Her Forever With Hero," *Pittsburgh Post-Gazette*, 22 September 2001, and in Wes Smith, "Operator Can't Forget Haunting Cries From Flight 93," *Orlando Sentinel*, 5 September 2002 (http://www.highbeam.com/doc/1G1-120211044.html).

769 Lisa Beamer and Ken Abraham, *Let's Roll!: Ordinary People, Extraordinary Courage* (Wheaton, IL: Tyndale House Publishers, 2002), 217.

770 Jefferson and Middlebrooks, *Called*, 47–48.

771 The graphics produced by the US prosecution for the trial of Zacarias Moussaoui in 2006 are readily accessed here: "Detailed Account of Telephone Calls From September 11th Flights: Todd Beamer" (http://911research.wtc7.net/planes/evidence/calldetail.html).

772 Jere Longman, *Among the Heroes* (Harper Perennial, 2003), 204.

773 Wendy Schuman, "'I Promised I Wouldn't Hang Up,'" Beliefnet, 2006 (http://www.beliefnet.com/Inspiration/2006/06/I-Promised-I-Wouldnt-Hang-Up.aspx?p=1).

774 Jefferson and Middlebrooks, *Called*, 33.

775　Beamer and Abraham, *Let's Roll!*, 211.

776　Jefferson and Middlebrooks, *Called*, 36.

777　Jefferson and Middlebrooks, *Called*, Ch. 1.

778　See the FBI Intelfiles page that lists Beamer-call interviews (http://news. intelwire.com/2008/03/911-commission-fbi-source-documents.html).

779　"Detailed Account of Telephone Calls From September 11th Flights: Todd Beamer" (http://911research.wtc7.net/planes/evidence/calldetail.html).

Primary sources: Letter and faxed telephone report from US Department of Justice to the National Commission on Terrorist Attacks, 26 April 2004 (http://www.scribd.com/doc/13499791/T7-B13-Flight-11-Calls-Fdr-Response-From-DOJ-to-Doc-Req-14-Calls-From-AA-11-and-77-and-UA-175-and-93-ATT-Wireless-UA-And-GTE-Airphone-Call-Record).

780　Wendy Schuman, "'I Promised I Wouldn't Hang Up,'" Beliefnet, 2006 (http://www.beliefnet.com/Inspiration/2006/06/I-Promised-1-Wouldnt-Hang-Up.aspx?p=1).

781　FBI Lead Control Number NK 5381, 29 September 2001 (http://intelfiles. egoplex.com/2001-09-29-FBI-phone-records.pdf). (Todd Beamer's cell phone area was in northern New Jersey [prefix 908], so the records reflect the Eastern Time zone; see http://phones.whitepages.com/908-930.)

782　"FBI Interview with Lisa Jefferson, 11 September 2011," Intelwire.com (http://intelfiles.egoplex.com/2001-09-11-FBI-FD302-lisa-jefferson.pdf).

783　Jim McKinnon, "The Phone Line from Flight 93 Was Still Open when a GTE Operator Heard Todd Beamer Say: 'Are You Guys Ready? Let's Roll,'" *Pittsburgh Post-Gazette*, 16 September 2001.

784　Great thanks are due to an essay by Shoestring 9/11, "Todd Beamer's Odd Phone Call and the Silent Crash of Flight 93," for several points (http:// shoestring911.blogspot.com/2007/10/todd-beamers-odd-phone-call-and-silent.html).

785　Lisa Beamer and Ken Abraham, *Let's Roll!: Ordinary People, Extraordinary Courage* (Tyndale House, 2002), 185.

786　Lisa D. Jefferson and Felicia Middlebrooks, *Called* (Northfield Publishing, 2006), 53; Jim McKinnon, "13-Minute Call Bonds Her Forever with Hero," *Pittsburgh Post-Gazette*, 22 September 2001.

787　"Bush: 'My Fellow Americans, Let's Roll,'" Jessica Reaves, *Time* magazine, 9 November 2001.

788　Peter Perl, "Hallowed Ground," *Washington Post*, 12 May 2002 (http:// www.washingtonpost.com/wp-srv/liveonline/02/magazine/magazine_ perl051302.htm).

789　*The 9/11 Commission Report*, 2004: 11.

790 Ibid., see note 70, "Commission Review of Aircraft Communication and Reporting System (ACARS) messages sent to and from Flight 93 (which indicate time of message transmission and receipt)"; see 456 note 71: "On flight data recording (FDR), see NTSB report, "Specialist's Factual Report of Investigation — Digital Flight Data Recorder" (www.gwu.edu/~nsar-chiv/NSAEBB/NSAEBB196/doc04.pdf). For United Airlines Flight 93, 15 February 2002, and on cockpit voice recording (CVR), see FBI report, "CVR from UA Flight #93," 4 December 2003 [http://intelfiles.egoplex.com/2003-12-04-FBI-cockpit-recorder-93.pdf]; FAA report, "Summary of Air Traffic Hijack Events: September 11, 2001," 17 September 2001; NTSB report, "Air Traffic Control Recording — United Airlines Flight 93," 21 December 2001 (http://www.ntsb.gov/doclib/foia/9_11/ATC_Report_UA93.pdf).

791 "Detailed Account of Telephone Calls from September 11th Flights: Todd Beamer" (http://911research.wtc7.net/planes/evidence/calldetail.html).

Primary sources: Letter and faxed telephone report from U.S. Department of Justice to the National Commission on Terrorist Attacks, 26 April 2004 (http://www.scribd.com/doc/13499791/T7-B13-Flight-11-Calls-Fdr-Re-sponse-From-DOJ-to-Doc-Req-14-Calls-From-AA-11-and-77-and-UA-175-and-93-ATT-Wireless-UA-And-GTE-Airphone-Call-Record).

792 Lisa Jefferson interview, 11 September 2001 (http://intelfiles.egoplex.com/2001-09-11-FBI-FD302-lisa-jefferson.pdf).

793 *The 9/11 Commission Report*, 11.

794 Lisa Jefferson FBI Interview.

795 *The 9/11 Commission Report*, 11.

796 Lisa Jefferson FBI Interview.

797 Wendy Schuman, "'I Promised I Wouldn't Hang Up,'" Beliefnet, 2006.

798 Tim O'Brien, "Wife of Solicitor General Alerted Him of Hijacking from Plane," CNN, 12 September 2001, 2:06 AM (http://archives.cnn.com/2001/US/09/11/pentagon.olson). Although this story, as now found in the CNN archives, indicates that the story was posted at 2:06 AM on September 12, reports of the story started appearing on blogs at 3:51 PM on the 11th (see http://www.fantasticforum.com/archive_2/911/11sep01_barbaraolsonkilled.pdf and http://forum.dvdtalk.com/archive/index.php/t-141263.html).

799 "Interview with Theodore Olsen [sic]," *9/11 Commission, FBI Source Documents, Chronological, September 11*, 2001Intelfiles.com, 14 March 2008 (http://intelfiles.egoplex.com/2001-09-11-FBI-FD302-theodore-olsen.pdf).

800 *Hannity & Colmes*, Fox News, 14 September 2001.

801 Ted Olson again gave the cell phone version on *Larry King Live*, CNN, 14 September 2001. He suggested the seatback phone version on three additional occasions: *Hannity & Colmes*, Fox News, 14 September 2001;

Theodore B. Olson, "Barbara K. Olson Memorial Lecture," 16 November 2001, Federalist Society, 15th Annual National Lawyers Convention (https://web.archive.org/web/20070912031207/http://www.fed-soc.org/resources/id.63/default.asp); and Toby Harnden, "She Asked Me How to Stop the Plane," *Daily Telegraph*, 5 March 2002.

802 "Interview with Theodore Olsen [sic]," *9/11 Commission, FBI Source Documents, Chronological, September 11*, 2001Intelfiles.com, 14 March 2008 (http://intelfiles.egoplex.com/2001-09-11-FBI-FD302-theodore-olsen.pdf).

803 "America's New War: Recovering from Tragedy," *Larry King Live*, CNN, 14 September 2001.

804 *The 9/11 Commission Report*, 455, n. 57.

805 "T7 B12 Flight 93 Calls- General Fdr-5-20-04 DOJ Briefing on Cell and Phone Calls From AA 77 408," Federal Bureau of Investigation, 20 May 2004 (http://www.scribd.com/doc/18886083/T7-B12-Flight-93-Calls-General-Fdr-52004-DOJ-Briefing-on-Cell-and-Phone-Calls From-AA-77-408).

806 The first three of the four calls attributed to Barbara Olson in *The 9/11 Commission Report* (p. 455, note 57) were, like all of the reported calls by Tom Burnett to his wife, far above an elevation at which cell phone calls might have been possible (National Transportation Safety Board, "Flight Path Study, American Airlines Flight 77," 19 February 2002). And the fourth call (reported by the 9/11 Commission as lasting 4 minutes and 20 seconds), was dialed at 9:30:56, when AA 77 was reportedly flying erratically up and down between 6,000 and 7,000 feet(see *NTSB Flight Path Study*, AA 77, as above).

807 This document is available at Pilots for 9/11 Truth (http://pilotsfor-911truth.org/AA757AMM.html).

808 Email letters to Rob Balsamo and David Griffin, 22 December 2009.

809 Letter from Ginger Gainer to David Griffin, 16 February 2011. The practice of using inoperative stickers for deactivated airphones was confirmed to Elizabeth Woodworth in a telephone call to a former AA mechanic, 7 January 2013. The time it would have taken to deactivate the phones on the ECO FO878 order, which involved pulling the circuit breakers and collaring them, was estimated by this mechanic to have taken 20–30 minutes.

810 See note 15, below.

811 United States v. Zacarias Moussaoui, Prosecution Trial Exhibit P200054. This FBI report on phone calls from AA 77 can be viewed more easily in an article by Jim Hoffman, "Detailed Account of Phone Calls from September 11th Flights" (http://911research.wtc7.net/planes/evidence/calldetail.html).

812   Whereas Ted Olson said that his wife called him twice, the Department of Justice and its FBI said in 2006 that the records show that she had attempted only one call to him, which was not connected. But the DOJ's records also indicate that there were three calls that *were* connected but were from an unknown caller to an unknown recipient, and the DOJ and the FBI declared, prior to the evidence it presented under oath at the 2006 Moussaoui trial, that they believed all of these to have been from Barbara Olson to her husband: See the previous note and also a DOJ memorandum for the record, "Briefing on cell and phone calls from Flight 77," 20 May 2004 (http://www.scribd.com/doc/18886083/T7-B12-Flight-93-Calls-General-Fdr-52004-DOJ-Briefing-on-Cell-and-Phone-Calls-From-AA-77-408). With regard to the question of whether this multi-call claim should be taken seriously, it is strange that the investigators, who went to great lengths to identify the phone call recipients for Flight 77, should have failed to retrieve from AT&T Wireless the recipients of four long operator-dialed (OSPS) calls from this flight. The information regarding Flight 77 calls reported by the Department of Justice was derived from "a study of all phone records from the flight, an examination of the cell phone records of each of the passengers aboard 9/11 [sic] who owned cell phones, and interviews with those who received calls from the flight, as well as with the family members of other passengers and crew. This work was conducted in support of the U.S. Justice Department's case against Zacarias Moussaoui [http://www.scribd.com/doc/18886083/T7-B12-Flight-93-Calls-General-Fdr-52004-DOJ-Briefing-on-Cell-and-Phone-Calls-From-AA-77-408]." This note has been taken from Elizabeth Woodworth, "9/11: What the Telephone Records Reveal about Calls from AA Flight 77: Did Barbara Olson Attempt Any Calls at All?" 16 September 2011.

813   Shoestring 9/11, "The Flight 77 Murder Mystery: Who Really Killed Charles Burlingame?" 2 February 2008 (http://shoestring911.blogspot.com/2008/02/flight-77-murder-mystery-who-really.html).

814   "Staff No. Statement 16: Outline of the 9/11 Plot," 9/11 Commission, 16 June 2004.

815   The evidence shows only that Barbara Olson did not call Ted Olson's office from aboard AA 77. That conclusion leaves open the possibility that Ted Olson's office may have received calls that people in this office *believed* to be from Barbara Olson while she was in the air on AA 77. This distinction is important because of evidence (1) that Lori Keyton, who was serving as a secretary in Ted Olson's office that morning, reported receiving two calls for him that morning (see Interview with Lori Lynn Keyton, Secretary, DOJ, 11 September 2001 [http://www.scribd.com/doc/15072623/T1A-B33-Four-Flights-Phone-Calls-and-Other-Data-Fdr-Entire-Contents-FBI-302s-843]), and (2) that these calls were forwarded to Ted Olson's special assistant, Helen Voss (see Interview with Helen Voss, Special Assistant to the Solicitor General, September 11, 2001 [http://www.scribd.com/doc/15072623/

T1A-B33-Four-Flights-Phone-Calls-and-Other-Data-Fdr-Entire-Con-tents-FBI-302s-843]). As to how these calls were really made, the publicly available evidence seems insufficient to answer that question.

816 "Were Hijackers Reported on Cell Phone Calls?" Chapter 17 of David Ray Griffin, *9/11 Contradictions: An Open Letter to Congress and the Press* (Interlink, 2008). The media did not investigate these cell phone reports at a time when the use of cell phones on airliners was not only highly unlikely but was also prohibited by regulations from both the Federal Aviation Authority and the Federal Communications Commission. See "In-Flight Phone-Free Zone May End," CNN, 3 October 2004.

817 "'I know we're All Going to Die,'" BBC, 12 September 2001.

818 Charles Lane and John Mintz, "Bid to Thwart Hijackers May Have Led to Pa. Crash," *Washington Post*, 13 September 2001.

819 Ibid.

820 Tim O'Brien, "Wife of Solicitor General Alerted Him of Hijacking from Plane," CNN, 12 September 2001, 2:06 AM (http://archives.cnn.com/2001/US/09/11/pentagon.olson). Although this story, as now found in the CNN archives, indicates that the story was posted at 2:06 AM on September 12, reports of the story started appearing on blogs at 3:51 PM on September 11 (see http://www.fantasticforum.com/archive_2/911/11sep01_bar-baraolsonkilled.pdf and http://forum.dvdtalk.com/archive/index.php/t-141263.html). On Fox News three days later, Olson suggested that she had been using the "airplane phone" (*Hannity & Colmes*, Fox News, 14 September 2001). Later that same day, Olson told Larry King that she must have used a cell phone ("America's New War: Recovering from Tragedy," *Larry King Live*, CNN, 14 September 2001. In November, he endorsed the onboard phone version of the story (Theodore B. Olson, "Barbara K. Olson Memorial Lecture," 16 November 2001, Federalist Society [http://www.fed-soc.org/resources/id.63/default.asp]), which he then repeated a few months later in an interview in what appears to have been his final public statement on this issue (Toby Harnden, "She Asked Me How to Stop the Plane," *Daily Telegraph*, March 5, 2002. A year after 9/11, however, CNN was still reporting that Barbara Olson had called her husband "on her cellular phone" ("On September 11, Final Words of Love," CNN, 10 September 2002.

821 For example, David Maraniss, in a *Washington Post* article four days after the attack, said: "By 9:25, one of the passengers, Barbara K. Olson, the television commentator, was on the cell phone with her husband, U.S. Solicitor General Theodore B. Olson." David Maraniss, "September 11, 2001," *Washington Post*, 16 September 2001; updated September 20, 2001 (story available with a new title "Another Workday Becomes a Surreal Plane of Terror", at (http://911research.wtc7.net/cache/planes/attack/startribune_surrealplane.html). Olson's FBI interview, carried out on 9/11, is available online (http://intelfiles.egoplex.com/2001-09-11-FBI-FD302-theodore-olsen.pdf).

822   Karen Gullo and John Solomon, "Experts, U.S. Suspect Osama bin Laden, Accused Architect of World's Worst Terrorist Attacks," Associated Press, 11 September 2001 (http://web.archive.org/web/20080930191242/http://www. sfgate.com/today/suspect.shtml). Mr. Hanson's FBI interview on 9/11, saying that he believed his son was calling from his cell phone, is available online (http://intelfiles.egoplex.com/2001-09-11-FBI-FD302-peter-hanson. pdf). Hanson's mother, Mrs. Eunice Hanson, reported the cell phone call to others interviewed by the FBI (http://www.scribd.com/doc/47935437/ T7-B13-DOJ-Doc-Req-35-13-Packet-8-Fdr-Entire-Contents).

823   Charles Lane and John Mintz, "Bid to Thwart Hijackers May Have Led to Pa. Crash," *Washington Post*, 13 September 2001 (http://www.highbeam. com/doc/1P2-459249.html).

824   David Maraniss, "September 11, 2001," *Washington Post*, 16 September 2001.

825   Julie Sweeney's FBI interview is available online (http://www.scribd.com/ doc/47935437/T7-B13-DOJ-Doc-Req-35-13-Packet-8-Fdr-Entire-Contents), see page 15. The elevation is shown on page 4 of the NTSB Flight Path Study.

826   Martha Raffaele, "Passengers May Have Thwarted Hijackers," Associated Press, 12 September 2001 (http://www.apnewsarchive. com/2001/Passengers-May-Have-Thwarted-Hijackers/id-7244be734c-7068713677e337bf9dd2f4. Deena Burnett's FBI interview is available online (http://intelfiles.egoplex.com/2001-09-11-FBI-FD302-deena-lynne-burnett.pdf).

827   See Greg Gordon, "Widow Tells of Poignant Last Calls," *Sacramento Bee*, 11 September 2002.

828   "Two Years Later...," *CBS News*, 10 September 2003 (http://www.cbsnews. com/2100-500168_162-572380.html).

829   Jim McKinnon, "13-Minute Call Bonds Her Forever with Hero," *Pittsburgh Post-Gazette*, 22 September 2001. An FBI interview conducted 20 September 2001 indicated that Britton had called using a "cellular telephone" during the hijacking of Flight 93 (http://intelfiles.egoplex.com/2001-09-22-FBI-United-93-marion-britton.pdf).

830   FBI, "Interview with Lee Hanson" (http://intelfiles.egoplex.com/2001-09-11-FBI-FD302-lee-hanson.pdf).

831   FBI, "Interview with Deena Lynne Burnett (re: phone call from hijacked flight)," 9/11 Commission, FBI Source Documents, Chronological, 11 September 2001, Intelfiles.com, 11 September 2001 (http://intelfiles. egoplex.com/2001-09-11-FBI-FD302-deena-lynne-burnett.pdf).

832   *The 9/11 Commission Report*, 12.

833   According to Marco Thompson, president of the San Diego Telecom Council, "Cell phones are not designed to work on a plane. Although

they do." The rough rule is that when the plane is slow and over a city, the phone will work up to 10,000 feet or so. "Also, it depends on how fast the plane is moving and its proximity to antennas," Thompson says. "At 30,000 feet, it may work momentarily while near a cell site, but it's chancy and the connection won't last." Also, the hand-off process from cell site to cell site is more difficult. It is created for a maximum speed of 60 mph to 100 mph. "They are not built for 400 mph airplanes." *San Diego Metropolitan*, October 2001 (http://web.archive.org/web/20120829085458/http://sandiegometro.archives.whsites.net:80/2001/oct/sdscene.html).

834 A. K. Dewdney, "Project Achilles Report: Parts One, Two and Three," Physics 911, 23 January 2003 (http://www.physics911.net/projectachilles); "The Cellphone and Airfone Calls from Flight UA93," Physics 911, 9 June 2003 (http://physics911.net/cellphoneflight93.htm).

835 The results of Dewdney's twin-engine experiments are reported in Barrie Zwicker, *Towers of Deception: The Media Cover-Up of 9/11* (New Society Publishers, 2006), 375.

836 For example: According to the 9/11 Commission's report, which reflected official documents, United Flight 93 was at 34,300 feet when passengers and crew members began making calls, and it soon climbed "to 40,700 feet" (*The 9/11 Commission Report*, 11–12, 29). The times of the reported calls (available at http://911research.wtc7.net/planes/evidence/calldetail.html) may be compared with the timed flight path elevations (available at http://911research.wtc7.net/planes/evidence/ntsb.html).

837 Betsy Harter, "Final Contact," *Telephony's Wireless Review*, 1 November 2001 (http://wirelessreview.com/ar/wireless final contact); "Will They Allow Cell Phones on Planes?" *The Travel Technologist*, 19 September 2001 (http://web.archive.org/web/20020405031059/http://elliott.org/technology/2001/cellpermit.htm); Michel Chossudovsky, "More Holes in the Official Story: The 911 Cell Phone Calls," *Global Research*, 10 August 2004; Ted Twietmeyer, "911 Cell Phone Calls from Planes? Not Likely," 23 August 2004 (http://www.rense.com/general56/cellpp.htm).

838 QUALCOMM Press Release, "American Airlines and QUALCOMM Complete Test Flight to Evaluate In-Cabin Mobile Phone Use," 15 July 2004 (http://www.qualcomm.com/news/releases/2004/07/15/american-airlines-and-qualcomm-complete-test-flight-evaluate-cabin-mobile-p).

839 Stephen Castle, "Era of In-Flight Mobile Phone Use Begins in Europe," *New York Times*, 18 April 2008. In contradiction with this report and those in the six previous notes, the *New York Times*, three days after 9/11, published a story stating that "cell phones can work in almost all phases of a commercial flight" (Simon Romero, "After the Attacks: Communications; New Perspective on the Issue of Cell Phone Use in Planes," *New York Times*, 14 September 2001. This story was evidently intended to tamp down doubts about whether the reported cell phone calls from the planes could have occurred.

840 For example, such data have been available (through a Texas law firm) since 2000 (https://web.archive.org/web/20130625190415/http://www. alexanderresources.com/Cell_Phone_Records_Billing_Usage_Expert_ Witness.htm?gclid=CPLXlvHk47UCFYpDMgod5lAAnQ).

841 These data would certainly have been sourced during the "study of all phone records from the flight, an examination of the cell phone records of each of the passengers aboard 9/11 [sic] who owned cell phones, and interviews with those who received calls from the flight, as well as with the family members of other passengers and crew. This work was conducted in support of the U.S. Justice Department's case against Zacarias Moussaoui" (http://www.scribd.com/doc/18886083/T7-B12-Flight-93-Calls-General-Fdr-52004-DOJ-Briefing-on-Cell-and-Phone-Calls-From-AA-77-408). However, these data have never been cited by officials to (1) justify changing the status of earlier reports of cell phone calls to seatback calls, or (2)support the status of the two alleged low-flying cell phone calls by Felt and Lyles.

842 *The 9/11 Commission Report*, 8 (Hanson and Brian Sweeney), 9 (Olson), 11, 28 (Burnett), and 456 (Bingham and Glick).

843 *The 9/11 Commission Report* disguised, perhaps deliberately, the fact that it was not affirming any cell phone calls other than the reported 9:58 calls from UA 93 by Edward Felt and CeeCee Lyles. Writing about this flight, for example, the commission said: "Shortly [after 9:32], the passengers and flight crew began a series of calls from GTE airphones and cellular phones" (*The 9/11 Commission Report*, 12). One could easily believe that the commissionhad thereby affirmed the occurrence of several cell phone calls (some of which would have been high-altitude calls). But a staff report for the 9/11 Commission dated 26 August 2004 (http://www. archives.gov/research/9-11/staff-report.pdf), by indicating that only the 9:58 calls by Felt and Lyles were made from cell phones (p. 45), made apparent that the only cell phone calls in the commission's alleged "series of calls from GTE airphones and cellular phones" were those of Felt and Lyles. The August 2004 Staff Report cited the FBI interviews with the recipients of the calls from Felt and Lyles, which the commission had cited in its July 2004 report.

844 Greg Gordon, "Prosecutors Play Flight 93 Cockpit Record-ing," KnoxNews.com, 12 April 2006 (http://web.archive.org/ web/20071130032831/http://www.knoxsingles.com/shns/story. cfm?pk=MOUSSAOUI-04-12-06&cat=WW).

845 Gordon, "Prosecutors Play Flight 93 Cockpit Recording."

846 "Flight Path Study: United Airlines Flight 93," National Transportation Safety Board, 19 February 2002.

847 United States v. Zacarias Moussaoui, Exhibit Number P200054 (http:// www.vaed.uscourts.gov/notablecases/moussaoui/exhibits/prosecution/ flights/P200054.html). These documents have been made more readily

accessible by 9/11 researcher Jim Hoffman in "Detailed Account of Phone Calls from September 11th Flights" (http://911research.wtc7.net/planes/evidence/calldetail.html).

848 See "Detailed Account of Phone Calls from September 11th Flights" (http://911research.wtc7.net/planes/evidence/calldetail.html).

849 Ibid.

850 A. K. Dewdney, "Project Achilles Report: Parts One, Two and Three," Physics 911, 23 January 2003 (http://www.physics911.net/projectachilles); "The Cellphone and Airfone Calls from Flight UA93," Physics 911, 9 June 2003 (http://physics911.net/cellphoneflight93.htm). For the results of Dewdney's twin-engine experiments. see Barrie Zwicker, *Towers of Deception: The Media Cover-Up of 9/11* (New Society Publishers, 2006), 375. According to Marco Thompson, president of the San Diego Telecom Council, "Cell phones are not designed to work on a plane. Although they do." The rough rule is that when the plane is slow and over a city, the phone will work up to 10,000 feet or so. "Also, it depends on how fast the plane is moving and its proximity to antennas," Thompson said. "At 30,000 feet, it may work momentarily while near a cell site, but it's chancy and the connection won't last." Also, the hand-off process from cell site to cell site is more difficult. It is created for a maximum speed of 60 mph to 100 mph. "They are not built for 400 mph airplanes." *San Diego Metropolitan*, October 2001 (http://sandiegometro.archives.whsites.net/2001/oct/sdscene.html).

851 E-mail letter of 21 November 2006 to David Ray Griffin. For confirmation, see the filmed 2010 experiment "9/11 Experiment: Do Cell Phones Work From an Airplane?" Part 1 (http://www.youtube.com/watch?v=wgQTVT-J2yIM); Part 2 (http://www.youtube.com/watch?v=iYOjkOmIn44); Part 3 (http://www.youtube.com/watch?v=ZJk8qdrv6AM).

852 The original Flight 93 phone call records are available at Scribd (http://www.scribd.com/doc/13499791/T7-B13-Flight-11-Calls-Fdr-Response-From-DOJ-to-Doc-Req-14-Calls-From-AA-11-and-77-and-UA-175-and-93-ATT Wireless-UA-And-GTE-Airphone-Call-Record).

853 The 9/11 Commission, "Memorandum for the Record: Department of Justice Briefing on Cell Phone Calls from UA Flight 93," 13 May 2004 (http://www.scribd.com/doc/19987615/Mfr-Nara-t7-Doj-Doj-Briefing-on-Ua93-Calls-51304-00217v).

854 David Maraniss, "September 11, 2001," *Washington Post*, 16 September 2001.

855 See Julie Sweeney's FBI interview, p. 15 (http://www.scribd.com/doc/47935437/T7-B13-DOJ-Doc-Req-35-13-Packet-8-Fdr-Entire-Contents). The elevation is shown on page 4 of the NTSB Flight Path Study.

856 See "Brian Sweeney," Telephone Calls, United Airlines Flight #175 (http://911research.wtc7.net/planes/evidence/docs/exhibit/BrianSweeney-Pic.png).

857 "Interview with Deena Lynne Burnett," Federal Bureau of Investigation, 11 September 2001, INTELWIRE (http://intelfiles.egoplex.com/2001-09-11-FBI-FD302-deena-lynne-burnett.pdf); also available at Scribd (http://www.scribd.com/doc/15072623/T1A-B33-Four-Flights-Phone-Calls-and-Other-Data-Fdr-Entire-Contents-FBI-302s-843) p. 65.

858 Jere Longman, *Among the Heroes: United 93 and the Passengers and Crew Who Fought Back* (HarperCollins, 2002), 107, 111; Deena L. Burnett (with Anthony F. Giombetti), *Fighting Back: Living Beyond Ourselves* (Advantage Inspirational Books, 2006), 61.

859 David Maraniss, "September 11, 2001," *Washington Post*, 16 September 2001, Greg Gordon, "Widow Tells of Poignant Last Calls," *Sacramento Bee*, 11 September 2002. This story is available with a new title, "Another Workday becomes a Surreal Plane of Terror" (http://911research.wtc7.net/cache/planes/attack/startribune_surrealplane.html).

860 *The 9/11 Commission Report*, 11, 29. According to the FBI's interview of Deena Burnett, the first call came at 6:30 AM PST, hence at 9:30 AM EST (http://intelfiles.egoplex.com/2001-09-11-FBI-FD302-deena-lynne-burnett.pdf). And at that time, UA 93 was said to have been at 36,000 feet: see "Flight Path Study: United Airlines Flight 93," National Transportation Safety Board, 19 February 2002.

861 Deena L. Burnett (with Anthony F. Giombetti), *Fighting Back*, 61. The calls were alleged to have lasted 28 seconds, 54 seconds, and 62 seconds—durations that in 2001 would have been unsustainable on cell phone calls at high altitudes.

862 United States v. Zacarias Moussaoui, Exhibit Number P200054 (http://www.vaed.uscourts.gov/notablecases/moussaoui/exhibits/prosecution/flights/P200054.html). This graphics presentation can be more easily viewed in Hoffman's "Detailed Account of Phone Calls from September 11th Flights."

863 The report (ibid.) indicated that Tom Burnett made these calls from phones located in rows 24 and 25 of this Boeing 757.

864 FBI, "Interview with Deena Lynne Burnett (re: phone call from hijacked flight)," 9/11 Commission, FBI Source Documents, Chronological, 11 September 2001, Intelfiles.com, 14 March 2008 (http://intelfiles.egoplex.com/2001-09-11-FBI-FD302-deena-lynne-burnett.pdf). John Raidt of the 9/11 Commission, who interviewed Deena Burnett by telephone in 2004, stated that she believed Tom had called her from first class: "She also thinks this was the one call he placed to her from his cell phone, because she recognized the number on the caller ID" (9/11 Commission, *Memorandum for the Record*, 26 April 2004)(https://web.archive.org/web/20130207095711/http://media.nara.gov/9-11/MFR/t-0148-911MFR-00260.pdf). This is a strange report, given that in her 2001 FBI interview, her 2006 book, and in all other reports, Deena believed that all of the calls came from Tom's cell phone. It seems possible that Raidt misunderstood her, that she said

"only one of the calls did not show on the caller identification" (as she told the FBI in 2001), but Raidt thought she said that only one of the calls was made from Tom's cell phone. In any case, whatever the accuracy of Raidt's statement, even one call shown to have been made from Tom's cell phone would be inconsistent with the FBI's new account.

865 Interview with Lorne Lyles, Federal Bureau of Investigation, 12 September 2001 (http://www.scribd.com/doc/15072623/T1A-B33-Four-Flights-Phone-Calls-and-Other-Data-Fdr-Entire-Contents-FBI-302s-843).

866 "Interview with Deena Lynne Burnett," Federal Bureau of Investigation, 11 September 2001, INTELWIRE (http://intelfiles.egoplex.com/2001-09-11-FBI-FD302-deena-lynne-burnett.pdf).

867 "Papers Salute New York Stock Exchange," BBC News, 18 September 2001.

868 For example, the BBC one week after 9/11 stated: "The City watchdog, the Financial Services Authority, has launched an inquiry into unusual share price movements in London before last week's atrocities. The Times reports that the American authorities are investigating unusually large sales of shares in airlines and insurance companies. There are said to be suspicions that the shares were sold by people who knew about the impending attacks" ("Papers Salute New York Stock Exchange," BBC News, 18 September, 2001).

869 The 9/11 Commission Report, 499 n. 130.

870 Ibid., 172.

871 Ibid., 499, n. 130.

872 Allen M. Poteshman, "Unusual Option Market Activity and the Terrorist Attacks of September 11, 2001," Journal of Business, 79 (2006): 1703-26 (http://www.jstor.org/stable/10.1086/503645?seq=1#page_scan_tab_contents).

873 Wing-Keung Wong, Howard E. Thompson, and Kweehong Teh, "Was there Abnormal Trading in the S&P 500 Index Options Prior to the September 11 Attacks?" Multinational Finance Journal 15/1-2 (2011): 1–46, at 43 (http://www.mfsociety.org/images/uploadFiles/photos/File/V15N12p1.pdf).

874 Marc Chesney, Remo Crameri, and Loriano Mancini, "Detecting Informed Trading Activities in the Options Markets," Swiss Finance Institute Research Paper, 7 September 2011 (https://papers.ssrn.com/sol3/papers.cfm?abstract_id=1522157).

875 See Table 2 of Paul Zarembka, "Evidence of Insider Trading Before September 11th Re-examined," International Hearings on the Events of September 11, 2001 (Ryerson University, Toronto), September 8-11, 2011 (http://web.archive.org/web/20111010192749/http://ithp.org/articles/septemberinsidertrading.html).

Index

time-change parts, 90
Tomb, Rex, 160
transponders, 84, 86, 142, 144
Tuohey, Michael, 170, 285n662
Twin Towers, ix, x, 1-2, 5, 6, 7, 8, 13-14, 17,
    23, 25-27, 29, 32, 34-35, 37-38, 43, 50,
    66, 87-90, 99, 105-06, 133, 142-43, 147,
    151, 153-54, 158, 226-27, 230nn22-23,
    279n604. *See also* World Trade Center
    1 (North Tower); World Trade Center 2
    (South Tower).

UA 93 (United 93), 81-85, 87, 103, 115-18,
    119-23, 125, 127, 131, 137, 140-42, 196-
    200, 201-04, 209-19, 252n259, 255n301,
    255n304, 257n322, 257n324, 265n420,
    265n433, 294n790, 295n805, 299n836,
    300n843, 301n852, 302n860
UA 175 (United 175), 82, 84-85, 87-88,
    210-11, 214, 217-18, 231n34, 293n779,
    256n321, 301n856
USGS (United States Geological Survey)
    report, 18-21
US Space Command, 95-97, 144
US Strategic Command, 95, 96,
    260nn359-60

vaporization, lead, 18, 22
Velasquez, José, 79
Vigilant Guardian, 95, 96, 98, 148,
    260nn355-58, 277n590
Von Essen, Commissioner Thomas, 157,
    280n613

Warzinski, Colonel Vic, 75
Weldon, Congressman Curt, 185-86, 189-
    93, 288n714, 289n721, 291n754
Westphal, Christopher, 188, 192
Whiskey 105 (military airspace): 97

White, Army Secretary Thomas, 104, 125,
    129, 131
Winfield, Brigadier General Montague,
    105-06, 117-18, 128, 136-41, 150,
    275n551, 275n556
Wittenberg, Russ, 70Wolfowitz, Deputy
    Defense Secretary Paul, 122-27, 131,
    268n454
Worcester Polytechnic Institute (WPI), 17,
    22, 51-53
World Trade Center (WTC), 1-3, 5, 11,
    14-15, 20, 24, 25, 72, 75, 76, 87, 97, 104,
    106, 108-09, 117, 121, 124, 129, 130,
    140, 151; attack on, 152, 163, 166, 176;
    collapse (destruction) of, 1, 2, 6, 19, 24,
    38, 151-53, 155-58; dust of, 18-22, 24,
    30, 33-34, 66, 23n129, 234n63; steel from
    destruction of, 7, 8, 14-23, 31-32, 50-53,
    55, 243n168; steel structure of, 1, 6, 8,
    13, 16, 33, 37, 39, 41, 42, 44, 47, 55, 58,
    154, 231n27, 244n178. *See also* World
    Trade Center 1 (North Tower); World
    Trade Center 2 (South Tower).
World Trade Center 1 (North Tower), 1, 6,
    25, 27-28, 30-33, 44, 52, 54, 55, 59-63,
    85, 148, 151, 156, 238n117, 238n122,
    239n125
World Trade Center 2 (South Tower), 6,
    9-13, 25, 27-8, 30, 31, 60-3, 66, 151-53,
    157, 231n34, 238n121, 279n604
World Trade Center 3: 231n31, 231n32
World Trade Center 5: 9
World Trade Center 7: 1, 14, 16, 22, 37, 39,
    42, 50-53, 54-58, 59-66, 151

Yardley, Jim, 69-70, 251n253

Zarrillo, Richard, 156, 280n606
Zelikow, Philip, 185, 189, 274n532